Information Security and Cryptography
Texts and Monographs

Series Editor
Ueli Maurer

Associate Editors
Martin Abadi
Ross Anderson
Mihir Bellare
Oded Goldreich
Tatsuaki Okamoto
Paul van Oorschot
Birgit Pfitzmann
Aviel D. Rubin
Jacques Stern

T0135132

Alon Rosen

Concurrent Zero-Knowledge

With Additional Background by Oded Goldreich

With 24 Figures

 Springer

Author

Alon Rosen
Harvard University DEAS
Maxwell Dworkin 110
33 Oxford Street
Cambridge, MA 02138
USA
alon@eecs.harvard.edu

Series Editor

Ueli Maurer
Inst. für Theoretische Informatik
ETH Zürich, 8092 Zürich
Switzerland

ACM Computing Classification (1998): E.3, E.4, F.1, F.2, C.2

ISSN 1619-7100

ISBN 978-3-642-06949-9   e-ISBN 978-3-540-32939-8

This work is subject to copyright. All rights are reserved, whether the whole or part of the material is concerned, specifically the rights of translation, reprinting, reuse of illustrations, recitation, broadcasting, reproduction on microfilm or in any other way, and storage in data banks. Duplication of this publication or parts thereof is permitted only under the provisions of the German Copyright Law of September 9, 1965, in its current version, and permission for use must always be obtained from Springer. Violations are liable for prosecution under the German Copyright Law.

Springer is a part of Springer Science+Business Media
springer.com

© Springer-Verlag Berlin Heidelberg 2006
Softcover reprint of the hardcover 1st edition 2006

The use of general descriptive names, registered names, trademarks, etc. in this publication does not imply, even in the absence of a specific statement, that such names are exempt from the relevant protective laws and regulations and therefore free for general use.

Cover Design: KünkelLopka, Heidelberg

To my parents, Kalman and Ora Rosen

Foreword

Zero-knowledge proofs are fascinating and extremely useful constructs. Their fascinating nature is due to their seemingly contradictory definition; zero-knowledge proofs are convincing and yet yield nothing beyond the validity of the assertion being proved. Their applicability in the domain of cryptography is vast; they are typically used to force malicious parties to behave according to a predetermined protocol. In addition to their direct applicability in cryptography, zero-knowledge proofs serve as a good benchmark for the study of various problems regarding cryptographic protocols (e.g., "secure composition of protocols").

A fundamental question regarding zero-knowledge protocols refers to the preservation of security (i.e., of the zero-knowledge feature) when many instances are executed concurrently, and in particular under a purely asynchronous model. The practical importance of this question, in the days of extensive Internet communication, seems clear. It turned out that this question is also very interesting from a theoretical point of view. In particular, this question served as a benchmark for the study of the security of concurrent executions of protocols and led to the development of techniques for coping with the problems that arise in that setting.

Protocols that remain zero-knowledge also when many instances are executed concurrently are called **concurrent zero-knowledge**, and the current book is devoted to their study. In view of the fact that the aforementioned generic application of zero-knowledge protocols relies on their existence for any NP-set, we focus on the construction of concurrent zero-knowledge for every NP-set. The book starts by establishing the mere existence of concurrent zero-knowledge protocols (for any NP-set). We stress that the mere existence of non-trivial concurrent zero-knowledge protocols was not clear for a couple of years, and was established by Richardson and Kilian (in the late 1990s). Once the existence of concurrent zero-knowledge protocols (for any NP-set) was established, the study turned to the complexity of such protocols, focusing on the round-complexity (which is arguably the most important complexity measure). The bulk of the book is devoted to the presentation of the results of that study. The main results presented in this book are:

1. Under standard intractability assumptions, concurrent zero-knowledge proofs with *almost-logarithmically many rounds* do exist (for any NP-set). As with all prior work, this result is established using a "black-box simulator".
2. Black-box simulators cannot establish the concurrent zero-knowledge property of non-trivial protocols having significantly *fewer than logarithmically many rounds*. Black-box simulators are the most natural way to establish the zero-knowledge feature of protocols, and until very recently they were (falsely) considered unavoidable (and so limitations concerning them were considered inherent to zero-knowledge itself).

Combined, these two results determine the round-complexity of concurrent zero-knowledge when restricted to black-box simulations. In doing so, these results make a significant contribution to the study of zero-knowledge and security of protocols at large.

We wish to stress that although we currently realize that "black-box zero-knowledge" is weaker than standard zero-knowledge, it is still important to determine the limits of "black-box" techniques. Firstly, asserting that some problem cannot be solved using "black-box" techniques means that, even in case it is solvable (by "non-black-box" techniques), this problem is inherently harder than others that can be solved using "black-box" techniques. Indeed, solutions that rely on "non-black-box" techniques tend to be more complex not only from a conceptual perspective but also in terms of the time and communication complexities of the resulting protocol. Furthermore, the latter tend to provide a lower level of security.

The focus of this book is on the study of concurrent zero-knowledge protocols. In addition, the book contains a brief introduction to zero-knowledge and a brief account of other developments in the study of zero-knowledge. The purpose of these two augmentations, written by me, is to provide an introduction to the basic concepts that underlie the main subject matter as well as a wider perspective on them.

Weizmann Institute of Science   Oded Goldreich
April 2006

Acknowledgements

I would like to express my deepest gratitude to Oded Goldreich and Moni Naor. Oded and Moni are very special individuals, and each of them has affected my scientific development in his own distinctive way.

I would like to thank Oded for making the writing and publication of this book possible. Oded has invested an unparalleled amount of time and effort to supply me with invaluable advice about technical issues, as well as on the way the results in this book should be presented. There is no doubt that Oded has had a significant impact both on my scientific taste and on my approach to research. For that and for his devotion I thank him very much.

I am deeply indebted to Moni for treating me as a peer from the first moment. The credit he has given me has greatly contributed to my self-confidence as a researcher. Moni has always been available to discuss scientific issues and has continuously provided me with extremely interesting ideas for research. I consider myself lucky for having spent so much time in the presence of someone as resourceful as Moni. I know that I have benefitted from it a lot.

I am most grateful to Ran Canetti, Cynthia Dwork, Shafi Goldwasser, Danny Harnik, Silvio Micali, Rafael Pass, Tal Rabin, Omer Reingold, Ronen Shaltiel and Salil Vadhan for their invaluable support. It would be hard to underestimate the contribution of their advice and encouragement to my development as a researcher.

The students and faculty members at the Weizmann Institute have taught me a great deal, and have made the Institute a great place to study in. Thanks to Adi Akavia, Boaz Barak, Itai Benjamini, Uri Feige, Tzvika Hartman, Robi Krauthgamer, Michael Langberg, Yehuda Lindell, Kobbi Nissim, Eran Ofek, Benny Pinkas, Ran Raz, Yoav Rodeh, Adi Shamir and Udi Wieder.

I would like to thank my co-researchers to the results that make up some of the chapters in this book. Chapter 7 was done jointly with Ran Canetti, Joe Kilian and Erez Petrank [30]. Chapter 5 is joint with Manoj Prabhakaran and Amit Sahai [93]. I would especially like to mention Joe for his generosity and for contributing so many key ideas to the field of concurrent zero-knowledge.

x

Thanks also to Alex Healy, Jonathan Katz, Shien Jin Ong and Salil Vadhan for their feedback on the presentation of the results in this book.

Most importantly, I would like to thank the members of my family for their love and encouragement throughout the years. My parents Ora and Kalman, my brothers Erez and Oren, my wife Vered and my sons Yoav and Itamar. I wish to express the deepest love to Vered, Yoav and Itamar. Being in their presence is a wonderful experience and I consider it the greatest privilege of them all. Finally, thanks to Rivka and Yossi for their much appreciated help with raising the kids.

Harvard University   Alon Rosen
April 2006

Contents

1   **A Brief Introduction to Zero-Knowledge (by O.G.)** 1
   1.1   Preliminaries.. 3
       1.1.1   Interactive Proofs and Argument Systems 4
       1.1.2   Computational Difficulty and One-Way Functions 6
       1.1.3   Computational Indistinguishability 7
   1.2   Definitional Issues 8
       1.2.1   The Simulation Paradigm 9
       1.2.2   The Basic Definition 10
       1.2.3   Variants.. 11
   1.3   Zero-Knowledge Proofs for Every NP-set 15
       1.3.1   Constructing Zero-Knowledge Proofs for NP-sets 15
       1.3.2   Using Zero-Knowledge Proofs for NP-sets 17
   1.4   Composing Zero-Knowledge Protocols..................... 18
       1.4.1   Sequential Composition 19
       1.4.2   Parallel Composition.............................. 20
       1.4.3   Concurrent Composition (With and Without Timing).. 22

2   **Introduction to Concurrent Zero-Knowledge**............... 25
   2.1   Zero-Knowledge Proof Systems.......................... 26
       2.1.1   Concurrent Composition of $\mathcal{ZK}$ 26
       2.1.2   On the Feasibility of $c\mathcal{ZK}$ 27
       2.1.3   The Round-Complexity of $c\mathcal{ZK}$ 27
   2.2   From Repetition to Composition 28
       2.2.1   A "Typical" $\mathcal{ZK}$ Protocol for $\mathcal{NP}$ 29
       2.2.2   Composition of $\mathcal{ZK}$ Protocols 32
   2.3   A Second Look at the Feasibility of $c\mathcal{ZK}$ 33
       2.3.1   A Troublesome Scheduling......................... 33
       2.3.2   The Richardson–Kilian Protocol and Its Analysis 35
       2.3.3   Improving the Analysis of the RK Protocol 36
       2.3.4   What About Non-Black-Box Simulation? 36
   2.4   Organization and the Rest of This Book.................... 37

3   Preliminaries 39
  3.1   General 39
     3.1.1   Basic Notation 39
     3.1.2   Probabilistic Notation 39
     3.1.3   Computational Indistinguishability 39
  3.2   Interactive Proofs 40
  3.3   Zero-Knowledge 41
  3.4   Witness Indistinguishability........................... 41
  3.5   Concurrent Zero-Knowledge 42
  3.6   Black-Box Concurrent Zero-Knowledge 43
  3.7   Conventions Used in Construction of Simulators 44
  3.8   Commitment Schemes................................. 46

4 $c\mathcal{ZK}$ Proof Systems for $\mathcal{NP}$ 49
  4.1   Blum's Hamiltonicity Protocol 50
  4.2   The Richardson–Kilian $c\mathcal{ZK}$ Protocol 51
  4.3   The Prabhakharan–Rosen–Sahai $c\mathcal{ZK}$ Protocol.............. 53
  4.4   Simulating the RK and PRS Protocols – Outline 55
  4.5   Analyzing the Simulation – Outline 58
     4.5.1   The Simulator Runs in Polynomial Time 59
     4.5.2   The Simulator's Output is "Correctly" Distributed 59
     4.5.3   The Simulator (Almost) Never Gets "Stuck" 59

5 $c\mathcal{ZK}$ in Logarithmically Many Rounds 67
  5.1   Detailed Description of the Simulator 67
     5.1.1   The Main Procedure and Ideas...................... 68
     5.1.2   The Actual Simulator 74
  5.2   The Simulator's Running Time........................... 75
  5.3   The Simulator's Output Distribution...................... 75
  5.4   The Probability of Getting "Stuck" 77
     5.4.1   Counting Bad Random Tapes 83
     5.4.2   Special Intervals Are Visited Many Times 90
  5.5   Extensions... 95
     5.5.1   Applicability to Other Protocols..................... 95
     5.5.2 $c\mathcal{ZK}$ Arguments Based on Any One-Way Function..... 96
     5.5.3   Applicability to Resettable Zero-Knowledge........... 98
     5.5.4 $c\mathcal{ZK}$ Arguments with Poly-Logarithmic Efficiency 99

6   A Simple Lower Bound 101
  6.1   Proof of Theorem 6.1 101
     6.1.1   Schedule, Adversary Verifiers and Decision Procedure .. 102
     6.1.2   Proof of Lemma 6.1.5 105
     6.1.3   Existence of Useful Initiation Prefixes 107
     6.1.4   The Structure of Good Subtrees 109

7   Black-Box *cZK* Requires Logarithmically Many Rounds . . . 111
  7.1   Proof Outline 112
      7.1.1   The High-Level Framework 112
      7.1.2   The Schedule and Additional Ideas 114
      7.1.3   The Actual Analysis 119
  7.2   The Actual Proof. 119
      7.2.1   The Concurrent Adversarial Verifier 119
      7.2.2   The Actual Verifier Strategy $V_{g,h}$ 126
      7.2.3   The Decision Procedure for L 130
  7.3   Performance on NO-instances. 132
      7.3.1   The Cheating Prover 133
      7.3.2   The Success Probability of the Cheating Prover 137
      7.3.3   Legal Transcripts Yield Useful Block Prefixes 142
      7.3.4   Existence of Potentially Useful Block Prefixes 144
      7.3.5   Existence of Useful Block Prefixes 152

8   Conclusions and Open Problems 161
  8.1   Avoiding the Lower Bounds of Chapter 7 161
  8.2   Open Problems 162

9   A Brief Account of Other Developments (by O.G.) 165
  9.1   Using the Adversary's Program in the Proof of Security 167
  9.2   Witness Indistinguishability and the FLS-Technique 169
  9.3   Proofs of Knowledge 171
      9.3.1   How to Define Proofs of Knowledge. 171
      9.3.2   How to Construct Proofs of Knowledge. 172
  9.4   Non-interactive Zero-Knowledge 173
  9.5   Statistical Zero-Knowledge 174
      9.5.1   Transformations. 175
      9.5.2   Complete Problems and Structural Properties. 176
  9.6   Resettability of a Party's Random-Tape (rZK and rsZK) 176
  9.7   Zero-Knowledge in Other Models 177

References 179

A Brief Introduction to Zero-Knowledge
(by Oded Goldreich)

Zero-knowledge proofs, introduced by Goldwasser, Micali and Rackoff [72], are fascinating and extremely useful constructs. Their fascinating nature is due to their seemingly contradictory definition; zero-knowledge proofs are both convincing and yet yield nothing beyond the validity of the assertion being proven. Their applicability in the domain of cryptography is vast: Following the results of Goldreich, Micali and Wigderson [65], zero-knowledge proofs are typically used to force malicious parties to behave according to a predetermined protocol. In addition to their direct applicability in cryptography, zero-knowledge proofs serve as a good benchmark for the study of various problems regarding cryptographic protocols (e.g., the "preservation of security under various forms of protocol composition" and the "use of the adversary's program within the proof of security").

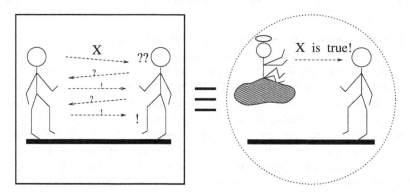

Fig. 1.1. Zero-knowledge proofs – an illustration.

We wish to highlight also the indirect impact of zero-knowledge on the definitional approach underlying the foundations of cryptography (cf. Sect. 1.2.1). In addition, zero-knowledge has served as a source of inspiration for complexity theory. In particular, it served as the main motivation towards the introduction of interactive proof systems [72] and multiprover interactive proof systems [17] (which, in turn, led to the exciting developments regarding PCP and the complexity of approximation [44, 4, 3]).

A Very Brief Summary of this Chapter. Loosely speaking, zero-knowledge proofs are proofs that yield nothing beyond the validity of the assertion. That is, a verifier obtaining such a proof only gains conviction in the validity of the assertion. This is formulated by saying that anything that is feasibly computable from a zero-knowledge proof is also feasibly computable from the (valid) assertion itself (by a so-called simulator). Variants on the basic definition include (see Sect. 1.2.3):

- consideration of auxiliary inputs;
- mandating of universal and black-box simulations;
- restricting attention to honest (or rather semi-honest) verifiers;
- the level of similarity required of the simulation.

It is well known (see Sect. 1.3) that *zero-knowledge proofs exist for any NP-set*, provided that one-way functions exist. This result is a powerful tool in the design of cryptographic protocols, because it can be used to force parties to behave according to a predetermined protocol (i.e., the protocol requires parties to provide zero-knowledge proofs of the correctness of their secret-based actions, without revealing these secrets).

A natural question regarding zero-knowledge proofs is whether the zero-knowledge condition is preserved under a variety of composition operations. Indeed, most of this book is devoted to the study of concurrent composition of zero-knowledge proofs, but more restricted types of composition are also of interest. The main facts regarding composition of zero-knowledge protocols are:

- Zero-knowledge is closed under sequential composition.
- In general, zero-knowledge is not closed under parallel composition. Yet, some zero-knowledge proofs (for NP) preserve their security when many copies are executed in parallel. Furthermore, some of these protocols use a constant number of rounds, and this result extends to restricted forms of concurrent composition (i.e., "bounded asynchronicity").
- Some zero-knowledge proofs (for NP) preserve their security when many copies are executed concurrently, but such a result is not known for constant-round protocols. Indeed, most of this book is devoted to the study of the round-complexity of concurrent zero-knowledge protocols.

Organization of this Chapter. In this chapter we present the basic definitions and results regarding zero-knowledge protocols. We start with some preliminaries (Sect. 1.1), which are central to the "mind-set" of the notion of zero-knowledge. In particular, we review the definitions of interactive proofs and arguments as well as the definitions of computational indistinguishability (which underlies the definition of general zero-knowledge) and of one-way functions (which are used in constructions). We then turn to the definitional treatment of zero-knowledge itself, provided in Sect. 1.2. In Sect. 1.3 we review the main feasibility result regarding zero-knowledge proofs and its typical applications. We conclude this chapter with a brief survey of results regarding sequential, parallel and concurrent composition (Sect. 1.4).

Suggestions for Further Reading. A brief account of other developments regarding zero-knowledge protocols is provided in Chap. 9. For further details regarding the material presented in Sect. 1.1–1.3, the reader is referred to [57, Chap. 4]. For a wider perspective on probabilistic proof systems, the reader is referred to [56, Chap. 2].

1.1 Preliminaries

Modern cryptography is concerned with the construction of *efficient* schemes for which it is *infeasible* to violate the security feature. The same concern underlies the main definitions of zero-knowledge. Thus, for starters, we need a notion of efficient computations as well as a notion of infeasible ones. The computations of the legitimate users of the scheme ought to be efficient, whereas violating the security features (via an adversary) ought to be infeasible.

Efficient computations are commonly modeled by computations that are polynomial-time in the security parameter. The polynomial bounding the running time of the legitimate user's strategy is fixed and typically explicit (and small). Here (i.e., when referring to the complexity of the legitimate users) we are in the same situation as in any algorithmic setting.

Things are different when referring to our assumptions regarding the computational resources of the adversary. A common approach is to postulate that the latter are polynomial-time too, where the polynomial is *not a priori specified*. In other words, the adversary is restricted to the class of efficient computations and anything beyond this is considered to be infeasible. Although many definitions explicitly refer to this convention, this convention is *inessential* to any of the results known in the area. In all cases, a more general statement can be made by referring to adversaries of running-time bounded by any super-polynomial function (or class of functions). Still, for sake of concreteness and clarity, we shall use the former convention in our treatment.

Actually, in order to simplify our exposition, we will often consider as infeasible any computation that cannot be conducted by a (possibly non-uniform) family of polynomial-size circuits. For simplicity we consider families of circuits $\{C_n\}$, where for some polynomials p and q, each C_n has exactly $p(n)$ input bits and has size at most $q(n)$.

Randomized computations play a central role in the definition of zero-knowledge (as well as in cryptography at large). That is, we allow the legitimate users to employ randomized computations, and likewise we consider adversaries that employ randomized computations. This brings up the issue of success probability: typically, we require that legitimate users succeed (in fulfilling their legitimate goals) with probability 1 (or negligibly close to this), whereas adversaries succeed (in violating the security features) with negligible probability. Thus, the notion of a negligible probability plays an important role in our exposition. One feature required of the definition of *negligible probability* is to yield a robust notion of rareness: A rare event should occur rarely even if we repeat the experiment for a feasible number of times. Likewise, we consider two events to occur "as frequently" if the absolute difference between their corresponding occurrence probabilities is negligible. For concreteness, we consider as negligible any function $\mu : N \to [0, 1]$ that vanishes faster than the reciprocal of any polynomial (i.e., for every positive polynomial p and all sufficiently big n, it holds that $\mu(n) < 1/p(n)$).

1.1.1 Interactive Proofs and Argument Systems

A proof is whatever convinces me.

Shimon Even, answering a student's question
in his Graph Algorithms class (1978)

Before defining zero-knowledge proofs, we have to define proofs. The standard notion of static (i.e., non-interactive) proofs will not do, because static zero-knowledge proofs exist only for sets that are easy to decide (i.e., are in $\mathcal{BPP}$) [67], whereas we are interested in zero-knowledge proofs for arbitrary NP-sets. Instead, we use the notion of an interactive proof (introduced exactly for that reason by Goldwasser, Micali and Rackoff [72]). That is, here a proof is a (multiround) randomized protocol for two parties, called *verifier* and *prover*, in which the prover wishes to convince the verifier of the validity of a given assertion. Such an *interactive proof* should allow the prover to convince the verifier of the validity of any true assertion, whereas NO prover strategy may fool the verifier to accept false assertions. Both the above *completeness* and *soundness* conditions should hold with high probability (i.e., a negligible error probability is allowed).

We comment that interactive proofs emerge naturally when associating the notion of efficient verification, which underlies the notion of a proof system, with probabilistic and interactive polynomial-time computations. This association is quite natural in light of the growing acceptability of randomized and distributed computations. Thus, a "proof" in this context is not a fixed and static object, but rather a randomized and dynamic (i.e., interactive) process in which the verifier interacts with the prover. Intuitively, one may think of this interaction as consisting of "tricky" questions asked by the verifier, to which the prover has to reply "convincingly". The above discussion, as well as the following definition, makes explicit reference to a prover, whereas a prover is only implicit in the traditional definitions of proof systems (e.g., NP-proofs).

Loosely speaking, an interactive proof is a game between a computationally bounded verifier and a computationally unbounded prover whose goal is to convince the verifier of the validity of some assertion. Specifically, the verifier is probabilistic polynomial-time. It is required that if the assertion holds then the verifier always accepts (i.e., when interacting with an appropriate prover strategy). On the other hand, if the assertion is false then the verifier must reject with "noticeable" probability, no matter what strategy is being employed by the prover. Indeed, the error probability (in the soundness condition) can be reduced by (either sequential or parallel) repetitions.

Definition 1.1.1 (Interactive proof systems and the class $\mathcal{IP}$ [72]) *An* interactive proof system *for a set S is a two-party game, between a* verifier *executing a probabilistic polynomial-time strategy* (denoted V) *and a* prover *which executes a computationally unbounded strategy* (denoted P), *satisfying:*

- Completeness: *For every $x \in S$ the verifier V always accepts after interacting with the prover P on common input x.*
- Soundness: *For some polynomial p, it holds that for every $x \notin S$ and every potential strategy P^*, the verifier V rejects with probability at least $1/p(|x|)$, after interacting with P^* on common input x.*

The class of problems having interactive proof systems is denoted $\mathcal{IP}$.

Note that by repeating such a proof system for $O(p(|x|)^2)$ times, we may decrease the probability that V accepts a false statement (from $1 - (1/p(|x|))$) to $2^{-p(|x|)}$. Thus, when constructing interactive proofs we sometimes focus on obtaining a noticeable rejection probability for NO-instances (i.e., obtaining a soundness error bounded away from 1), whereas when using interactive proofs we typically assume that their soundness error is negligible.

Variants. Arthur–Merlin games (a.k.a. *public-coin* proof systems), introduced by Babai [5], are a special case of interactive proofs in which the verifier must send the outcome of any coin it tosses (and thus need not send any other information). Yet, as shown in [74], this restricted case has essentially the same power as the general case (introduced by Goldwasser, Micali and Rackoff [72]). Thus, in the context of interactive proof systems, *asking random questions is as powerful as asking "tricky" questions*. (As we shall see, this does not necessarily hold in the context of zero-knowledge proofs.) Also, in some sources interactive proofs are defined so that two-sided error probability is allowed (rather than requiring "perfect completeness" as done above); yet, this does not increase their power [52].

Arguments (or Computational Soundness). A fundamental variant on the notion of interactive proofs was introduced by Brassard, Chaum and Crépeau [23], who relaxed the soundness condition so that it only refers to feasible ways of trying to fool the verifier (rather than to all possible ways). Specifically, the soundness condition was replaced by the following computational soundness condition that asserts that it is infeasible to fool the verifier into accepting false statements. That is:

> *For every polynomial p, every prover strategy that is implementable by*
> *a family of polynomial-size circuits $\{C_n\}$, and every sufficiently large*
> *$x \in \{0,1\}^* \setminus S$, the probability that V accepts x when interacting with*
> *$C_{|x|}$ is less than $1/p(|x|)$.*

We warn that although the computational-soundness error can always be reduced by sequential repetitions, it is not true that this error can always be reduced by parallel repetitions (cf. [15]). Protocols that satisfy the computational-soundness condition are called arguments.[1] We mention that argument systems may be more efficient than interactive proofs (see [80, 61]).

Terminology. Whenever we wish to blur the distinction between proofs and arguments, we will use the term protocols. We will consider such a protocol trivial if it establishes membership in a BPP-set (because membership in such a set can be determined by the verifier itself). On the other hand, we will sometimes talk about "protocols for $\mathcal{NP}$", when what we actually mean is protocols for each set in $\mathcal{NP}$. (The latter terminology is quite common in the area; see [10] for further discussion of the distinction.)

1.1.2 Computational Difficulty and One-Way Functions

Most positive results regarding zero-knowledge proofs are based on intractability assumptions. Furthermore, the very notion of a zero-knowledge proof is interesting only in case the assertion being proven to be valid is hard to verify in probabilistic polynomial-time. Thus, our discussion always assumes (at least implicitly) that $\mathcal{IP}$ is not contained in $\mathcal{BPP}$, and often we explicitly assume more than that.

In general, modern cryptography is concerned with the construction of schemes that are easy to operate (properly) but hard to foil. Thus, a complexity gap (i.e., between the complexity of proper usage and the complexity of defeating the prescribed functionality) lies at the heart of modern cryptography. However, gaps as required for modern cryptography are not known to exist; they are only widely believed to exist. Indeed, almost all of modern cryptography rises or falls with the question of whether one-way functions exist. One-way functions are functions that are easy to evaluate but hard (on the average) to invert (cf. [37]). That is, a function $f : \{0,1\}^* \to \{0,1\}^*$ is called one-way if there is an efficient algorithm that on input x outputs $f(x)$, whereas any feasible algorithm that tries to find a preimage of $f(x)$ under f may succeed only with negligible probability (where the probability is taken uniformly over the choices of x and the algorithm's coin tosses). Associating feasible computations with (possibly non-uniform) families of polynomial-size circuits, we obtain the following definition.

---

[1] A related notion not discussed here is that of CS-proofs, introduced by Micali [86].

Definition 1.1.2 (One-way functions) *A function $f : \{0,1\}^* \to \{0,1\}^*$ is called* one-way *if the following two conditions hold:*

1. Easy to evaluate: *There exists a polynomial-time algorithm A such that $A(x) = f(x)$ for every $x \in \{0,1\}^*$.*
2. Hard to invert: *For every family of polynomial-size circuits $\{C_n\}$, every polynomial p, and all sufficiently large n,*

$$\Pr[C_n(f(x)) \in f^{-1}(f(x))] < \frac{1}{p(n)}$$

where the probability is taken uniformly over all the possible choices of $x \in \{0,1\}^n$.

Some of the most popular candidates for one-way functions are based on the conjectured intractability of computational problems in number theory. One such conjecture is that it is infeasible to factor large integers. Consequently, the function that takes as input two (equal length) primes and outputs their product is widely believed to be a one-way function.

Terminology. Some of the known (positive) results (regarding zero-knowledge) require stronger forms of one-way functions (e.g., one-way permutations with (or without) trapdoor [57, Sect. 2.4.4] and claw-free permutation pairs [57, Sect. 2.4.5]). Whenever we wish to avoid the specific details, we will talk about standard intractability assumptions. In all cases, the conjectured intractability of factoring will suffice.

1.1.3 Computational Indistinguishability

> Indistinguishable things are identical
> (or should be considered as identical).
>
> The Principle of Identity of Indiscernibles[2]
> G.W. Leibniz (1646–1714)

A central notion in modern cryptography is that of "effective similarity" (introduced by Goldwasser, Micali and Yao [71, 102]). The underlying thesis is that we do not care whether or not objects are equal, all we care is whether or not a difference between the objects can be observed by a feasible computation. In case the answer is negative, the two objects are equivalent as far as any practical application is concerned. Indeed, like in many other cryptographic definitions, in the definition of general/computational zero-knowledge we will freely interchange such (computationally indistinguishable) objects.

The asymptotic formulation of computational indistinguishability refers to (pairs of) probability ensembles, which are infinite sequences of finite distributions, rather than to (pairs of) finite distributions. Specifically, we consider

---

[2]Leibniz admits that counterexamples to this principle are conceivable but will not occur in real life because God is much too benevolent.

sequences indexed by strings, rather than by integers (in unary representation). For $S \subseteq \{0,1\}^*$, we consider the probability ensembles $X = \{X_\alpha\}_{\alpha \in S}$ and $Y = \{Y_\alpha\}_{\alpha \in S}$, where each X_α (resp., Y_α) is a distribution that ranges over strings of length polynomial in $|\alpha|$. We say that X and Y are computationally indistinguishable if for every feasible algorithm A the difference $d_A(n) \stackrel{\text{def}}{=} \max_{\alpha \in \{0,1\}^n} \{|\Pr[A(X_\alpha) = 1] - \Pr[A(Y_\alpha) = 1]|\}$ is a negligible function in $|\alpha|$. That is:

Definition 1.1.3 (Computational indistinguishability [71, 102]) *We say that $X = \{X_\alpha\}_{\alpha \in S}$ and $Y = \{Y_\alpha\}_{\alpha \in S}$ are* computationally indistinguishable *if for every family of polynomial-size circuits $\{D_n\}$, every polynomial p, all sufficiently large n and every $\alpha \in \{0,1\}^{\text{poly}(n)} \cap S$,*

$$|\Pr[D_n(X_\alpha) = 1] - \Pr[D_n(Y_\alpha) = 1]| < \frac{1}{p(n)}$$

where probabilities are taken over the relevant distribution (either X_n or Y_n).

That is, we think of $D = \{D_n\}$ as of somebody who wishes to distinguish two distributions (based on a sample given to it), and think of 1 as of D's verdict that the sample was drawn according to the first distribution. Saying that the two distributions are computationally indistinguishable means that if D is an efficient procedure then its verdict is not really meaningful (because the verdict is almost as often 1 when the input is drawn from the first distribution as when the input is drawn from the second distribution).

We comment that indistinguishability by a single sample (as defined above) implies indistinguishability by multiple samples. Also note that the definition would not have been stronger if we were to provide the distinguisher (i.e., D) with the index (i.e., α) of the distribution pair being tested.[3]

1.2 Definitional Issues

> A: Please.
> B: Please.
> A: I insist.
> B: So do I.
> A: OK then, thank you.
> B: You are most welcome.

A protocol for two Italians to pass through a door.[4]

Source: Silvio Micali, 1985.

---

[3] Furthermore, the definition would not have been stronger if we were to consider a specialized polynomial-size circuit for each $\alpha \in S$ (i.e., consider the difference $|\Pr[D_\alpha(X_\alpha) = 1] - \Pr[D_\alpha(Y_\alpha) - 1]|$ for any set of circuits $D = \{D_\alpha\}_{\alpha \in S}$ such that the size of D_α is polynomial in $|\alpha|$).

[4] The protocol is zero-knowledge because it can be simulated without knowing any of the secrets of these Italians; in fact, the execution is independent of their secrets as well as of anything else.

Loosely speaking, zero-knowledge proofs are proofs that yield nothing beyond the validity of the assertion. That is, a verifier obtaining such a proof only gains conviction in the validity of the assertion. This is formulated by saying that anything that can be feasibly obtained from a zero-knowledge proof is also feasibly computable from the (valid) assertion itself. The latter formulation follows the simulation paradigm, which is discussed next.

1.2.1 The Simulation Paradigm

In defining zero-knowledge proofs, we view the verifier as a potential adversary that tries to gain knowledge from the (prescribed) prover. We wish to state that no (feasible) adversary strategy for the verifier can gain anything from the prover (beyond conviction in the validity of the assertion). Let us consider the desired formulation from a wide perspective.

A key question regarding the modeling of security concerns is how to express the intuitive requirement that an adversary "gains nothing substantial" by deviating from the prescribed behavior of an honest user. Our approach is that the adversary *gains nothing* if whatever it can obtain by unrestricted adversarial behavior can be obtained within essentially the same computational effort by a benign behavior. The definition of the "benign behavior" captures what we want to achieve in terms of security, and is specific to the security concern to be addressed. For example, in the previous paragraph, we said that a proof is zero-knowledge if it yields nothing beyond the validity of the assertion (i.e., the benign behavior is any computation that is based (only) on the assertion itself, while assuming that the latter is valid). Thus, in a zero-knowledge proof no feasible adversarial strategy for the verifier can obtain more than a "benign verifier", which believes the assertion, can obtain from the assertion itself. We comment that the simulation paradigm, which was first developed in the context of zero-knowledge [72], is pivotal also to the definition of the security of encryption schemes (cf. [58, Chap. 5]) and cryptographic protocols (cf. [26] and [58, Chap. 7]).

A notable property of defining security (or zero-knowledge) via the simulation paradigm is that this approach is "overly liberal" with respect to its view of the abilities of the adversary as well as to what might constitute a gain for the adversary. Thus, the approach may be considered overly cautious, because it prohibits also "non-harmful" gains of some "far fetched" adversaries. We warn against this impression. Firstly, there is nothing more dangerous in cryptography than to consider "reasonable" adversaries (a notion which is almost a contradiction in terms): typically, the adversaries will try exactly what the system designer has discarded as "far fetched". Secondly, it seems impossible to come up with definitions of security that distinguish "breaking the scheme in a harmful way" from "breaking it in a non-harmful way": what is harmful is application-dependent, whereas a good definition of security ought to be application-independent (as otherwise using the scheme in any new application will require a full re-evaluation of its security). Furthermore, even with respect to a specific application, it is typically very hard to classify the set of "harmful breakings".

1.2.2 The Basic Definition

Zero-knowledge is a property of some prover strategies. More generally, zero-knowledge is a property of some interactive machines. Fixing an interactive machine (e.g., a prescribed prover), we consider what can be computed by an *arbitrary* feasible adversary (e.g., a verifier) that interacts with the fixed machine on a common input taken from a predetermined set (in our case the set of valid assertions). This is compared against what can be computed by an *arbitrary* feasible algorithm that is only given the input itself. An interactive strategy A is zero-knowledge on (inputs from) the set S if, for every feasible (interactive) strategy B^*, there exists a feasible (non-interactive) computation C^* such that the following two probability ensembles are computationally indistinguishable:

1. $\{(A, B^*)(x)\}_{x \in S} \stackrel{\text{def}}{=}$ the output of B^* after interacting with A on common input $x \in S$; and
2. $\{C^*(x)\}_{x \in S} \stackrel{\text{def}}{=}$ the output of C^* on input $x \in S$.

We stress that the first ensemble represents an actual execution of an interactive protocol, whereas the second ensemble represents the computation of a stand-alone procedure (called the "simulator"), which does not interact with anybody. Thus, whatever can be feasibly extracted from interaction with A on input $x \in S$ can also be feasibly extracted from x itself. This means that nothing was gained by the interaction itself (beyond confidence in the assertion $x \in S$).

The above definition does NOT account for auxiliary information that an adversary may have prior to entering the interaction. Accounting for such auxiliary information is essential for using zero-knowledge proofs as subprotocols inside larger protocols (see [63, 67]). This is taken care of by a more strict notion called auxiliary-input zero-knowledge.[5]

Definition 1.2.1 (Zero-knowledge [72], revisited [67]) *A strategy A is* auxiliary-input zero-knowledge *on inputs from S if for every probabilistic polynomial-time strategy B^* and every polynomial p there exists a probabilistic polynomial-time algorithm C^* such that the following two probability ensembles are computationally indistinguishable:*

---

[5] We note that Definition 1.2.1 seems stronger than merely allowing the verifier and simulator to be arbitrary polynomial-size circuits. The issue is that the latter formulation does not guarantee that the simulator can be easily derived from the cheating verifier nor that the length of the simulator's description is related to the length of the description of the verifier. Both issues are important when trying to use zero-knowledge proofs as subprotocols inside larger protocols or to compose them (even sequentially). For further discussion, see Sect. 1.4.

1. $\{(A, B^*(z))(x)\}_{x \in S, z \in \{0,1\}^{p(|x|)}} \overset{\text{def}}{=}$ *the output of B^* when having auxiliary-input z and interacting with A on common input $x \in S$; and*

2. $\{C^*(x, z)\}_{x \in S, z \in \{0,1\}^{p(|x|)}} \overset{\text{def}}{=}$ *the output of C^* on inputs $x \in S$ and $z \in \{0,1\}^{p(|x|)}$.*

An interactive proof (resp., an argument) *system for S is called* auxiliary-input zero-knowledge *if the prescribed prover strategy is auxiliary-input zero-knowledge on inputs from S.*[6]

The more basic definition of zero-knowledge is obtained by eliminating the auxiliary-input z from Definition 1.2.1. We comment that almost all known zero-knowledge proofs are in fact auxiliary-input zero-knowledge. (Notable exceptions are zero-knowledge proofs constructed on purpose in order to show a separation between these two notions (e.g., in [63]) and protocols having only "non-black-box simulators" (see warm-up in [8]).) As hinted above, *auxiliary-input zero-knowledge is preserved under sequential composition* [67].

We stress that the zero-knowledge property of an interactive proof (resp., argument) refers to all feasible *adversarial strategies that the verifier may employ* (in an attempt to extract knowledge from the prescribed prover that tries to convince the verifier to accept a valid assertion). In contrast, the soundness property of an interactive proof (resp., the computational-soundness property of an argument) refers to all possible (resp., feasible) *adversarial strategies that the prover may employ* (in an attempt to fool the prescribed verifier to accept a false assertion). Finally, the completeness property (only) refers to the behavior of both prescribed strategies (when given, as common input, a valid assertion).

1.2.3 Variants

The reader may skip the current subsection and return to it whenever encountering (especially in Chap. 9) a notion that was not defined above.

Universal and Black-Box Simulation

We have already discussed two variants of the basic definition (i.e., with or without auxiliary-inputs). Further strengthening of Definition 1.2.1 is obtained by requiring the existence of a universal simulator, denoted C, that is given the program of the verifier (i.e., B^*) as an auxiliary-input; that is, in terms of Definition 1.2.1, one should replace $C^*(x, z)$ by $C(x, z, \langle B^* \rangle)$, where

---

[6] Note that the *prescribed* verifier strategy (which is a probabilistic polynomial-time strategy that only depends on the common input) is always auxiliary-input zero-knowledge. In contrast, typical prover strategies are implemented by probabilistic polynomial-time algorithms that are given an auxiliary input (which is not given to the verifier), but not by probabilistic polynomial-time algorithms that are only given the common input.

$\langle B^* \rangle$ denotes the description of the program of B^* (which may depend on x and on z).[7] That is, we effectively restrict the simulation by requiring that it be a uniform (feasible) function of the verifier's program (rather than arbitrarily depend on it). This restriction is very natural, because it seems hard to envision an alternative way of establishing the zero-knowledge property of a given protocol.

Taking another step, one may argue that since it seems infeasible to reverse-engineer programs, the simulator may as well just use the verifier strategy as an oracle (or as a "black-box"). This reasoning gave rise to the notion of black-box simulation, which was introduced and advocated in [62] and further studied in numerous works (see, e.g., [30]). The belief was that impossibility results regarding black-box simulation represent inherent limitations of zero-knowledge itself. However, this belief has been refuted recently by Barak [8]. For further discussion, see Sect. 9.1.

Knowledge Tightness

Intuitively, knowledge tightness is a refinement of zero-knowledge that is aimed at measuring the "actual security" of the proof system; namely, how much harder does the verifier need to work, when not interacting with the prover, in order to compute something that it can compute after interacting with the prover. Thus, knowledge tightness is the ratio between the running time of the simulator and the running time of the verifier in the real interaction simulated by the simulator. (For more details, see [57, Sect. 4.4.4.2].)

Note that black-box simulators guarantee that the underlying zero-knowledge protocol has knowledge tightness that is bounded by some fixed polynomial. In fact, in some cases, the knowledge tightness can be bounded by a constant (e.g., 2). In contrast, the general definition of zero-knowledge (i.e., Definition 1.2.1) does not guarantee that the knowledge tightness can be bounded by some fixed polynomial. In fact, the non-black-box simulators of Barak [8] seem to have a running time that is polynomially (but not linearly) related to the running time of the verifier that they simulate.

Honest Verifier Versus General Cheating Verifier

The (general) definition of zero-knowledge (i.e., Definition 1.2.1) refers to all feasible verifier strategies. This choice is most natural since zero-knowledge is supposed to capture the robustness of the prover under *any feasible* (i.e., adversarial) attempt to gain something by interacting with it. Thus, we typically view the verifier as an adversary that is trying to cheat.

---

[7] Actually, we may incorporate x and z in $\langle B^* \rangle$, and thus replace $C(x, z, \langle B^* \rangle)$ by $C(\langle B^* \rangle)$.

A weaker and still interesting notion of zero-knowledge refers to what can be gained by an "honest verifier" (or rather a semi-honest verifier)[8] that interacts with the prover as directed, with the exception that it may maintain (and output) a record of the entire interaction (i.e., even if directed to erase all records of the interaction). Although such a weaker notion is not satisfactory for standard cryptographic applications, it yields a fascinating notion from a conceptual as well as a complexity-theoretic point of view. Furthermore, as shown in [68], every public-coin proof system that is *zero-knowledge with respect to the honest-verifier* can be transformed into a *standard zero-knowledge* proof that maintains many of the properties of the original protocol (and without increasing the prover's powers or using any intractability assumptions).

We stress that the definition of zero-knowledge with respect to the honest-verifier V is derived from Definition 1.2.1 by considering a single verifier strategy B that is equal to V except that B also maintains a record of the entire interaction (including its own coin tosses) and outputs this record at the end of the interaction. (In particular, the messages sent by B are identical to the corresponding messages that would have been sent by V.)

Statistical Versus Computational Zero-Knowledge

Recall that the definition of zero-knowledge postulates that for every probability ensemble of one type (i.e., representing the verifier's output after interaction with the prover) there exists a "similar" ensemble of a second type (i.e., representing the simulator's output). One key parameter is the interpretation of "similarity". Three interpretations, yielding different notions of zero-knowledge, have been commonly considered in the literature (cf., [72, 50]):

1. Perfect zero-knowledge (PZK) requires that the two probability ensembles be identical.[9]
2. Statistical zero-knowledge (SZK) requires that these probability ensembles be statistically close (i.e., the variation distance between them is negligible).
3. Computational (or rather general) zero-knowledge (CZK) requires that these probability ensembles be computationally indistinguishable.

Indeed, computational zero-knowledge (CZK) is the most liberal notion, and is the notion considered in Definition 1.2.1 as well as in most of this book. (In particular, whenever we fail to qualify the type of zero-knowledge, we mean

---

[8] The term "honest verifier" is more appealing when considering an alternative (equivalent) formulation of Definition 1.2.1. In the alternative definition, the simulator is "only" required to generate the verifier's view of the real interaction, when the verifier's view includes its inputs, the outcome of its coin tosses, and all messages it has received.

[9] The actual definition of PZK allows the simulator to fail (while outputting a special symbol) with some probability that is bounded away from 1, and the output distribution of the simulator is conditioned on its not failing.

computational zero-knowledge.) The only exception is Sect. 9.5, which is devoted to a discussion of statistical (or almost-perfect) Zero-Knowledge (SZK). We note that the class SZK contains several problems that are considered intractable.

Strict Versus Expected Probabilistic Polynomial-Time

So far, we did not specify what we exactly mean by the term probabilistic polynomial-time. Two common interpretations are:

1. Strict probabilistic polynomial-time. That is, there exists a (polynomial in the length of the input) bound on the *number of steps in each possible run* of the machine, regardless of the outcome of its coin tosses.
2. Expected probabilistic polynomial-time. The standard approach is to look at the running time as a random variable and *bound its expectation* (by a polynomial in the length of the input). As observed by Levin [84] (cf. [54]), this definitional approach is quite problematic (e.g., it is not model-independent and is not closed under algorithmic composition), and an alternative treatment of this random variable is preferable.[10]

The notion of expected polynomial-time raises a variety of conceptual and technical problems. For that reason, whenever possible, one should prefer to use the more robust (and restricted) notion of strict (probabilistic) polynomial-time. Thus, with the *exception of constant-round* zero-knowledge protocols, whenever we talk of a probabilistic polynomial-time verifier (resp., simulator) we mean one in the strict sense. In contrast, with the exception of [8, 12],[11] all results regarding *constant-round* zero-knowledge protocols refer to a strict polynomial-time verifier and an expected polynomial-time simulator, which is indeed a small cheat. For further discussion, the reader is referred to [12].

---

[10] Specifically, it is preferable to define expected polynomial-time as having running time that is polynomially related to a function that has linear expectation. That is, rather than requiring that $e[X_n] = \text{poly}(n)$, one requires that for some Y_n it holds that $X_n = \text{poly}(Y_n)$ and $e[Y_n] = O(n)$. The advantage of the latter approach is that if X_n is deemed *polynomial on the average* then so is X_n^2, which is not the case under the former approach (e.g., $X_n = 2^n$ with probability 2^{-n} and $X_n = n$ otherwise).

[11] Specifically, in [8, 12] both the verifier and the simulator run in strict polynomial-time. We comment that, as shown in [12], the use of non-black-box is necessary for the non-triviality of constant-round zero-knowledge protocols under the strict definition.

1.3 Zero-Knowledge Proofs for Every NP-set

A question avoided so far is whether zero-knowledge proofs exist at all. Clearly, every set in $\mathcal{P}$ (or rather in $\mathcal{BPP}$)[12] has a "trivial" zero-knowledge proof (in which the verifier determines membership by itself); however, what we seek is zero-knowledge proofs for statements that the verifier cannot decide by itself.

1.3.1 Constructing Zero-Knowledge Proofs for NP-sets

Assuming the existence of commitment schemes,[13] which in turn exist if one-way functions exist [87, 77], *there exist* (auxiliary-input) *zero-knowledge proofs of membership in any NP-set* (i.e., sets having efficiently verifiable static proofs of membership). These zero-knowledge proofs, first constructed by Goldreich, Micali and Wigderson [65] (and depicted in Figure 1.2), have the following important property: the prescribed prover strategy is efficient, provided it is given as auxiliary-input an NP-witness to the assertion (to be proven). That is:

Theorem 1.1 ([65], using [77, 87]) *If one-way functions exist then every set $S \in \mathcal{NP}$ has a zero-knowledge interactive proof. Furthermore, the prescribed prover strategy can be implemented in probabilistic polynomial-time, provided it is given as auxiliary-input an NP-witness for membership of the common input in S.*

Theorem 1.1 makes zero-knowledge a very powerful tool in the design of cryptographic schemes and protocols (see below). We comment that the intractability assumption used in Theorem 1.1 seems essential; see [91].

Analyzing the Protocol of Fig. 1.2. Let us consider a single execution of the main loop (and rely on the fact that zero-knowledge is preserved under sequential composition). Clearly, the prescribed prover is implemented in probabilistic polynomial-time, and always convinces the verifier (provided that it is given a valid 3-coloring of the common input graph). In case the graph is not 3-colorable then, no matter how the prover behaves, the verifier will reject with probability at least $1/|E|$ (because at least one of the edges must be improperly colored by the prover). We stress that the verifier selects uniformly which edge to inspect after the prover has committed to the colors of all vertices. Thus, Fig. 1.2 depicts an interactive proof system for Graph 3-colorability. As can be expected, the zero-knowledge property is the hardest

---

[12] Trivial zero-knowledge proofs for sets in $\mathcal{BPP} \setminus \text{co}\mathcal{RP}$ require modifying the definition of interactive proofs so as to allow a negligible error also in the completeness condition. Alternatively, zero-knowledge proofs for sets in $\mathcal{BPP}$ can be constructed by having the prover send a single message that is distributed almost uniformly (cf. [52]).

[13] Loosely speaking, commitment schemes are digital analogues of non-transparent sealed envelopes. See further discussion in Fig. 1.2.

Commitment schemes are digital analogies of sealed envelopes (or, better, locked boxes). Sending a commitment means sending a string that binds the sender to a unique value without revealing this value to the receiver (as when getting a locked box). Decommitting to the value means sending some auxiliary information that allows the receiver to read the uniquely committed value (as when sending the key to the lock).

Common Input: *A graph $G(V, E)$. Suppose that $V \equiv \{1, ..., n\}$ for $n \stackrel{\text{def}}{=} |V|$.*
Auxiliary Input (to the prover): *A 3-coloring $\phi : V \to \{1, 2, 3\}$.*
The following four steps are repeated $t \cdot |E|$ many times to obtain soundness-error $\exp(-t)$.
Prover's first step (P1): *Select uniformly a permutation π over $\{1, 2, 3\}$. For $i = 1$ to n, send the verifier a commitment to the value $\pi(\phi(i))$.*
Verifier's first step (V1): *Select uniformly an edge $e \in E$ and send it to the prover.*
Prover's second step (P2): *Upon receiving $e = (i, j) \in E$, decommit to the i-th and j-th values sent in Step (P1).*
Verifier's second step (V2): *Check whether or not the decommitted values are different elements of $\{1, 2, 3\}$ and whether or not they match the commitments received in Step (P1).*

Fig. 1.2. The zero-knowledge proof of graph 3-colorability (of [65]). Zero-knowledge proofs for other NP-sets can be obtained using the standard reductions.

to establish, and we will confine ourselves to presenting a simulator (which we hope will convince the reader without a detailed analysis). We start with three simplifying conventions (which are useful in general):

1. Without loss of generality, we may assume that the cheating verifier strategy is implemented by a *deterministic* polynomial-size circuit (or, equivalently, by a polynomial-time algorithm with an auxiliary input). This is justified by fixing any outcome of the verifier's coins, and observing that our (uniform) simulation of the various (residual) deterministic strategies yields a simulation of the original probabilistic strategy.

2. Without loss of generality, it suffices to consider cheating verifiers that (only) output their view of the interaction (i.e., their input, coin tosses, and the messages they received). This is justified by observing that the output of the original verifier can be computed by an algorithm of comparable complexity that is given the verifier's view of the interaction. Thus, it suffices to simulate the view that cheating verifiers have of the real interaction.

3. Without loss of generality, it suffices to construct a "weak simulator" that produces output with some noticeable probability. This is the case because, by repeatedly invoking this weak simulator (polynomially) many

times, we may obtain a simulator that fails to produce an output with negligible probability, whereas the latter yields a simulator that never fails (as required).

The simulator starts by selecting uniformly and independently a random color (i.e., element of $\{1, 2, 3\}$) for each vertex, and feeding the verifier strategy with random commitments to these random colors. Indeed, the simulator feeds the verifier with a distribution that is very different from the distribution that the verifier sees in a real interaction with the prover. However, being computationally restricted the verifier cannot tell these distributions apart (or else we obtain a contradiction to the security of the commitment scheme in use). Now, if the verifier asks to inspect an edge that is properly colored then the simulator performs the proper decommitment action and outputs the transcript of this interaction. Otherwise, the simulator halts proclaiming failure. We claim that failure occurs with probability approximately $1/3$ (or else we obtain a contradiction to the security of the commitment scheme in use). Furthermore, based on the same hypothesis (but via a more complex proof), conditioned on not failing, the output of the simulator is computationally indistinguishable from the verifier's view of the real interaction.

Zero-Knowledge Proofs for Other NP-Sets. By using the standard Karp-reductions to 3-colorability, the protocol of Fig. 1.2 can be used for constructing zero-knowledge proofs for any set in $\mathcal{NP}$. We comment that this is probably the first time that an NP-completeness result was used in a "positive" way (i.e., in order to construct something rather than in order to derive a hardness result). Subsequent positive uses of completeness results have appeared in the context of interactive proofs [85, 100], probabilistically checkable proofs [6, 44, 4, 3], "hardness versus randomness trade-offs" [7], and statistical zero-knowledge [99].

Efficiency Considerations. The protocol in Fig. 1.2 calls for invoking some constant-round protocol for a non-constant number of times. At first glance, it seems that one can derive a constant-round zero-knowledge proof system (of negligible soundness error) by performing these invocations in parallel (rather than sequentially). Unfortunately, as demonstrated in [62], this intuition is not sound. See further discussions in Sects. 1.4 and 9.1. We comment that the number of rounds in a protocol is commonly considered the most important efficiency criterion (or complexity measure), and typically one desires to have it be a constant. We mention that, under standard intractability assumptions (e.g., the intractability of factoring), constant-round zero-knowledge proofs (of negligible soundness error) exist for every set in $\mathcal{NP}$ (cf. [62]).

1.3.2 Using Zero-Knowledge Proofs for NP-sets

We stress two important aspects regarding Theorem 1.1. Firstly, it provides a zero-knowledge proof for every NP-set, and secondly the prescribed prover can be implemented in probabilistic polynomial-time when given an adequate NP-witness. These properties are essential to the wide applicability of zero-knowledge protocols.

A Generic Application. In a typical cryptographic setting, a user referred to as U has a secret and is supposed to take some action depending on its secret. The question is how can other users verify that U indeed took the correct action (as determined by U's secret and the publicly known information). Indeed, if U discloses its secret then anybody can verify that U took the correct action. However, U does not want to reveal its secret. Using zero-knowledge proofs we can satisfy both conflicting requirements (i.e., having other users verify that U took the correct action without violating U's interest in not revealing its secrets). That is, U can prove in zero-knowledge that it took the correct action. Note that U's claim to having taken the correct action is an NP-assertion (since U's legal action is determined as a polynomial-time function of its secret and the public information), and that U has an NP-witness to its validity (i.e., the secret is an NP-witness to the claim that the action fits the public information). Thus, by Theorem 1.1, it is possible for U to efficiently prove the correctness of its action without yielding anything about its secret. Consequently, it is fair to ask U to prove (in zero-knowledge) that it behaves properly, and so to force U to behave properly. Indeed, "forcing proper behavior" is the canonical application of zero-knowledge proofs (see [66, 55]).

This general principle (i.e., "forcing proper behavior" via zero-knowledge proofs), which is based on the fact that zero-knowledge proofs can be constructed for any NP-set, has been utilized in numerous different settings. Indeed, this general principle is the basis for the wide applicability of zero-knowledge protocols in cryptography.

Zero-Knowledge Proofs for All IP. We mention that under the same assumption used in the case of $\mathcal{NP}$, it holds that *any set that has an interactive proof also has a zero-knowledge interactive proof* (cf. [78, 16]).

1.4 Composing Zero-Knowledge Protocols

A natural question regarding zero-knowledge proofs (and arguments) is whether the zero-knowledge condition is preserved under a variety of composition operations. Three types of composition operation were considered in the literature: *sequential composition, parallel composition* and *concurrent composition*. We note that the preservation of zero-knowledge under these forms of composition is not only interesting for its own sake, but rather also sheds light on the preservation of the security of general protocols under these forms of composition.

We stress that when we talk of composition of protocols (or proof systems) we mean that the honest users are supposed to follow the prescribed program (specified in the protocol description) that refers to a single execution. That is, the actions of honest parties in each execution are independent of the messages they received in other executions. The adversary, however, may coordinate the actions it takes in the various executions, and in particular its actions in one execution may depend also on messages it received in other executions.

Let us motivate the asymmetry between the independence of executions assumed of honest parties but not of the adversary. Coordinating actions in different executions is possible but quite difficult. Thus, it is desirable to use composition (as defined above) rather than to use protocols that include inter-execution coordination-actions, which require users to keep track of all executions that they perform. Actually, trying to coordinate honest executions is even more problematic than it seems because one may need to coordinate executions of *different* honest parties (e.g., all employees of a big cooperation or an agency under attack), which in many cases is highly unrealistic. On the other hand, the adversary attacking the system may be willing to go to the extra trouble of coordinating its attack in the various executions of the protocol.

For $T \in \{\texttt{sequential}, \texttt{parallel}, \texttt{concurrent}\}$, we say that a protocol is T-zero-knowledge if it is zero-knowledge under a composition of type T. The definitions of T-zero-knowledge are derived from Definition 1.2.1 by considering appropriate adversaries (i.e., adversarial verifiers); that is, adversaries that can initiate a polynomial number of interactions with the prover, where these interactions are scheduled according to the type T.[14] The corresponding simulator (which, as usual, interacts with nobody) is required to produce an output that is computationally indistinguishable from the output of such a type T adversary.

1.4.1 Sequential Composition

In this case, the protocol is invoked (polynomially) many times, where each invocation follows the termination of the previous one. At the very least, security (e.g., zero-knowledge) should be preserved under sequential composition, or else the applicability of the protocol is highly limited (because one cannot safely use it more than once).

Referring to Definition 1.2.1, we mention that whereas the "simplified" version (i.e., without auxiliary inputs) is not closed under sequential composition (cf. [63]), the actual version (i.e., with auxiliary inputs) is closed under sequential composition (cf. [67]). We comment that the same phenomena arises when trying to use a zero-knowledge proof as a subprotocol inside larger

---

[14] Without loss of generality, we may assume that the adversary never violates the scheduling condition; it may instead send an illegal message at the latest possible adequate time. Furthermore, without loss of generality, we may assume that all the adversary's messages are delivered at the latest possible adequate time.

protocols. Indeed, it is for these reasons that the augmentation of the "most basic" definition by auxiliary inputs was adopted in all subsequent works.[15]

Bottom-Line. Every protocol that is zero-knowledge (under Definition 1.2.1) is sequential-zero-knowledge.

1.4.2 Parallel Composition

In this case, (polynomially) many instances of the protocol are invoked at the same time and proceed at the same pace. That is, we assume a synchronous model of communication, and consider (polynomially) many executions that are totally synchronized so that the i-th message in all instances is sent exactly (or approximately) at the same time. (Natural variants on this model are discussed below as well as at the end of Sect. 1.4.3.)

It turns out that, in general, zero-knowledge is not closed under parallel composition. A simple counter-example (to the "parallel composition conjecture") is depicted in Fig 1.3. This counter-example, which is adapted from [63], consists of a simple protocol that is zero-knowledge (in a strong sense), but is not closed under parallel composition (not even in a very weak sense).

We comment that, in the 1980s, the study of parallel composition was interpreted mainly in the context of *round-efficient error reduction* (cf. [47, 63]); that is, the construction of full-fledge zero-knowledge proofs (of negligible soundness error) by composing (in parallel) a basic zero-knowledge protocol of high (but bounded away from 1) soundness error. Since alternative ways of constructing constant-round zero-knowledge proofs (and arguments) were found (cf. [62, 48, 25]), interest in parallel composition (of zero-knowledge protocols) has died. In retrospect, this was a conceptual mistake, because parallel composition (and mild extensions of this notion) capture the preservation of security in a fully synchronous (or almost-fully synchronous) communication network. We note that the almost-fully synchronous communication model is quite realistic in many settings, although it is certainly preferable not to assume even weak synchronism.

Although, in general, zero-knowledge is not closed under parallel composition, under standard intractability assumptions (e.g., the intractability of factoring), there exist zero-knowledge protocols for $\mathcal{NP}$ that are closed under parallel composition. Furthermore, these protocols have a constant number of rounds (cf. [59] for proofs and [39] for arguments).[16] Both results extend also

---

[15] Interestingly, the preliminary version of Goldwasser, Micali and Rackoff's work [72] used the "most basic" definition, whereas the final version of this work used the augmented definition. In some works, the "most basic" definition is used for simplicity, but typically one actually needs and means the augmented definition.

[16] In case of parallel-zero-knowledge *proofs*, there is no need to specify the soundness error because it can always be reduced via parallel composition. As mentioned above, this is not the case with respect to arguments, which were therefore defined to have negligible soundness error.

Consider a party P holding a random (or rather pseudorandom) function f: $\{0,1\}^{2n} \to \{0,1\}^n$, and willing to participate in the following protocol (with respect to security parameter n). The other party, called A for adversary, is supposed to send P a binary value $v \in \{1,2\}$ specifying which of the following cases to execute:

For $v = 1$: Party P uniformly selects $\alpha \in \{0,1\}^n$, and sends it to A, which is supposed to reply with a pair of n-bit long strings, denoted (β,γ). Party P checks whether or not $f(\alpha\beta) = \gamma$. In case equality holds, P sends A some secret information.

For $v = 2$: Party A is supposed to uniformly select $\alpha \in \{0,1\}^n$, and sends it to P, which selects uniformly $\beta \in \{0,1\}^n$, and replies with the pair $(\beta, f(\alpha\beta))$.

Observe that P's strategy is zero-knowledge (even w.r.t. auxiliary-inputs as defined in Definition 3.3.1): Intuitively, if the adversary A chooses the case $v = 1$, then it is infeasible for A to guess a passing pair (β,γ) with respect to the random α selected by P. Thus, except with negligible probability (when it may get secret information), A does not obtain anything from the interaction. On the other hand, if the adversary A chooses the case $v = 2$, then it obtains a pair that is indistinguishable from a uniformly selected pair of n-bit long strings (because β is selected uniformly by P, and for any α the value $f(\alpha\beta)$ looks random to A).

In contrast, if the adversary A can conduct two concurrent[a] executions with P, then it may learn the desired secret information: In one session, A sends $v = 1$ while in the other it sends $v = 2$. Upon receiving P's message, denoted α, in the first session, A sends α as its own message in the second session, obtaining a pair $(\beta, f(\alpha\beta))$ from P's execution of the second session. Now, A sends the pair $(\beta, f(\alpha\beta))$ to the first session of P, this pair passes the check, and so A obtains the desired secret.

---

[a]Dummy messages may be added (in both cases) in order to make the above scheduling fit the perfectly parallel case.

Fig. 1.3. A counter-example (adapted from [62]) to the parallel repetition conjecture for zero-knowledge protocols.

to concurrent composition in a synchronous communication model, where the extension is in allowing protocol invocations to start at different (synchronous) times (and in particular executions may overlap but not run simultaneously).

We comment that parallel composition is problematic also in the context of reducing the soundness error of arguments (cf. [15]), but our focus here is on the zero-knowledge aspect of protocols regardless of whether they are proofs, arguments or neither.

Bottom-Line. Under standard intractability assumptions, every NP-set has a constant-round parallel-zero-knowledge proof.

1.4.3 Concurrent Composition (With and Without Timing)

Concurrent composition generalizes both sequential and parallel composition. Here (polynomially) many instances of the protocol are invoked at arbitrary times and proceed at arbitrary pace. That is, we assume an asynchronous (rather than synchronous) model of communication.

In the 1990s, when extensive two-party (and multiparty) computations became a reality (rather than a vision), it became clear that it is (at least) desirable that cryptographic protocols maintain their security under concurrent composition (cf. [38]). In the context of zero-knowledge, concurrent composition was first considered by Dwork, Naor and Sahai [39]. Actually, two models of concurrent composition were considered in the literature, depending on the underlying model of communication (i.e., a *purely asynchronous model* and an *asynchronous model with timing*). Both models cover sequential and parallel composition as special cases.

Concurrent Composition in the Pure Asynchronous Model. Here we refer to the standard model of asynchronous communication. In comparison to the timing model, the pure asynchronous model is a simpler model and using it requires no assumptions about the underlying communication channels. However, it seems harder to construct concurrent zero-knowledge protocols for this model. In particular, for a while it was not known whether concurrent zero-knowledge proofs for $\mathcal{NP}$ exist at all (in this model). Under standard intractability assumptions (e.g., the intractability of factoring), this question was affirmatively resolved by Richardson and Kilian [94]. Following their work, research has focused on determining the round-complexity of concurrent zero-knowledge proofs for $\mathcal{NP}$. This question is still open, and the current state of the art regarding it is as follows:

- Under standard intractability assumptions, every language in $\mathcal{NP}$ has a concurrent zero-knowledge proof with *almost-logarithmically* many rounds (cf. [93], building upon [82], which in turn builds over [94]). Furthermore, the zero-knowledge property can be demonstrated using a black-box simulator (see definition in Sects. 1.2.3 and 9.1). This result is presented in Chap. 5.
- Black-box simulators cannot demonstrate the concurrent zero-knowledge property of non-trivial proofs (or arguments) having significantly less than logarithmically many rounds (cf. Canetti et al. [30]).[17] This result is presented in Chap. 7.
- Recently, Barak [8] demonstrated that the "black-box simulation barrier" can be bypassed. With respect to concurrent zero-knowledge he only obtains partial results: constant-round zero-knowledge arguments (rather

---

[17] By *non-trivial* proof systems we mean ones for languages outside $\mathcal{BPP}$, whereas by *significantly less than logarithmic* we mean any function $f : N \rightarrow N$ satisfying $f(n) = o(\log n / \log \log n)$. In contrast, by *almost-logarithmic* we mean any function f satisfying $f(n) = \omega(\log n)$.

than proofs) for $\mathcal{NP}$ that maintain security as long as an a priori bounded (polynomial) number of executions take place concurrently. (The length of the messages in his protocol grows linearly with this a priori bound.)

Thus, it is currently unknown whether or not *constant-round* protocols for $\mathcal{NP}$ may be concurrent zero-knowledge (in the pure asynchronous model).

We comment that the result of Canetti et al. [30] was proven at a time when it was (falsely) believed that limitations concerning "black-box simulators" are inherent to zero-knowledge itself. This belief turned out to be wrong; see Sect. 9.1 for further discussion. Still black-box simulators are the natural way to demonstrate the zero-knowledge feature of protocols, and it is still important to determine the limits of "black-box" techniques. One reason is that asserting that some problem cannot be solved using "black-box" techniques means that, even in case it is solvable (by "non-black-box" techniques), this problem is inherently harder than others that can be solved using "black-box" techniques. Indeed, solutions that rely on "non-black-box" techniques tend to be more complex not only from a conceptual perspective but also in terms of the time and communication complexities of the resulting protocol. Furthermore, the latter tend to provide a lower level of security (e.g., in terms of knowledge tightness, as discussed in Sect. 1.2.3).

Concurrent Composition Under the Timing Model. A model of naturally-limited asynchronousness (which certainly covers the case of parallel composition) was introduced by Dwork, Naor and Sahai [39]. Essentially, they assume that each party holds a local clock such that the relative clock rates are bounded by an a priori known constant, and consider protocols that employ time-driven operations (i.e., `time-out` in-coming messages and `delay` outgoing messages). The benefit of the timing model is that it is known to construct concurrent zero-knowledge protocols in it. Specifically, using standard intractability assumptions, *constant-round* arguments and proofs that are concurrent zero-knowledge under the timing model do exist (cf. [39] and [59], respectively). The disadvantages of the timing model are discussed next.

The timing model consists of the *assumption* that talking about the actual timing of events is meaningful (at least in a weak sense) and of the *introduction of time-driven operations*. The timing assumption amounts to postulating that each party holds a local clock and knows a global bound, denoted $\rho \geq 1$, on the relative rates of the local clocks.[18] Furthermore, it is postulated that the parties know a (pessimistic) bound, denoted Δ, on the message delivery time (which also includes the local computation and handling times). In our opinion, these timing assumptions are most reasonable, and are unlikely to restrict the scope of applications for which concurrent zero-knowledge is relevant. We are more concerned about the effect of the time-driven operations introduced in the timing model. Recall that these operations are the

---

[18] The rate should be computed with respect to reasonable intervals of time; for example, for Δ as defined below, one may assume that a time period of Δ units is measured as Δ' units of time on the local clock, where $\Delta/\rho \leq \Delta' \leq \rho\Delta$.

`time-out` of in-coming messages and the `delay` of out-going messages. Furthermore, typically the delay period is at least as long as the time-out period, which in turn is at least Δ (i.e., the time-out period must be at least as long as the pessimistic bound on message-delivery time as so not to disrupt the proper operation of the protocol). This means that the use of these time-driven operations yields a slowing down of the execution of the protocol (i.e., running it at the rate of the pessimistic message-delivery time rather than at the rate of the actual message-delivery time, which is typically much faster). Still, in the absence of more appealing alternatives (i.e., a constant-round concurrent zero-knowledge protocol for the pure asynchronous model), the use of the timing model may be considered reasonable. (We comment that other alternatives to the timing-model include various set-up assumptions; cf. [28, 34].)

Back to Parallel Composition. Given our opinion about the timing model, it is not surprising that we consider the problem of parallel composition almost as important as the problem of concurrent composition in the timing model. Firstly, it is quite reasonable to assume that the parties' local clocks have approximately the same rate, and that drifting is corrected by occasional clock synchronization. Thus, it is reasonable to assume that the parties have approximately-good estimate of some global time. Furthermore, the global time may be partitioned into phases, each consisting of a constant number of rounds, so that each party wishing to execute the protocol just delays its invocation to the beginning of the next phase. Thus, concurrent execution of (constant-round) protocols in this setting amounts to a sequence of (time-disjoint) almost-parallel executions of the protocol. Consequently, proving that the protocol is parallel zero-knowledge suffices for concurrent composition in this setting.

Relation to Resettable Zero-Knowledge. Going to the other extreme, we mention that there exists a natural model of zero-knowledge that is even stronger than concurrent zero-knowledge (even in the pure asynchronous model). Specifically, "resettable zero-knowledge" as defined in Sect. 9.6, implies concurrent zero-knowledge.

2

Introduction to Concurrent Zero-Knowledge

The past two and a half decades have witnessed unprecedented progress in the field of cryptography. During these years, many cryptographic tasks have been subject to rigorous treatment and numerous constructions realizing these tasks have been proposed. By now, the scope of cryptographic constructions ranges from simple schemes that realize "atomic" tasks such as authentication, identification, encryption and digital signatures, to fairly complex protocols that realize "high-level" tasks such as general secure two-party computation (the latter being so general that it captures almost any conceivable cryptographic task in which two mutually distrustful parties interact).

The original setting in which cryptographic protocols were investigated consisted of a single execution of the protocol at a time (this is the so-called *stand-alone* setting). A more realistic setting, especially in the era of the Internet, is one that allows the *concurrent* execution of protocols. In the concurrent setting many protocols are executed at the same time, involving multiple parties that may be talking with the same (or many) other parties simultaneously. The concurrent setting presents the new risk of a coordinated attack in which an adversary controls many parties, interleaving the executions of the protocols while trying to extract knowledge based on the existence of multiple concurrent executions. It would be most desirable to have cryptographic protocols retain their security properties even when executed concurrently. This would enable the realization of cryptographic tasks in a way that preserves security in a setting that is closer to the "real world".

Unfortunately, security of a specific protocol in the stand-alone setting does not necessarily imply its security in the (more demanding) concurrent setting. It is thus of great relevance to examine whether the original feasibility results for cryptographic protocols still hold when many copies of the protocol are executed concurrently.

2.1 Zero-Knowledge Proof Systems

In the course of developing tools for the design of complex cryptographic tasks, many innovative notions have emerged. One of the most basic (and important) examples for such notions is the one of *zero-knowledge interactive proofs*. Interactive proofs, introduced by Goldwasser, Micali and Rackoff [72], are efficient protocols that enable one party, known as the *prover*, to convince another party, known as the *verifier*, of the validity of an assertion. In the process of proving the assertion, the prover and the verifier exchange messages for a predetermined number of rounds. Throughout the interaction, both prover and verifier may employ probabilistic strategies and toss coins in order to determine their next message. At the end of the process, the verifier decides whether to accept or reject the proof based on his view of the interaction (as well as on his coin-tosses).

The basic requirement is that whenever the assertion is true, the prover always convinces the verifier (this is called the *completeness* condition), whereas if the assertion is false, then no matter what the prover does, the verifier is convinced with very small probability, where the probability is taken over the verifier's coin-tosses (this is called the *soundness* condition).

An interactive proof is said to be *zero-knowledge* ($\mathcal{ZK}$) if it yields nothing beyond the validity of the assertion being proved. This is formalized by requiring that the view of every probabilistic polynomial-time adversary interacting with the prover can be simulated by a probabilistic polynomial-time machine (a.k.a. the *simulator*). The idea behind this definition is that whatever an adversary verifier might have learned from interacting with the prover, he could have actually learned by himself (by running the simulator).

The concept of zero-knowledge was originally introduced by Goldwasser, Micali and Rackoff [72]. The generality of $\mathcal{ZK}$ has been demonstrated by Goldreich, Micali and Wigderson [65], who showed that every language in $\mathcal{NP}$ can be proved in $\mathcal{ZK}$, provided that one-way functions exist (cf. Naor [87], Håstad et al. [77]). Since then, $\mathcal{ZK}$ proof systems have turned out to be an extremely useful tool in the realization of increasingly many cryptographic tasks.

2.1.1 Concurrent Composition of $\mathcal{ZK}$

The wide applicability of $\mathcal{ZK}$ proofs makes them a very useful "test case" for examining the behavior of cryptographic protocols in the concurrent setting. On the one hand, many of the difficulties that arise in the concurrent setting already appear in the (relatively basic) case of $\mathcal{ZK}$. On the other hand, positive solutions for the case of $\mathcal{ZK}$ may translate to positive solutions for much more complex cryptographic tasks (that use $\mathcal{ZK}$ protocols as a subroutine).

The scenario that is typically considered in the context of $\mathcal{ZK}$ involves a single (or many) honest provers that are running many concurrent executions of the same $\mathcal{ZK}$ protocol. The honest prover is trying to protect itself from a malicious adversary that controls a subset (or all) of the verifiers it is interacting with. Since it seems unrealistic (and certainly undesirable) for honest provers to coordinate their actions so that security is preserved, one must assume that in each instance of the protocol the prover acts independently.

A $\mathcal{ZK}$ protocol is said to be *concurrent zero-knowledge* ($c\mathcal{ZK}$) if it remains zero-knowledge in the above scenario. Recall that in order to demonstrate the $\mathcal{ZK}$ property of a protocol it is required to demonstrate that the view of every probabilistic polynomial-time adversary interacting with the prover can be simulated in probabilistic polynomial-time. In the concurrent setting, the verifiers' view may include multiple sessions running at the same time. Furthermore, the verifiers may have control over the scheduling of the messages in these sessions (i.e., the order in which the interleaved execution of these sessions should be conducted). As a consequence, the simulator's task becomes considerably more complicated.

2.1.2 On the Feasibility of $c\mathcal{ZK}$

Concurrent composition of $\mathcal{ZK}$ protocols was first mentioned by Feige [42]. A more extensive treatment was given by Dwork, Naor and Sahai [39], who also argued that the task of proving the $\mathcal{ZK}$ property of a protocol in the concurrent setting might encounter technical difficulties if approached in a straightforward manner. The intuition from [39] was transformed into an impossibility result by Kilian, Petrank and Rackoff [83], who proved that "standard" (i.e., black-box simulation) techniques would fail in demonstrating the $c\mathcal{ZK}$ property of four-message protocols. This ruled out a large class of candidate protocols (which included most known constant-round $\mathcal{ZK}$ protocols).

For a while, it was not even clear whether $c\mathcal{ZK}$ protocols exist. The feasibility of $c\mathcal{ZK}$ was first established by Richardson and Kilian [94], who showed that every $\mathcal{NP}$-statement can be proved in $c\mathcal{ZK}$. This was done by introducing a new class of protocols, and by showing how to simulate the verifiers' view in multiple concurrent executions of these protocols.

2.1.3 The Round-Complexity of $c\mathcal{ZK}$

A bothersome property of the Richardson–Kilian solution was that the number of messages in their proposed protocols was required to grow with the number of concurrent executions (i.e., it had high *round-complexity*). This is in contrast to the original (stand-alone) $\mathcal{ZK}$ protocols, which only required the exchange of a constant number of messages. It thus became natural to ask whether the high number of messages exchanged in the Richardson–Kilian protocol was "inherent" to the notion of $c\mathcal{ZK}$, or whether it was possible to come up with protocols that allowed for the exchange of fewer messages. Consequently, the attention of research in the area has shifted towards the study of the *round-complexity* of $c\mathcal{ZK}$.

In the context of $c\mathcal{ZK}$, the round-complexity of a protocol is measured as a function of some predetermined "security" parameter $n \in N$. The requirement is that the protocol will remain secure as long as the number of concurrent executions is bounded by some polynomial in n (we stress that the protocol is constructed *before* the polynomial bound is determined). A protocol is regarded as having "high" round complexity if the number of messages exchanged in this protocol depends on the value of n. This should be contrasted to constant-round protocols in which the number of messages is *not* required to increase as n grows.

The intensive focus on the round-complexity of $c\mathcal{ZK}$ has resulted in an almost full understanding of the round-complexity of *black-box* $c\mathcal{ZK}$ protocols. That is, protocols for which the $c\mathcal{ZK}$ property is established via black-box simulation. (Loosely speaking, a black-box simulator is a simulator that has only black-box access to the adversary verifier.) The results obtained can be summarized as follows:

- Assuming that statistically hiding commitments exist, every language in $\mathcal{NP}$ has a $c\mathcal{ZK}$ proof system with $O(\alpha(n) \cdot \log n)$ rounds of interaction, where $\alpha(n)$ is any super-constant function. Moreover, the $c\mathcal{ZK}$ property of this proof system is proved using black-box simulation [93].
- Any $c\mathcal{ZK}$ proof system for a language outside $\mathcal{BPP}$, whose $c\mathcal{ZK}$ property is proved using black-box simulation, requires $\Omega(\log n / \log \log n)$ rounds of interaction [30].

The above results are the main foci of this book. The first result is presented in Chapter 5, whereas the second result is presented in Chapter 7.

The rest of the introduction is devoted to the presentation of the main technical difficulties that are encountered when trying to prove the $c\mathcal{ZK}$ property of a protocol using a black-box simulator. It also contains a more detailed account of the developments that have led to the full characterization of the round-complexity of black-box $c\mathcal{ZK}$, as well as of subsequent developments.

2.2 From Repetition to Composition

The notion of protocol composition should not be confused with that of protocol *repetition*. Whereas in the case of composition multiple executions of the protocol are assumed to be conducted *independently*, in the case of repetition the multiple executions are "linked" together. The assumed independence of the executions is what makes protocol composition suitable for modelling the behavior of interactive protocols in the "real world". Protocol repetition, on the other hand, is predominantly used in the context of error reduction (but other uses are conceivable as well).

The difference between the above two notions is best understood through the presentation of the "typical" construction of a $\mathcal{ZK}$ protocol for $\mathcal{NP}$. The presentation of such a construction also facilitates the understanding of the main technical difficulties that are encountered when trying to establish the $c\mathcal{ZK}$ property of a protocol via black-box simulation.

2.2.1 A "Typical" $\mathcal{ZK}$ Protocol for $\mathcal{NP}$

A central tool in all known constructions of $\mathcal{ZK}$ protocols for $\mathcal{NP}$ is the one of *commitment schemes* [87]. Commitment schemes are the "digital" analog of sealed envelopes. They are used to enable a party, known as the *sender*, to commit itself to a value while keeping it secret from the *receiver* (this property is called *hiding*). Furthermore, the commitment is *binding* in the sense that in a later stage, when the commitment is opened, it is guaranteed that the "opening" can yield only a single value determined in the committing phase.

For our purposes, it will be convenient to think of commitments as a non-interactive process in which the sender sends a single message to the receiver (somewhat analogously to an encryption scheme). The sender can then open the commitment by sending an additional message that reveals the value committed to.

Constructing a $\mathcal{ZK}$ Protocol for $\mathcal{NP}$. At a high-level, the typical $\mathcal{ZK}$ protocol for $\mathcal{NP}$ is constructed by combining many atomic $\mathcal{ZK}$ protocols that proceed as follows.[1] Given a specific $\mathcal{NP}$ assertion, A, and a "proof" for the validity of this assertion (typically, an $\mathcal{NP}$-witness w for the validity of A), the prover uses his coin-tosses to generate two (related) messages M_0 and M_1 that depend on A and w. Letting P denote the prover and V denote the verifier, the protocol proceeds as follows:

> $P \rightarrow V$: Commit to M_0 and M_1.
> $V \rightarrow P$: Send a random $\sigma \in \{0,1\}$.
> $P \rightarrow V$: Reveal M_σ.

The verifier accepts if and only if the revealed message M_σ is "valid" (i.e., if it passes a prespecfied validity inspection that is related to the commonly known assertion A). To insure that the resulting protocol is indeed an interactive proof, it is required that M_0, M_1 satisfy the following properties:

- If A is true, it is possible to make sure that both M_0 and M_1 are "valid".
- If A is false, then no matter what P does, either M_0 or M_1 is "invalid".

Thus if A is true then V always accepts, whereas if A is false then V accepts with probability at most $1/2$. (Here we rely on the binding property of the commitment used by P.) To insure that the protocol is also $\mathcal{ZK}$, the following property is required:

- Given the value of σ, it is always possible to make sure that M_σ is "valid".

---

[1]The type of protocols considered here resemble Blum's protocol for Hamiltonicity [18] (see Construction 4.1.1 on page 50), and not the protocol by Goldreich, Micali and Wigderson for graph 3-coloring [65].

Indeed, the soundness property of the protocol heavily relies on the fact that P does not know the value of σ before the protocol starts (and so V can always "surprise" P by choosing σ at random). Otherwise, P (knowing σ in advance) would have always been able to make V accept in the protocol.

However, knowing σ in advance is the key for proving the $\mathcal{ZK}$ property of the protocol. Consider an adversary verifier V^* that is trying to extract knowledge from the interaction (by possibly deviating from the honest verifier strategy). All that has to be done in order to simulate the view of V^* is to let the simulator "guess" the value of σ in advance and generate M_0, M_1 so that M_σ is valid. The simulator can then "feed" V^* with a commitment to M_0, M_1 and obtain the value of some σ' that depends on this commitment. If indeed $\sigma' = \sigma$ then the simulator has succeeded in his task and will output a "valid" transcript in which V^* accepts. The hiding property of the commitment guarantees us that, no matter what the strategy applied by V^*, the probability that $\sigma' = \sigma$ is $1/2$. In particular, after two attempts the simulator is expected to succeed in its task. Notice that the resulting simulator is "black-box" in the sense that the only way in which V^*'s strategy is used is through the examination of its input/output behavior.

Reducing the Error via Repetition. To make the above protocol useful, however, one must make sure that whenever A is false, V accepts only with small probability (rather than $1/2$). To achieve this, the atomic protocol is repeated many (say, k) times independently. V accepts if and only if it has accepted in all k repetitions. The probability of having V accept a false statement is now reduced to $1/2^k$ (by the independence of the repetitions).

The straightforward way to conduct the repetitions would be to perform the atomic protocols *sequentially* (i.e., one protocol after the other, see Fig. 2.1a). This approach suffers from the drawback that the resulting protocol has a fairly high round-complexity. To overcome this problem, the repetitions may be conducted in *parallel* (i.e., the jth message of the atomic protocol is sent together in all the k repetitions, see Fig. 2.1b).

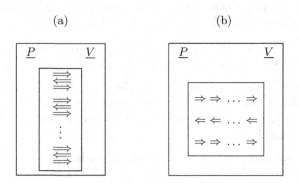

Fig. 2.1. Sequential and parallel repetition.

Unfortunately, repeating the protocol many times in parallel brings up the following difficulty. Whereas in the case of a single execution, the probability that the $\mathcal{ZK}$ simulator "guesses" the value of σ correctly is at least $1/2$, the probability that he does so *simultaneously* for all k repetitions is $1/2^k$. For large k, this probability will be very small and might cause the simulator to run for too long. Thus, it is not clear that the $\mathcal{ZK}$ property of the protocol is preserved.

The solution to this problem is to let the verifier commit to all his "challenges" in advance. Specifically, consider the following protocol [62]:

$V \to P$ (v1): Commit to random $\sigma_1, \ldots, \sigma_k \in \{0, 1\}$.
$P \to V$ (p1): Commit to $(M_0^1, M_1^1), (M_0^2, M_1^2), \ldots, (M_0^k, M_1^k)$.
$V \to P$ (v2): Reveal $\sigma_1, \ldots, \sigma_k$.
$P \to V$ (p2): Reveal $M_{\sigma_1}^1, M_{\sigma_2}^2, \ldots, M_{\sigma_k}^k$.

The verifier accepts if and only if for all j, the message M_σ^j is "valid". By the hiding property of the commitment used in (v1), we are guaranteed that when sending (p1), the prover P has "no idea" about the values of $\sigma_1, \ldots, \sigma_k$, and so the soundness of the original protocol is preserved.

To see that the resulting protocol is $\mathcal{ZK}$, consider the following simulation technique. Start by obtaining the (v1) message from the verifier V^*. Then, playing the role of the prover, generate a sequence of k pairs $\{M_0^j, M_1^j\}_{j=1}^k$ each containing "garbage" (i.e., not necssarily "valid"). Feed V^* with the commitments to these pairs and obtain the values of $\sigma_1, \ldots, \sigma_k$. Once these values are obtained, "rewind" the interaction to Step (p1) and recompute the values of $\{M_0^j, M_1^j\}_{j=1}^k$ so that for all j, the value of $M_{\sigma_j}^j$ is "valid". Since we have not rewound past (v1) (and thus did not modify its value), and since the commitment used in (v1) is binding, we are guaranteed that when reaching (v2) for the second time, the revealed values of $\sigma_1, \ldots, \sigma_k$ are identical to the ones revealed in the first time (v2) was reached (here we also use the fact that the commitment used in (p1) is hiding and so V^* cannot distinguish a commitment to "garbage" from a commitment to "valid" $M_{\sigma_j}^j$'s). Using the values of the $M_{\sigma_j}^j$'s, the simulator can thus output a "valid" transcript in which V^* accepts, as required.

But what if V^* refuses to reveal some (or all) of the committed values in Step (v2)? (Recall that V^* may behave in any adversarial manner.) In such a case, the simulator does not obtain all of the values of $\sigma_1, \ldots, \sigma_k$ and will supposedly fail in its task. Luckily, if V^* deviates from his prescribed strategy and does not reveal some σ_j value in (v2), then the prover in the protocol is not obligated to continue in the interaction (in particular, it aborts all k repetitions altogether). Using this fact, it is then possible to show (with some compications) that the simulator can eventually succeed in obtaining all of the values $\sigma_1, \ldots, \sigma_k$ and thus complete its task (cf. [62]).

2.2.2 Composition of $\mathcal{ZK}$ Protocols

Protocol composition involves a single (or many) honest provers that are running many executions (sessions) of the same $\mathcal{ZK}$ protocol. Similarly to the case of protocol repetition, in the case of protocol composition the honest prover is trying to protect itself from a malicious adversary V^* that controls a subset (or all) of the verifiers it is interacting with. However, unlike the case of protocol repetition, the honest prover is not assumed to coordinate its actions between different executions. As a consequence, a verifier in one execution of the protocol is not held accountable for the "misbehavior" of a verifier in another execution. Thus, even if the verifier refuses to reveal the committed values in some of the executions, the prover is still obligated to continue the interaction in the other executions. In particular, techniques used for analyzing protocol repetition do not apply in the case of composition.

As in the case of repetition, composition of protocols is classified according to the scheduling of messages amongst the various executions. The schedules considered are sequential, parallel and concurrent.

Sequential and Parallel Composition. The most "basic" case of protocol composition is the one of sequential composition (Fig. 2.2a). This case has been treated in full generality by Goldreich and Oren [67], who showed that *any* protocol that is (auxiliary input) $\mathcal{ZK}$ in a single execution will remain $\mathcal{ZK}$ under sequential composition. A more complicated case is the one of parallel composition (Fig. 2.2b). Here, a composition theorem is not known (and in fact does hold in general [63, 42]). Still, as recently shown by Goldreich [59], there exists a *specific $\mathcal{ZK}$ protocol* for $\mathcal{NP}$ (specifically, the protocol of [62]) that remains $\mathcal{ZK}$ under parallel composition.

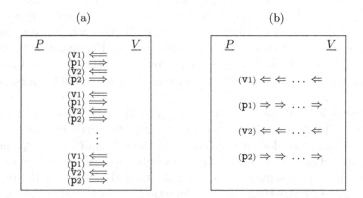

Fig. 2.2. Sequential and parallel composition of a four-round protocol.

Concurrent Composition. A more general notion of protocol composition is the one of *concurrent* composition. Unlike the case of sequential and parallel composition (in which the scheduling of messages is defined in advance), the scheduling of messages is controlled by the adversary verifier, who determines the order in which the interleaved execution of the various sessions should be conducted. As first observed by Dwork, Naor and Sahai [39], letting V^* control the scheduling and coordinate between sessions introduces technical difficulties that black-box simulation does not seem to handle very well. In light of these difficulties, it is not a priori clear that concurrent zero-knowledge is *at all* achievable.

2.3 A Second Look at the Feasibility of $c\mathcal{ZK}$

2.3.1 A Troublesome Scheduling

The difficulties arising in the setting of concurrent zero-knowledge were first observed when considering the scheduling of messages for a four-round protocol (originally suggested by Dwork, Naor and Sahai in [39]), shown in fig. 2.3.

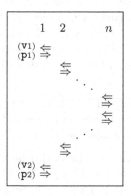

Fig. 2.3. A concurrent schedule for n sessions of a four-round protocol.

In this scheduling, the prover starts by sending the first two messages (i.e., (p1), (v1)) in all n sessions, only then proceeding to send the last two messages (i.e., (p2), (v2)) in the reverse order of sessions (i.e., starting at the nth session and ending at the first). Suppose now that an adversary verifier V^* is sending messages according to the above schedule while applying the following "coordinated" strategy for all n sessions:

- V^* produces the various verifier messages according to the honest verifier strategy.
- The verifier coin-tosses used in a specific session depend on previous messages in the schedule.[2]

---

[2] For example, V^* could obtain random coins by applying a $poly(n)$-wise independent hash function (or even a pseudorandom function) to the previous messages in the schedule. This would imply that the modification of even one of the previous messages yields "fresh" randomness for the current session.

- Whenever V^* is not convinced in one session, he aborts the whole interaction altogether.[3]

Since the view of V^* consists of the concurrent interaction in all n sessions
in the schedule and since in each session V^* sends messages according to the
honest verifier strategy, the simulator's task is to produce a transcript that
contains n sessions in which V^* accepts (notice that the honest prover P
would never cause V^* to reject, and so the simulator must do so as well).

The straightforward approach for simulation would be to use the four-
round protocol described above and let the simulator "rewind" the interaction with V^* in each session (just as it has done in the "stand-alone" case).
However, by doing so the following problem is encountered. In order to succeed in the rewinding of the ith session, the simulator must obtain the (v2)
message in this session. Since by the above scheduling, this message occurs
after the end of session i' for all $i' > i$, the simulator has to make V^* accept
(and thus rewind) in all sessions $i' > i$ (otherwise, V^* would have aborted
the interaction at the moment session i' ends, and the simulator would never
obtain (v2) in session i). Moreover, whenever the simulator rewinds session i,
it modifies the value of (p1) in this session. This causes the randomness of all
subsequent sessions (and so the verifier's "challenges" in sessions $i' > i$) to be
modified. In particular, the simulation work done for all sessions $i' > i$ is lost.
To conclude:

- The simulator must rewind all n sessions.
- To rewind session i, the simulator must rewind session i' for all $i' > i$.
- By rewinding session i, the work invested in sessions $i' > i$ is lost.

Denoting by $W(m)$ the amount of work that the simulator invests in m
sessions, we obtain the recursion $W(m) \geq 2 \cdot W(m-1)$, which solves to
$W(n) \geq 2^n$ (because $W(1) = 2$). This is clearly a too high running time for
the simulator to afford.

Transforming the Intuition into a Lower Bound: The above example
gives intuition to the difficulties that a "rewinding" simulator will encounter
in the concurrent setting. At first glance it may seem that this still leaves
open the possibility that an alternative black-box simulation technique might
be found. Unfortunately, the technique of rewinding the interaction with V^*
turns out to be inherent to black-box simulation. (Intuitively, this follows
from the fact that rewinding is the only advantage that a black-box simulator
might have over the honest prover.) Using this fact, and building on the work
of Goldreich and Krawczyk [63], Kilian, Petrank and Rackoff [83] have been
able to transform the above argument into an impossibility result, and to
prove that for every language outside $\mathcal{BPP}$ there is no four-round protocol
whose concurrent execution is simulatable in polynomial-time using black-
box simulation. This impossibility result has been extended to seven rounds

---

[3]This behavior deviates from the honest verifier strategy, where the decision on
whether to reject or not is taken for each session independently of other sessions.

by Rosen [97], and eventually raised to $\Omega(\log n / \log \log n)$ rounds by Canetti, Kilian, Petrank and Rosen [30].

The latter result is presented in Chap. 7 of this book. It is obtained by employing a new scheduling of messages (more sophisticated than the one described in Fig. 2.3) and by having the adversary verifier V^* occasionally *abort* sessions (i.e., refuse to continue the interaction) depending on the history of the interaction thus far.

2.3.2 The Richardson–Kilian Protocol and Its Analysis

For a while, it was not even clear whether there exist $c\mathcal{ZK}$ protocols for languages outside of $\mathcal{BPP}$. Several works have (successfully) attempted to overcome the above difficulties by augmenting the communication model with the so-called *timing assumption* [39, 41] or, alternatively, by using various set-up assumptions (such as various *public-key models* [28, 34]). However, it remained open whether "non-trivial" $c\mathcal{ZK}$ is possible in a model where no set-up assumptions are made (a.k.a. the *plain model*).

The feasibility of $c\mathcal{ZK}$ in the plain model has been first established by Richardson and Kilian (RK) [94], who exhibited a family of $c\mathcal{ZK}$ protocols (parameterized by the number of rounds) for all languages in $\mathcal{NP}$. The idea underlying the RK protocol is to transform a given constant-round $\mathcal{ZK}$ protocol into $c\mathcal{ZK}$ by adding a k-round "preamble" to it. This preamble (i.e., messages $(V0), (P1), (V1), \ldots, (Pj), (Vj)$) is completely independent of the common input and its sole purpose is to enable a successful simulation in the concurrent setting. Every round in the preamble (i.e., every $(Pj), (Vj)$ pair) is viewed as a "rewinding opportunity". Having "successfully rewound" even one of the rounds in the preamble is sufficient in order to cheat arbitrarily in the actual proof (i.e., messages $(p1), (v1), (v2)$) and thus complete the simulation. The transformation is made possible through the usage of the well-known Feige–Shamir paradigm [47, 48] (frequently referred to as the Feige–Lapidot–Shamir (FLS) paradigm [46]).

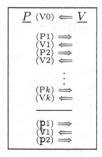

Fig. 2.4. The structure of the Richardson–Kilian k-round protocol.

The RK transformation reduces the problem of proving that the resulting protocol is $c\mathcal{ZK}$ to coming up with a simulator that, with overwhelming probability, manages to successfully rewind every session in the concurrent schedule (no matter what the strategy applied by the verifier). Clearly, the larger the number of rounds in the preamble, the easier the simulation task is. However, the main goal is to minimize the number of rounds in the protocol. The original analysis of the RK protocol showed how to simulate in polynomial-time $n^{O(1)}$ concurrent sessions as long as the number of rounds in the protocol is at least n^{ϵ} (for some arbitrary $\epsilon > 0$). This implied that for any $\epsilon > 0$, every language in $\mathcal{NP}$ has an n^{ϵ}-round $c\mathcal{ZK}$ proof system.

2.3.3 Improving the Analysis of the RK Protocol

The RK analysis has been subsequently improved by Kilian and Petrank [82], who have employed a more sophisticated simulation technique (see Sects. 4.4 and 5.1.1) to show that the RK protocol remains concurrent zero-knowledge even if it has $O(\alpha(n)\cdot\log^2 n)$ rounds, where $\alpha(\cdot)$ is any super-constant function (e.g., $\alpha(n) = \log\log n$). On a high level, the key idea underlying the Kilian–Petrank simulation strategy is that the order and timing of the simulator's rewindings are determined *obliviously* of the concurrent scheduling (which is determined "on the fly" by the adversary verifier). This is in contrast to the RK simulation strategy which heavily depends on the schedule as it is being revealed.

The Kilian–Petrank analysis was eventually improved by Prabhakharan, Rosen and Sahai (PRS) [93], who conducted a more sophisticated analysis of the Kilian–Petrank simulation technique, as well as presented a new $c\mathcal{ZK}$ protocol that is more amenable to analysis than the RK one. The improved analysis established that $O(\alpha(n)\cdot\log n)$ rounds of interaction are in fact sufficient for proving any language in $\mathcal{NP}$ in $c\mathcal{ZK}$. We note that the PRS analysis is not restricted to their protocol, and could also be applied to the RK protocol (the main reason to analyze the former is that it admits a somewhat simpler proof of security). The PRS proof is presented in Chap. 5.

2.3.4 What About Non-Black-Box Simulation?

In a recent breakthrough result, Barak [8] constructs a constant-round protocol for all languages in $\mathcal{NP}$ whose zero-knowledge property is proved using a *non-black-box* simulator. Such a method of simulation enables him to prove results known impossible for black-box simulation. Specifically, for every (predetermined) polynomial $p(\cdot)$, there exists a constant-round protocol that preserves its zero-knowledge property even when it is executed $p(n)$ times concurrently (where n denotes the "security" parameter). As we show in Chap. 7, even this weaker notion of concurrency is impossible to achieve when using black-box simulation, unless $\mathcal{NP} \subseteq \mathcal{BPP}$.

A major drawback of Barak's protocol is that the (polynomial) number of concurrent sessions relative to which the protocol should be secure must be fixed *before* the protocol is specified. Moreover, the length of the messages in the protocol grows linearly with the number of concurrent sessions. Thus, from both a theoretical and a practical point of view, Barak's protocol is still not satisfactory. What we would like to have is a *single* protocol that preserves its zero-knowledge property even when it is executed concurrently for *any* (not predetermined) polynomial number of times. Such a property is indeed satisfied by the Richardson–Kilian, and Prabhakharan–Rosen–Sahai protocols [94, 82, 93].

2.4 Organization and the Rest of This Book

Below is a brief summary of the material presented in the various chapters of the book. The central results are presented in Chaps. 5 and 7.

Chapter 3 – Preliminaries. Includes formal definitions of interactive proofs, zero-knowledge and witness indistinguishability. Defines concurrent zero-knowledge, as well as black-box concurrent zero-knowledge. Also specifies some conventions that are used in the proofs of the lower bound and the upper bound. Finally, defines the notion of bit-commitment, which will be used in the constructions of the $c\mathcal{ZK}$ protocols.

Chapter 4 – $c\mathcal{ZK}$ Proof Systems for $\mathcal{NP}$. Contains a full description of the Richardson–Kilian and Prabhakharan–Rosen–Sahai protocols, as well as a high-level exposition of the ideas underlying the simulation of these protocols and its analysis in the concurrent setting. A full exposition of the simulation of the Prabhakharan–Rosen–Sahai protocol (which implicitly contains an almost full analysis of the Richardson–Kilian protocol) appears in Chap. 5.

Chapter 5 – $c\mathcal{ZK}$ in Logarithmically Many Rounds. Contains a full analysis of the PRS $c\mathcal{ZK}$ protocol. As a consequence, every language in $\mathcal{NP}$ can be proved in $c\mathcal{ZK}$ using only $O(\alpha(n) \cdot \log n)$ rounds of interaction, where $\alpha(n)$ is any super-constant function (Theorem 5.1). The PRS protocol retains its zero-knowledge property no matter how many times it is executed concurrently (as long as the number of concurrent sessions is polynomial in the size of the input). By considering so-called zero-knowledge arguments, it is also shown how to achieve a similar result assuming only the existence of one-way functions (Theorem 5.3). The result presented in fact yields a generic transformation that takes any "standard" $\mathcal{ZK}$ protocol and transforms it into $c\mathcal{ZK}$ while paying only a "logarithmic" penalty in the round-complexity (Theorem 5.2). Additional results include the construction of a *resettable $\mathcal{ZK}$* protocol with "logarithmic" number of rounds (Theorem 5.4), and of $c\mathcal{ZK}$ arguments with polylogarithmic efficiency (Theorem 5.5).

Chapter 6 – A Simple Lower Bound. In this chapter we make a preliminary step towards demonstrating that the protocol presented in Chap. 5

is round-optimal (at least as far as black-box simulation is concerned). We show that the $c\mathcal{ZK}$ property of "non-trivial" 4-message protocols cannot be demonstrated via black-box simulation. Chapter 6 can serve as a "gentle" introduction to the considerably more complex result presented in Chap. 7.

Chapter 7 – Black-box $c\mathcal{ZK}$ Requires Logarithmically Many Rounds. The main result presented in this chapter is that $\Omega(\log n/\log n \log n)$ rounds of interaction are essential for black-box simulation of $c\mathcal{ZK}$ proof systems for languages outside of $\mathcal{BPP}$ (Theorem 7.1). The lower bound that is presented holds also for the case of $c\mathcal{ZK}$ arguments. In fact, it will hold even if the simulator knows the schedule in advance (in particular, it knows the number of concurrent sessions, which may just equal the security parameter), and even if the scheduling of the messages is fixed.

Chapter 8 - Conclusions and Open Problems. The chapter discusses the issues arising from the known results on $c\mathcal{ZK}$, as well as some open problems arising from Barak's non-black-box simulation techniques [8]. We also suggest investigating the round-complexity of $c\mathcal{ZK}$ without aborts as an interesting open–problem.

3

Preliminaries

3.1 General

3.1.1 Basic Notation

We let N denote the set of all integers. For any integer $k \in N$, denote by $[k]$ the set $\{1, 2, \ldots, k\}$. For any $x \in \{0, 1\}^*$, we let $|x|$ denote the size of x (i.e., the number of bits used in order to write it). For two machines M, A, we let $M^A(x)$ denote the output of machine M on input x and given oracle access to A. The term negligible is used for denoting functions that are (asymptotically) smaller than one over any polynomial. More precisely, a function $\nu(\cdot)$ from non-negative integers to reals is called negligible if for every constant $c > 0$ and all sufficiently large n, it holds that $\nu(n) < n^{-c}$.

3.1.2 Probabilistic Notation

Denote by $x \overset{\text{R}}{\leftarrow} X$ the process of uniformly choosing an element x in a set X. If $B(\cdot)$ is an event depending on the choice of $x \overset{\text{R}}{\leftarrow} X$, then $\Pr_{x \leftarrow X}[B(x)]$ (alternatively, $\Pr_x[B(x)]$) denotes the probability that $B(x)$ holds when x is chosen with probability $1/|X|$. Namely,

$$\Pr_{x \leftarrow X}[B(x)] = \sum_x \frac{1}{|X|} \cdot \chi(B(x))$$

where χ is an indicator function so that $\chi(B) = 1$ if event B holds, and equals zero otherwise. We denote by U_n the uniform distribution over the set $\{0, 1\}^n$.

3.1.3 Computational Indistinguishability

Let $S \subseteq \{0, 1\}^*$ be a set of strings. A probability ensemble indexed by S is a sequence of random variables indexed by S. Namely, any $X = \{X_w\}_{w \in S}$ is a random variable indexed by S.

Definition 3.1.1 (Computational indistinguishability) *Two ensembles* $X = \{X_w\}_{w \in S}$ *and* $Y = \{Y_w\}_{w \in S}$ *are said to be* computationally indistinguishable *if for every probabilistic polynomial-time algorithm* D, *there exists a negligible function* $\nu(\cdot)$ *so that for every* $w \in S$:

$$|\Pr[D(X_w, w) = 1] - \Pr[D(Y_w, w) = 1]| < \nu(|w|)$$

The algorithm D is often referred to as the distinguisher. For more details on computational indistinguishability see Sect. 3.2 of [56].

3.2 Interactive Proofs

We use the standard definitions of interactive proofs (and interactive Turing machines) [72, 56] and arguments (a.k.a. computationally sound proofs) [23]. Given a pair of interactive Turing machines, P and V, we denote by $\langle P, V \rangle(x)$ the random variable representing the (local) output of V when interacting with machine P on common input x, when the random input to each machine is uniformly and independently chosen.

Definition 3.2.1 (Interactive proof system) *A pair of interactive machines* $\langle P, V \rangle$ *is called an* interactive proof system *for a language* L *if machine* V *is polynomial-time and the following two conditions hold with respect to some negligible function* $\nu(\cdot)$:

- Completeness: *For every* $x \in L$,

$$\Pr[\langle P, V \rangle(x) = 1] \geq 1 - \nu(|x|).$$

- Soundness: *For every* $x \notin L$, *and every interactive machine* B,

$$\Pr[\langle B, V \rangle(x) = 1] \leq \nu(|x|).$$

In case that the soundness condition is required to hold only with respect to a computationally bounded prover, the pair $\langle P, V \rangle$ *is called an interactive* argument *system.*

Definition 3.2.1 can be relaxed to require only soundness error that is bounded away from $1 - \nu(|x|)$. This is so, since the soundness error can always be made negligible by sufficiently many parallel repetitions of the protocol (as such may occur anyhow in the concurrent model). However, in the context of our lower bound, we do not know whether this condition can be relaxed when dealing with computationally sound proofs (i.e., when the soundness condition is required to hold only for machines B that are implementable by poly-size circuits). In particular, in this case parallel repetitions do not necessarily reduce the soundness error (cf. [15]).

Definition 3.2.2 (Round-complexity) *Let $\langle P, V \rangle$ be an interactive proof system for a language L and let $r : N \to N$ be an integer function. We say that $\langle P, V \rangle$ has round-complexity $r(\cdot)$ if for every input x the number of messages exchanged is at most $r(|x|)$. In such a case, we sometimes refer to $\langle P, V \rangle$ as an $r(\cdot)$-round interactive proof system.*

3.3 Zero-Knowledge

An interactive proof is said to be *zero-knowledge* ($\mathcal{ZK}$) if it yields nothing beyond the validity of the assertion being proved. This is formalized by requiring that the view of every probabilistic polynomial-time adversary V^* interacting with the honest prover P can be simulated by a probabilistic polynomial-time machine S_{V^*} (a.k.a. the *simulator*). The idea behind this definition is that whatever V^* might have learned from interacting with P, he could have actually learned by himself (by running the simulator S). The transcript of an interaction consists of the common input x, followed by the sequence of prover and verifier messages exchanged during the interaction. We denote by $\mathrm{view}_{V^*}^P(x)$ a random variable describing the content of the random tape of V^* and the transcript of the interaction between P and V^* (that is, all messages that V^* sends and receives during the interaction with P, on common input x).

Definition 3.3.1 (Zero-knowledge) *Let $\langle P, V \rangle$ be an interactive proof system for a language L. We say that $\langle P, V \rangle$ is zero-knowledge, if for every probabilistic polynomial-time interactive machine V^* there exists a probabilistic polynomial-time algorithm S_{V^*} such that the ensembles $\{\mathrm{view}_{V^*}^P(x)\}_{x \in L}$ and $\{S_{V^*}(x)\}_{x \in L}$ are computationally indistinguishable.*

To make Definition 3.3.1 useful in the context of protocol composition, Goldreich and Oren [67] suggested augmenting the definition so that the corresponding conditions hold also with respect to all $z \in \{0, 1\}^*$, where both V^* and S_{V^*} are allowed to obtain z as auxiliary input. Jumping ahead, we comment that in the context of black-box simulation,, the original definition implies the augmented one (i.e., any black-box $\mathcal{ZK}$ protocol is also $\mathcal{ZK}$ w.r.t. auxiliary inputs). Since in this work we only consider the notion of black-box $\mathcal{ZK}$, we may ignore the issue of auxiliary inputs while being guaranteed that all results hold with respect to the augmented definition as well.

3.4 Witness Indistinguishability

An interactive proof is said to be *witness indistinguishable* ($\mathcal{WI}$) if the verifier's view is "computationally independent" of the witness used by the prover for proving the statement. In this context, we focus our attention on languages

$L \in \mathcal{NP}$ with a corresponding witness relation R_L. Namely, we consider inter-actions in which on common input x the prover is given a witness in $R_L(x)$. By saying that the view is computationally independent of the witness, we mean that for any two possible $\mathcal{NP}$-witnesses that could be used by the prover to prove the statement $x \in L$, the corresponding views are computationally indistinguishable. Let V^* be a probabilistic polynomial-time adversary inter-acting with the prover, and let $\mathrm{view}_{V^*}^P(x, w)$ denote V^*'s view of an interaction in which the witness used by the prover is w (where the common input is x).

Definition 3.4.1 (Witness-indistinguishability) *Let $\langle P, V \rangle$ be an interactive proof system for a language $L \in \mathcal{NP}$. We say that $\langle P, V \rangle$ is witness-indistinguishable for R_L, if for every probabilistic polynomial-time interactive machine V^* and for every two sequences $\{w_x^1\}_{x \in L}$ and $\{w_x^2\}_{x \in L}$, such that $w_x^1, w_x^2 \in R_L(x)$, the ensembles $\{\mathrm{view}_{V^*}^P(x, w_x^1)\}_{x \in L}$ and $\{\mathrm{view}_{V^*}^P(x, w_x^2)\}_{x \in L}$ are computationally indistinguishable.*

3.5 Concurrent Zero-Knowledge

Let $\langle P, V \rangle$ be an interactive proof (resp. argument) for a language L, and consider a concurrent adversary (verifier) V^* that, given input $x \in L$, interacts with an unbounded number of independent copies of P (all on common input x). The concurrent adversary V^* is allowed to interact with the various copies of P concurrently, without any restrictions over the scheduling of the messages in the different interactions with P (in particular, V^* has control over the scheduling of the messages in these interactions). In order to control the scheduling, the concurrent adversary V^* concatenates every message that it sends with the session and round number to which the next scheduled message belongs. The convention is that the reply sent by the prover should have session and message indices as specified in the preceding verifier message (in case it does not, the verifier V^* is allowed to reject the corresponding session). As before, the transcript of a concurrent interaction consists of the common input x, followed by the sequence of prover and verifier messages exchanged during the interaction. We denote by $\mathrm{view}_{V^*}^P(x)$ a random variable describing the content of the random tape of V^* and the transcript of the *concurrent* in-teraction between P and V^* (that is, *all* messages that V^* sends and receives during the concurrent interactions with P, on common input x).

Definition 3.5.1 (Concurrent Zero-Knowledge) *Let $\langle P, V \rangle$ be an interactive proof system for a language L. We say that $\langle P, V \rangle$ is concurrent zero-knowledge, if for every probabilistic polynomial-time concurrent adversary V^* there exists a probabilistic polynomial-time algorithm S_{V^*} such that the ensembles $\{\mathrm{view}_{V^*}^P(x)\}_{x \in L}$ and $\{S_{V^*}(x)\}_{x \in L}$ are computationally indistinguishable.*

In the context of concurrent $\mathcal{ZK}$, the round-complexity of a protocol is measured as a function of some predetemined "security" parameter $n \in N$.

The requirement is that the protocol will remain secure as long as the number of concurrent executions is bounded by some polynomial in n (we stress that the protocol is constructed *before* the polynomial bound is determined). In this book, we use the convention that the "security" paramter n is equal (or polynomially related) to $|x|$.

3.6 Black-Box Concurrent Zero-Knowledge

Loosely speaking, the definition of black-box zero-knowledge requires that there exists a "universal" simulator, S, so that for every $x \in L$ and every probabilistic polynomial-time adversary V^*, the simulator S produces a distribution that is indistinguishable from $\text{view}_{V^*}^P(x)$ while using V^* as an oracle (i.e., in a "black-box" manner). Essentially, the definition of black-box simulation says that the black-box simulator mimics the interaction of the prover P with any polynomial-time verifier V^* relative to any random input r it might choose. The simulator does so merely by using oracle calls to $V^*(x; r)$ (which specifies the next message that V^* sends on input x and random input r). The simulation is indistinguishable from the true interaction even if the distinguisher (i.e., D) is given access to the oracle $V^*(x; r)$. For more details see Sect. 4.5.4.2 of [57].

Before we proceed with the formal definition for the case of $c\mathcal{ZK}$, we will have to overcome a technical difficulty arising from an inherent difference between the concurrent setting and "stand-alone" setting. In "stand-alone" zero-knowledge the length of the output of the simulator depends only on the protocol and the size of the common input x. It is thus reasonable to require that the simulator runs in time that depends only on the size of x, regardless of the running time of its black-box. However, in black-box concurrent zero-knowledge the output of the simulator is an entire schedule, and its length depends on the running time of the concurrent adversary. Therefore, if we naively require that the running time of the simulator is a fixed polynomial in the size of x, then we end up with an unsatisfiable definition. (As for any simulator S there is an adversary V^* that generates a transcript that is longer than the running time of S.)

One way to solve the above problem is to have for *each* fixed polynomial $q(\cdot)$, a simulator S_q that "only" simulates all $q(\cdot)$-sized circuits V^*. Clearly, the running time of the simulator now depends on the running time of V^* (which is an upper bound on the size of the schedule), and the above problem does not occur anymore. Another (less restrictive) way to overcome the above problem would be to consider a simulator S_q that "only" simulates all adversaries V^* which run at most $q(|x|)$ sessions during their execution (we stress that $q(\cdot)$ is chosen *after* the protocol is determined). Such simulators should run in worst-case time that is a fixed polynomial in $q(|x|)$ and in the size of the common input x. In the sequel we choose to adopt the latter formalization.

Definition 3.6.1 (Black-Box Concurrent Zero-Knowledge) *Let $\langle P, V \rangle$ be an interactive proof system for a language L. We say that $\langle P, V \rangle$ is black-box concurrent zero-knowledge, if for every polynomial $q(\cdot)$, there exists a probabilistic polynomial-time algorithm S_q, so that for every concurrent adversary circuit V^* that runs at most $q(|x|)$ concurrent sessions, $S_q(x)$ runs in time polynomial in $q(|x|)$ and $|x|$, and satisfies that the ensembles $\{\text{view}_{V^*}^P(x)\}_{x \in L}$ and $\{S_q^{V^*}(x)\}_{x \in L}$ are computationally indistinguishable.*

3.7 Conventions Used in Construction of Simulators

Deviation Gap and Expected Polynomial-Time Simulators. The deviation gap of a simulator S for a proof-system $\langle P, V \rangle$ is defined as follows. Consider a distinguisher D that is required to decide whether its input consists of $\text{view}_{V^*}^P(x)$ or of the transcript that was produced by S. The deviation gap of D is the difference between the probability that D outputs 1 given an output of S, and the probability that D outputs 1 given $\text{view}_{V^*}^P(x)$. The deviation gap of S is the deviation gap of the best polynomial-time distinguisher D. In our definitions of concurrent zero-knowledge (Definitions 3.5.1 and 3.6.1) the deviation gap of the simulator is required to be negligible in $|x|$.

For our lower bound, we allow simulators that run in strict (worst-case) polynomial time, and have deviation gap at most $1/4$. As for expected polynomial-time simulators, one can use a standard argument to show that any simulator running in expected polynomial time, and having deviation gap at most $1/8$ can be transformed into a simulator that runs in strict (worst-case) polynomial time, and has deviation gap at most $1/4$. In particular, our lower bound (on simulators that run in strict polynomial time, and have deviation gap at most $1/4$) extends to a lower bound on simulators running in expected polynomial time (and have deviation gap as large as $1/8$).

Query Conventions. In the lower bound presented in Chap. 7, k-round protocols will consist of protocols in which $2k + 2$ messages are exchanged subject to the following conventions. The first message will be a fixed initiation message by the verifier, denoted v_1, which is answered by the prover's first message denoted p_1. The following verifier and prover messages are denoted $v_2, p_2, \ldots, v_{k+1}, p_{k+1}$, where v_{k+1} is an ACCEPT/REJECT message indicating whether the verifier has accepted its input, and the last message (i.e., p_{k+1}) is a fixed acknowledgment message sent by the prover.[1] Clearly, any protocol in which $2k$ messages are exchanged can be modified to fit this form (by adding at most two messages).

Both in the lower bound and the upper bound, we impose the following technical restrictions on the simulator (we claim that each of these restrictions

---

[1] The p_{k+1} message is an artificial message included in order to "streamline" the description of the adversarial schedule (the schedule will be defined in Sect. 7.2.1).

can be satisfied by any simulator): As in [63], the queries of the simulator are prefixes of possible execution transcripts (in the concurrent setting).[2] Such a prefix is a sequence of alternating prover and verifier messages (which may belong to different sessions as determined by the fixed schedule) that ends with a prover message. The answer to the queries made by the simulator consists of a single verifier message (which belongs to the next scheduled session), and is determined by the output of the machine V^* when applied to the corresponding query (that is, the answer to query $\bar{q}$ is the message $V^*(\bar{q})$). In the case of the upper bound, we assume that the verifier's answers are always sent along with the identifiers of the next scheduled message (as determined by V^*). That is, every verifier message is concatenated with the session and round number to which the next scheduled message belongs. In the case of the lower bound, this is not necessary since we are considering a fixed scheduling that is determined in advance and known to everybody. We assume that the simulator never repeats the same query twice. In addition, we assume that before making a query $\bar{q} = (b_1, a_1, \ldots, b_t, a_t)$, where the a's are prover messages, the simulator has made queries to all relevant prefixes (i.e., $(b_1, a_1, \ldots, b_i, a_i)$, for every $i < t$), and has obtained the b_i's as answers. Finally, we assume that before producing output $(b_1, a_1, \ldots, b_T, a_T)$, the simulator makes the query $(b_1, a_1, \ldots, b_T, a_T)$.

On the Simulator's "Behavior". Similarly to all known black-box simulators, the simulator presented in Chap. 5 will go about the simulation task by means of "rewinding" the adversary V^* to past points in the interaction. That is, the simulator will explore many possible concurrent interactions with V^* by feeding it with different queries of the same length (while examining V^*'s output on these queries).[3] As will turn out from our proof, before making a query $\bar{q} = (p_1, v_1, \ldots, v_{t-1}, p_t)$, where the p's are prover messages, the simulator will always make queries to all relevant prefixes (i.e., $(p_1, v_1, \ldots, v_{i-1}, p_i)$, for every $i < t$), and will obtain the v_i's as answers. In addition, the simulator will never make an illegal query (except with negligible probability). That is, the simulator will always feed the verifier with messages in the prescribed format, and will make sure that the session and message numbers of any prover message in the query are indeed consistent with the identifiers appearing in the preceding verifier message. Actually, in order to succeed, the simulator *does* deviate from the prescribed prover strategy (and indeed sends messages that would have not been sent by an honest prover). However, it will do so in a way that cannot be noticed by any probabilistic polynomial-time procedure (unless computationally hiding commitments do not exist). What we actually mean by saying that illegal queries are never made is that the simulator will

---

[2] For sake of simplicity, we choose to omit the input x from the transcript's representation (as it is implicit in the description of the verifier anyway).

[3] Recall that every query made by the simulator corresponds to a specific execution transcript, and that the query's length corresponds to the number of messages exchanged so far.

never send an ill-formed message (i.e., one that would cause an honest verifier V to immediately reject the protocol).

Dealing with ABORT Messages. Since the adversary verifier V^* may arbitrarily deviate from the prescribed strategy, it may be the case that throughout its interaction with the prover (simulator), V^* occasionally sends ill-formed messages (in other words, V^* may potentially refuse to decommit to a previous commitment). Clearly, such an action on behalf of the verifier is considered illegal, and the interaction in the relevant session stops (i.e., there is no need to continue exchanging messages in this session). Without loss of generality, such ill-formed messages are always interpreted as some predetermined ABORT message. For the sake of concreteness, we assume that whenever an ABORT message is sent by the verifier, the prover and verifier keep exchanging ABORT messages until the relevant session is completed. We stress that, as far as the prover (simulator) is concerned, illegal actions on behalf of the verifier in one session do not have any effect on the interaction in other sessions (since in the concurrent setting each prover/verifier pair is assumed to act independently).

3.8 Commitment Schemes

Commitment schemes are used to enable a party, known as the *sender*, to commit itself to a value while keeping it secret from the *receiver* (this property is called hiding). Furthermore, the commitment is binding, and thus in a later stage when the commitment is opened, it is guaranteed that the "opening" can yield only a single value determined in the committing phase.

Perfectly Binding Commitment Schemes. In a perfectly binding commitment scheme, the binding property holds even for an all-powerful sender, while the hiding property is only guaranteed with respect to a polynomial-time bounded receiver. For simplicity, we present the definition for a non-interactive, commitment scheme for a single bit. String commitment can be obtained by separately committing to each bit in the string.

We denote by $\mathrm{Com}(b;r)$ the output of the commitment scheme C upon input $b \in \{0,1\}$ and using the random string $r \in_R \{0,1\}^n$ (for simplicity, we assume that Com uses n random bits where $n \in N$ is the security parameter).

Definition 3.8.1 (Perfectly Binding Commitment) *A perfectly binding bit commitment scheme* is a probabilistic algorithm Com satisfying the following two conditions:

- Perfect binding: $\mathrm{Com}(0;r) \neq \mathrm{Com}(1;s)$ *for every* $r,s \in \{0,1\}^n$ *and* $n \in N$.
- Computational hiding: *The ensemble* $\{\mathrm{Com}(0;U_n)\}_{n \in N}$ *is computationally indistinguishable from the ensemble* $\{\mathrm{Com}(1;U_n)\}_{n \in N}$.

Non-interactive perfectly binding commitment schemes can be constructed using any 1–1 one-way function (see Sect. 4.4.1 of [57]). Allowing some minimal interaction (in which the receiver first sends a single message), (almost) perfectly binding commitment schemes (a.k.a. statistically binding) can be obtained from any one-way function [87, 77].

Perfectly Hiding Commitment Schemes. In a perfectly hiding commitment scheme, the binding property is guaranteed to hold only with respect to a probabilistic polynomial-time sender. On the other hand, the hiding property is information-theoretic. That is, the distributions of commitments to 0 and commitments to 1 are identical (statistically close), and thus even an all-powerful receiver cannot know the value committed to by the sender. We stress that the binding property guarantees that a cheating probabilistic polynomial-time sender can find only one decommitment, even though decommitments to both 0 and 1 exist (which in particular means that an all-powerful sender can always decommit both to 0 and to 1). See [57] (Sect. 4.8.2) for a full definition.

Perfectly hiding commitment schemes can be constructed from any one-way permutation [88]. However, *constant-round* schemes are only known to exist under stronger assumptions; specifically, assuming the existence of collision-resistant hash functions [89, 35] or the existence of a collection of certified clawfree functions [62] (see also [57], Sect. 4.8.2.3).

$c\mathcal{ZK}$ Proof Systems for $\mathcal{NP}$

This chapter describes the construction of the Richardson–Kilian (RK) and the Prabhakharan–Rosen–Sahai (PRS) $c\mathcal{ZK}$ protocols (introduced in [94] and [93] respectively). It also gives a high-level description of the ideas used for the analysis of these protocols in the concurrent setting. A full analysis of the PRS protocol (which implicitly contains an almost full analysis of the RK protocol) appears in Chap. 5.

Both the RK and PRS protocols follow the same paradigm of adding a "preamble" to some underlying constant-round protocol (cf. [94]). This preamble is completely independent of the common input, and its sole purpose is to enable a successful simulation in the concurrent setting. The two protocols implement the above paradigm in different ways, where each of the approaches has both advantages and disadvantages compared to the other. While the RK approach has the advantage of being somewhat easier to describe, the PRS approach is easier to analyze and yields more efficient protocols.

The approaches also differ in the properties required by the underlying constant-round protocol. For the RK construction, it is required that the underlying protocol is *witness indistinguishable*, whereas for the PRS construction, it is required that the protocol enables simulation whenever the verifier's "challenge" is known in advance (a.k.a. *special simulation*).

In our exposition we have chosen to make use of Blum's Hamiltonicity protocol (cf. [18]) as the underlying protocol for both the RK and PRS constructions. As it turns out, Blum's protocol satisfies both the witness indistinguishability and special simulation properties. This makes it suitable for both constructions. We mention that the choice of Blum's protocol is arbitrary, and is made only for convenience. In particular, Blum's protocol could be conceivably replaced by any constant-round protocol that satisfies either one of the above properties.

4.1 Blum's Hamiltonicity Protocol

Blum's protocol consists of n parallel repetitions of the following basic proof system for the *Hamiltonian Cycle* (HC) problem. since HC is $\mathcal{NP}$-complete this yields a proof system for any language in $\mathcal{NP}$ [18, 57]. We consider directed graphs (and the existence of directed Hamiltonian cycles).

Construction 4.1.1 (Basic proof system for HC)

Common input: *a directed graph* $G = (V, E)$ *with* $n \stackrel{\text{def}}{=} |V|$.

Auxiliary input to prover: *a directed Hamiltonian cycle,* $C \subset E$, *in* G.

Prover's first step ($\widehat{p1}$): *Select a random permutation,* π, *of the vertices* V, *and commit (using a statistically-binding commitment scheme) to the entries of the adjacency matrix of the resulting permuted graph. That is, send an n-by-n matrix of commitments so that the* $(\pi(u), \pi(v))^{\text{th}}$ *entry is a commitment to 1 if* $(u, v) \in E$, *and is a commitment to 0 otherwise.*

Verifier's first step ($\widehat{v1}$): *Uniformly select* $\sigma \in \{0, 1\}$ *and send it to the prover.*

Prover's second step ($\widehat{p2}$): *If* $\sigma = 0$, *send* π *to the verifier along with the revealing (i.e., preimages) of all commitments. Otherwise, reveal only the commitments to entries* $(\pi(u), \pi(v))$ *with* $(u, v) \in C$. *In both cases also supply the corresponding decommitments.*

Verifier's second step ($\widehat{v2}$): *If* $\sigma = 0$, *check that the revealed graph is indeed isomorphic, via* π, *to* G. *Otherwise, just check that all revealed values are 1 and that the corresponding entries form a simple n-cycle. In both cases check that the decommitments are proper (i.e., that they fit the corresponding commitments). Accept if and only if the corresponding condition holds.*

We start by showing that Construction 4.1.1 satisfies the special simulation property. Namely if the prover knows the contents of verifier's "challenge" message σ (determined in Step ($\widehat{v1}$)) prior to sending its own first message (determined in Step ($\widehat{p1}$)), then it is able to convince the verifier that G contains a Hamiltionian cycle even without knowing such a cycle (actually, it will convince the verifier even if the graph does not contain a cycle).

Claim 4.1.2 *Construction 4.1.1 satisfies the special simulation property.*

Proof Sketch Consider a single execution of Construction 4.1.1. We show that if the prover knows σ in advance, it can set up its first message according to σ in a way that will always make the verifier accept in Step ($\widehat{v2}$). Specifically, knowing in advance that $\sigma = 0$, the prover will commit to the entries of the adjacency matrix of the permuted graph (as specified in Step ($\widehat{p1}$) of Construction 4.1.1), thus being able to reveal a permutation π and the preimages of all commitments in Step ($\widehat{p2}$). On the other hand, knowing in advance that $\sigma = 1$, the prover will commit to the full graph K_n, thus being able to open an arbitrary cycle in the supposedly permuted graph. The above argument can be easily extended to the case of n parallel repetitions. ∎

Claim 4.1.3 ([18, 47, 57]) *Construction 4.1.1 is witness indistinguishable.*

Proof Sketch Observe that the special simulation property is in fact sufficient in order to prove that a single execution of Construction 4.1.1 is (black-
box) zero-knowledge.[1] All that the simulator has to do is to try and "guess"
the value of σ prior to determining the value of the prover's first message
(and keep trying until it succeeds). Since $\mathcal{ZK}$ implies witness indistinguishability [57] then Construction 4.1.1 is $\mathcal{WI}$. As for n parallel repetitions of
Construction 4.1.1, these are also $\mathcal{WI}$ since witness indistinguishability is
preserved under parallel repetition [57, 47]. ∎

4.2 The Richardson–Kilian $c\mathcal{ZK}$ Protocol

The RK protocol consists of two stages. In the *first stage*, which is independent of the common input, the verifier commits to k random n-bit strings,
$v_1, ..., v_k \in \{0,1\}^n$, where n is the "security" parameter of the protocol and k
is a special parameter that determines the number of rounds. This is followed
by k iterations so that in each iteration the prover commits to a random n-bit
string, p_j, and the verifier decommits to the corresponding v_j.

In the *second stage*, the prover provides a witness indistinguishable proof
that either the common input is in the language or that $v_j = p_j$ for some
$j \in \{1, ..., k\}$. Intuitively, since the latter case is unlikely to happen in an
actual execution of the protocol, the protocol constitutes a proof system for
the language. However, the latter case is the key to the simulation of the
protocol in the concurrent setting. Whenever the simulator may cause $v_j = p_j$
to happen for some i (this is done by the means of *rewinding* the verifier after
the value v_i has been revealed), it can simulate the rest of the protocol (and
specifically Stage 2) by merely running the witness indistinguishable proof
system with v_i (and the prover's coins) as a witness.

The Actual Protocol. Consider the following $\mathcal{NP}$-relation, denoted $R_{\sf sim}$,
and its corresponding $\mathcal{NP}$-language $L_{\sf sim}$.

Construction 4.2.1 (The RK $\mathcal{NP}$-relation $R_{\sf sim}$)

Instance: *a tuple* $\langle c_1, ..., c_k, v_1 ..., v_k \rangle$.
Witness: *an index* $j \in \{1, ..., k\}$ *and a pair of strings* $p_j, r_j \in \{0,1\}^n$.
Relation: $R_{\sf sim}(\langle c_1, ..., c_k, v_1, ..., v_k \rangle, \langle j, p_j, r_j \rangle) = 1$ *if and only if:*
   1. $c_j = \mathrm{Com}(p_j; r_j)$.
   2. $p_j = v_j$.

Using $R_{\sf sim}$, and Construction 4.1.1, the RK protocol proceeds as follows.

---

[1]This is in contrast to the protocol obtained by conducting n parallel repetitions
of the basic Hamiltonicity proof system (from Construction 4.1.1), which cannot be
proved to be black-box zero-knowledge (unless $\mathcal{NP} \subseteq \mathcal{BPP}$) [63].

Construction 4.2.2 (The RK $c\mathcal{ZK}$ proof system for HC)

Common input: *a directed graph $G = (V, E)$ with $n \stackrel{\text{def}}{=} |V|$, and a parameter $k = k(n)$ (used for determining the number of rounds).*
Auxiliary input to prover: *a directed Hamiltonian Cycle, $C \subset E$, in G.*
First stage: *This stage involves $2k + 2$ rounds and is independent of G.*

1. Prover's preliminary step (P0): *Uniformly select a first message for a (two-round) statistically hiding commitment scheme and send it to the verifier.*
2. Verifier's preliminary step (V0): *Uniformly select a sequence, $\{v_j\}_{j=1}^{k}$, of k random n-bit strings. Commit (using the statistically hiding commitment scheme) to all k selected strings.*
3. For $j = 1, \ldots, k$:
   a) Prover's j^{th} step (Pj): *Uniformly select a random n-bit string r_j and send $c_j = \text{Com}(0^n; r_j)$ to the verifier (where Com denotes a statistically-binding commitment).*
   b) Verifier's j^{th} step (Vj): *Reveal the value of v_j (by sending the decommitment information for the corresponding commitment in (V0)).*
4. *The prover proceeds with the execution if and only if for every $j \in \{1, \ldots, k\}$, the verifier has properly decommitted to the values of v_j (i.e., that for every $j \in \{1, \ldots, k\}$, v_j is a valid decommitment of β_j).*

Second stage: *The prover and verifier engage in a witness-indistinguishable proof of knowledge (e.g. n parallel executions of Construction 4.1.1) for the OR of the following $\mathcal{NP}$-statements:*
   1. *G has a Hamiltonian cycle (i.e. $G \in HC$).*
   2. *$\langle c_1, \ldots, c_k, v_1 \ldots, v_k \rangle \in L_{\text{sim}}$.*

Completeness. Completeness of Construction 4.2.2 follows from the perfect completeness of the Hamiltonicity proof system. All that the prover has to do in order to convince the verifier that $G \in HC$ is to send an initialization message for the statistically hiding commitments scheme, and k commitments to the all-zero string, one commitment per each round in the first stage. As for the second stage, since the prover knows a Cycle $C \subset E$ in G, then no matter what is the "challenge" sent by the verifier in Step (v1), the perfect completeness of Construction 4.1.1 guarantees that the prover will be always able to answer properly in Step (p2) (thus making the verifier accept).

Soundness. Soundness of Construction 4.2.2 follows from soundness of the basic Hamiltonicity proof system, from the statistically-hiding property of the commitment used by the verifier in Step (V0) and from the statistical binding property of the commitments used by the prover in Steps (P1), ..., (Pk).

Claim 4.2.3 *Suppose that the commitment used in Step (V0) is statistically hiding. Further suppose that the commitments used in Steps (P1), ..., (Pk) are statistically binding. Then, Construction 4.2.2 is sound.*

Proof Sketch Suppose that the input graph G is not Hamiltonian. Since the commitment scheme used by the verifier in Step (V0) is statistically hiding, we deduce that when reaching Step (Pj) the prover has "no idea" about the value of v_j that is about to be revealed in Step (Vj) (i.e., as far as the information available to the prover is concerned each possibility is almost equally likely). Thus, the value p_j committed to by the prover in Step (Pj) is (almost) independent of the value of v_j. As a consequence, when the interaction reaches Stage 2 it is the case that with overwhelming probability $p_j \neq v_j$ for all $j \in \{1, \ldots, k\}$. Now, the commitment scheme used by the prover in Step (Pj) is statistically binding, and so once the prover sends c_j, the value of p_j is (almost) completely determined. This means that with overwhelming probability (over the verifier's coin tosses) $\langle c_1, \ldots, c_k, v_1 \ldots, v_k \rangle \notin L_{\mathsf{sim}}$. A standard argument can be then used to demonstrate how a cheating prover for Construction 4.3.1 is transformed into an (all-powerful) cheating prover for Construction 4.1.1 (with only a negligible difference in the cheating probability), in contradiction to the soundness property of Construction 4.1.1. ∎ We thus get:

Proposition 4.2.4 ([94]) *Construction 4.2.2 constitutes an interactive proof system for Hamiltonicity.*

4.3 The Prabhakharan–Rosen–Sahai $c\mathcal{ZK}$ Protocol

Similarly to the RK protocol, the PRS protocol consists of two stages. In the first stage, which is independent of the actual common input, the verifier commits to a random n-bit string σ, and to two sequences, $\{\sigma_{i,j}^0\}_{i,j=1}^k$, and $\{\sigma_{i,j}^1\}_{i,j=1}^k$, each consisting of k^2 random n-bit strings (this first message is called the initial commitment of the protocol). The sequences are chosen under the constraint that for every i, j the value of $\sigma_{i,j}^0 \oplus \sigma_{i,j}^1$ equals σ. This is followed by k iterations so that in the jth iteration the prover sends a random k-bit string, $r_j = r_{1,j}, \ldots, r_{k,j}$, and the verifier decommits to $\sigma_{1,j}^{r_{1,j}}, \ldots, \sigma_{k,j}^{r_{k,j}}$.

In the second stage, the prover and verifier engage in the three-round protocol for Hamiltonicity (with soundness error 2^{-n}), where the "challenge" sent by the verifier in the second round of the Hamiltonicity protocol equals σ (at this point the verifier also decommits to all the values $\sigma, \{\sigma_{i,j}^{1-r_{i,j}}\}_{i,j=1}^k$ that were not revealed in the first stage).

Intuitively, since in an actual execution of the protocol, the prover does not know the value of σ, the protocol constitutes a proof system for Hamiltonicity (with soundness error 2^{-n}). However, knowing the value of σ in advance allows the simulation of the protocol: whenever the simulator may cause the verifier to reveal both $\sigma_{i,j}^0$ and $\sigma_{i,j}^1$ for some i, j (as in the RK protocol, this is done by the means of *rewinding* the verifier after the values $\sigma_{1,j}^{r_{1,j}}, \ldots, \sigma_{k,j}^{r_{k,j}}$ have been revealed), it can simulate the rest of the protocol (and specifically Stage 2) by adjusting the first message of the Hamiltonicity protocol according to the value of $\sigma = \sigma_{i,j}^0 \oplus \sigma_{i,j}^1$ (which, as we said, is obtained before entering Stage 2).

The Actual Protocol. We assume the existence of commitment schemes with security 2^{-k}, where $k \in N$ is an appropriately chosen "security" parameter. The parameter k is also used in order to determine the number of rounds in the protocol. In principle, the security of the commitment schemes does not have to be linked to the number of rounds. Indeed, the above choice is arbitrary and was done only for convenience of presentation.

Construction 4.3.1 (The PRS c$\mathcal{ZK}$ proof system for HC)

Common input: *a directed graph $G = (V, E)$ with $n \overset{\text{def}}{=} |V|$, and a parameter $k = k(n)$ (used for determining the number of rounds, as well as the security of the commitment schemes used in the protocol).*

Auxiliary input to prover: *a directed Hamiltonian cycle, $C \subset E$, in G.*

First stage: *This stage involves $2k + 2$ rounds and is independent of G.*

1. Prover's preliminary step (P0): *Uniformly select a first message for a (two-round) statistically hiding commitment scheme and send it to the verifier.*
2. Verifier's preliminary step (V0): *Uniformly select $\sigma \in \{0,1\}^n$, and two sequences, $\{\sigma_{i,j}^0\}_{i,j=1}^k$, $\{\sigma_{i,j}^1\}_{i,j=1}^k$, each consisting of k^2 random n-bit strings. The sequences are chosen under the constraint that for every i,j the value of $\sigma_{i,j}^0 \oplus \sigma_{i,j}^1$ equals σ. Commit (using the statistically hiding commitment scheme) to all $2k^2 + 1$ selected strings. The commitments are denoted $\beta, \{\beta_{i,j}^0\}_{i,j=1}^k, \{\beta_{i,j}^1\}_{i,j=1}^k$.*
3. For $j = 1, \dots, k$:
   a) Prover's j^{th} step (Pj): *Uniformly select a k-bit string $r_j = r_{1,j}, \dots, r_{k,j} \in \{0,1\}^k$ and send it to the verifier.*
   b) Verifier's j^{th} step (Vj): *Reveal the values (preimages) of $\beta_{1,j}^{r_{1,j}}, \dots, \beta_{k,j}^{r_{k,j}}$.*
4. *The prover proceeds with the execution if and only if for every $j \in \{1, \dots, k\}$, the verifier has properly decommitted to the values of $\sigma_{1,j}^{r_{1,j}}, \dots, \sigma_{k,j}^{r_{k,j}}$ (i.e., that for every $i \in \{1, \dots, k\}$, $\sigma_{i,j}^{r_{i,j}}$ is a valid decommitment of $\beta_{i,j}^{r_{i,j}}$).*

Second stage: *The prover and verifier engage in n (parallel) executions of a slightly modified version of the basic Hamiltonicity protocol (described in Construction 4.1.1):*

1. Prover's first step (p1): *Send the first message in the Hamiltonicity proof system (i.e., n parallel copies of Step (p̂1) in Construction 4.1.1).*
2. Verifier's first step (v1): *Reveal the value (i.e., preimage) of β (which is supposed to be equal to σ). Also reveal the value of all k^2 commitments that have not been revealed in the first stage (i.e., the values of all $\{\beta_{i,j}^{1-r_{i,j}}\}_{i,j=1}^k$).*
3. Prover's second step (p2): *Check that the verifier has properly decommited to the values of σ and $\{\sigma_{i,j}^{1-r_{i,j}}\}_{i,j=1}^k$ (in particular, check that $\sigma_{i,j}^0 \oplus \sigma_{i,j}^1$ indeed equals σ for all j). If so, send the third message in the basic Hamiltonicity proof system (i.e., n parallel copies of Step (p̂2) in Construction 4.1.1).*
4. Verifier's second step (v2): *Conduct the verification of the prover's proofs (i.e., as described in Step (v̂2) of Construction 4.1.1), and accept if and only if all corresponding conditions hold.*

Completeness. Completeness of Construction 4.3.1 follows from the perfect completeness of the Hamiltonicity proof system. All that the prover has to do in order to convince the verifier that $G \in HC$ is to send an initialization message for the statistically hiding commitments scheme, and k uniformly and independently chosen k-bit strings, one string per each round in the first stage (this can be done even without knowing a Hamiltonian cycle in G). As for the second stage, since the prover knows a Hamiltionian cycle $C \subset E$ in G, then no matter what the "challenge" sent by the verifier in Step (v1) is, the perfect completeness of Construction 4.1.1 guarantees that the prover will be always able to answer properly in Step (p2).

Soundness. Soundness of Construction 4.3.1 follows from soundness of the basic Hamiltonicity proof system, and from the statistically hiding property of the commitment sent by the verifier in Step (V0).

Claim 4.3.2 *Suppose that the commitment used in Step* (V0) *is statistically hiding. Then, Construction 4.3.1 is sound.*

Proof Sketch Suppose that the input graph G is not Hamiltonian. Observe that no matter what the prover does, the k^2 values, $\{\sigma_{i,1}^{r_{i,1}}\}_{i=1}^k, \ldots, \{\sigma_{i,k}^{r_{i,k}}\}_{i=1}^k$, which are revealed by the verifier in the first stage, are uniformly and independently chosen (and so reveal no information about the actual value of σ). Since the commitment scheme used by the verifier in Step (V0) is statistically hiding, we deduce that when reaching Step (p1) the prover has "no idea" about the value of the "challenge" σ that is about to be revealed in Step (v2) (i.e., as far as the information available to the prover is concerned each possibility is almost equally likely). In other words, even though the cheating prover reaches the second stage (i.e., Step (p1)) after seeing all messages in the first stage, the messages in the second stage are (almost) statistically independent of the verifier's messages in the first stage. A standard argument can be then used to demonstrate how a cheating prover for Construction 4.3.1 is transformed into an (all-powerful) cheating prover for Construction 4.1.1 (with only a negligible difference in the cheating probability), in contradiction to the soundness property of Construction 4.1.1. ∎
We thus get:

Proposition 4.3.3 ([93]) *Construction 4.3.1 constitutes an interactive proof system for Hamiltonicity.*

4.4 Simulating the RK and PRS Protocols – Outline

We next give a high-level description of the ideas used to analyze the $c\mathcal{ZK}$ property of the PRS and RK protocols. Since the analysis of the RK protocol involves some complications that are not directly related to the issue of concurrency, we choose to focus our attention on the PRS protocol. A fully detailed exposition of the analysis of the PRS protocol appears in Chap. 5.

Let $(V0), (P1), (V1), \ldots, (Pk), (Vk)$ denote the $2k + 1$ first stage messages in the PRS protocol and let $(p1), (v1), (p2)$ denote the three (second stage) messages in the Hamiltonicity proof system. Loosely speaking, the simulator is said to rewind the the jth round if after receiving a (Vj) message, it "goes back" to some point preceding the corresponding (Pj) message and "re-executes" the relevant part of the interaction until (Vj) is reached again.

The simulator is said to successfully rewind the jth round, if it manages to receive (Vj) as answer to two *different* (Pj) messages. Note that, once this happens, the simulator has obtained both $\sigma_{i,j}^0$ and $\sigma_{i,j}^1$ for some $i \in \{1, \ldots, k\}$. Thus, if the simulator successfully rewinds even one of the rounds in the first stage then it reveals the verifier's "challenge" (which is equal to $\sigma_{i,j}^0 \oplus \sigma_{i,j}^1$). Once the "challenge" is revealed, the simulator can cheat arbitrarily in the second stage of the protocol.

To simplify the analysis, we let the simulator always pick the (Pj)'s uniformly at random. Since the length of the (Pj) messages is super-logarithmic, the probability that *any* two (Pj) messages sent during the simulation are equal is negligible.

Motivating Discussion. The binding property of the initial commitment guarantees us that, once $\sigma_{i,j}^0$ and $\sigma_{i,j}^1$ have been revealed, the verifier cannot "change his mind" and decommit to $\sigma \neq \sigma_{i,j}^0 \oplus \sigma_{i,j}^1$ at a later stage. However, this remains true *only* if we have not rewound past the initial commitment. As observed by Dwork, Naor and Sahai [39], rewinding a specific session in the concurrent setting may result in rewinding past the initial commitment of other sessions. This means that the "work" done for these sessions may be lost (since once we rewind past the initial commitment of a session all $\sigma_{i,j}^{r_{i,j}}$ values that we have gathered in this session become irrelevant). Consequently, the simulator may find himself doing the same amount of "work" again.

The Richardson–Kilian Simulator [94]. The big question is how to design a simulation strategy that will manage to overcome the above difficulty. One possible approach would be to try and rewind every session at the location that will "minimize the damage". This is the approach taken in the original analysis by Richardson and Kilian [94]. Specifically, for every specific session (out of m concurrent sessions), there must be a $j \in \{1, \ldots, k\}$ so that at most $(m - 1)/k$ other sessions start in the interval corresponding to the jth iteration (of this specific session). So if we try to rewind on the correct j, we will invest (and so waste) only work proportional to $(m - 1)/k$ sessions. The idea is to avoid the rewinding attempt on the jth iteration if more than $(m - 1)/k$ sessions are initiated in the corresponding interval (this will rule out the incorrect j's). The same reasoning applies *recursively* (i.e., to the rewinding in these $(m - 1)/k$ sessions).

The drawback of this approach is that it works only when the number of iterations in the preamble is polynomially related to the number of concurrent sessions. Specifically, denoting by $W(m)$ the amount of work invested in m sessions, we obtain the recursion $W(m) = \text{poly}(m) \cdot W(\frac{m-1}{k})$, which solves to $W(m) = m^{\Theta(\log_k m)}$. Thus, whenever $k = n$, we get $W(m) = m^{O(1)}$, whereas taking k to be a constant (or even poly-logarithmic) will cause $W(m)$ to be quasi-polynomial. Despite the apparent drawbacks, the RK simulation and its analysis are important. This is mainly (but not only) due to the fact that they were the ones originally used to establish the *feasibility* of $c\mathcal{ZK}$. We also mention that the RK ideas also seem to be somewhat relevant to the construction of $c\mathcal{ZK}$ protocols with a *quasi-polynomial* time simulation guarantee (a notion considered in [92], but not fully explored in the context of $c\mathcal{ZK}$).

Theorem 4.1 ([94]) *Suppose that there exist statistically hiding commitment schemes. Then, for any $\epsilon > 0$ there exists an n^{ϵ}-round black-box concurrent zero-knowledge proof system for every language $L \in \mathcal{NP}$.*

The Kilian–Petrank Simulator [82]. A totally different approach is taken by Kilian and Petrank (KP). Rather than concentrating on each session separately and decide on the rewindings according to the schedule as it is being revealed, determine the rewindings *obliviously* of the concurrent scheduling (which is determined "on the fly" by the adversary verifier). Specifically, the order and timing of the simulator's rewindings are determined recursively and depend only on: (1) the length of the execution transcript determined so far; (2) the total number of concurrent sessions (which, by definition, is determined prior to the simulation process). This is also the approach taken by Prabhakharan, Rosen and Sahai [93].

The Rewinding Strategy. The rewinding strategy of the KP simulator is specified by the SOLVE procedure. The goal of the SOLVE procedure is to supply the simulator with V^*'s "challenges" before reaching the second stage in the protocol. As discussed above, this is done by rewinding the interaction with V^* while trying to achieve two "different" answers to some (Vj) message.

The timing of the rewinds performed by the SOLVE procedure depends only the number of first stage verifier messages received so far (and on the size of the schedule). For the sake of simplicity, we currently ignore second stage messages and refrain from specifying the way they are handled. On a very high level, the SOLVE procedure splits the (first stage) messages it is about to explore into two halves and invokes itself recursively twice for each half (completing the two runs of the first half before proceeding to the two runs of the second half).

At the top level of the recursion, the messages that are about to be explored consist of the entire schedule, whereas at the bottom level the procedure explores only a single message (at this level, the verifier message explored is stored in a special "data structure", denoted $\mathcal{T}$). The solve procedure always outputs the sequence of "most recently explored" messages.

The input to the SOLVE procedure consists of a triplet $(\ell, \text{hist}, \mathcal{T})$. The parameter ℓ corresponds to the number of verifier messages to be explored, the string hist consists of the messages in the "most recently visited" history of interaction, and $\mathcal{T}$ is a table containing the contents of all the messages explored so far (to be used whenever the second stage is reached in some session).[2]

The simulation is performed by invoking the SOLVE procedure with the appropriate parameters. Specifically, whenever the schedule contains $m = \text{poly}(n)$ sessions, the SOLVE procedure is invoked with input $(m(k+1), \phi, \phi)$, where $m(k+1)$ is the total number of first stage verifier messages in a schedule of size m, and is assumed (without loss of generality) to be a power of 2. The SOLVE procedure is depicted in Fig. 4.1.

Procedure SOLVE($\ell, \text{hist}, \mathcal{T}$):
Bottom level ($\ell = 1$):

1. If session s does not appear in hist, delete all session s messages from $\mathcal{T}$.
2. Uniformly choose a first stage prover message p, and feed V^* with (hist, p).
3. Store V^*'s answer v, in $\mathcal{T}$.
4. Output $\mathcal{T}, (\text{p}, \text{v})$.

Recursive step ($\ell > 1$):

1. Set $\mathcal{T}_1, (\tilde{\text{p}}_1, \tilde{\text{v}}_1, \ldots, \tilde{\text{p}}_{\ell/2}, \tilde{\text{v}}_{\ell/2}) \leftarrow$ SOLVE($\ell/2, \text{hist}, \mathcal{T}$).
2. Set $\mathcal{T}_2, (\text{p}_1, \text{v}_1, \ldots, \text{p}_{\ell/2}, \text{v}_{\ell/2}) \leftarrow$ SOLVE($\ell/2, \text{hist}, \mathcal{T}_1$).
3. Set $\mathcal{T}_3, (\tilde{\text{p}}_{\ell/2+1}, \tilde{\text{v}}_{\ell/2+1}, \ldots, \tilde{\text{p}}_\ell, \tilde{\text{v}}_\ell) \leftarrow$ SOLVE($\ell/2, (\text{hist}, \text{p}_1, \text{v}_1, \ldots, \text{p}_{\ell/2}, \text{v}_{\ell/2}), \mathcal{T}_2$).
4. Set $\mathcal{T}_4, (\text{p}_{\ell/2+1}, \text{v}_{\ell/2+1}, \ldots, \text{p}_\ell, \text{v}_\ell) \leftarrow$ SOLVE($\ell/2, (\text{hist}, \text{p}_1, \text{v}_1, \ldots, \text{p}_{\ell/2}, \text{v}_{\ell/2}), \mathcal{T}_3$).
5. Output $\mathcal{T}_4, (\text{p}_1, \text{v}_1, \ldots, \text{p}_\ell, \text{v}_\ell)$.

Fig. 4.1. The rewinding strategy of the KP and PRS simulators. We stress that the actual "work" is done at the bottom level of the recursion. Even though messages $(\tilde{\text{p}}_1, \tilde{\text{v}}_1, \ldots, \tilde{\text{p}}_\ell, \tilde{\text{v}}_\ell)$ do not explicitly appear in the output, some of them (i.e., the ones that are still "relevant") do appear in the table $\mathcal{T}_4$. Notice that the timing of the rewinds is *oblivious* of the scheduling.

4.5 Analyzing the Simulation – Outline

In order to prove the correctness of the simulation, it will be sufficient to show that for every adversary verifier V^*, the three conditions corresponding to the following subsections are satisfied.

---

[2]The messages stored in $\mathcal{T}$ are used in order to determine the verifier's "challenge" according to "different" answers to (Vj). They are kept "relevant" by constantly keeping track of the sessions that are rewound past their initial commitment. That is, whenever the SOLVE procedure rewinds past the (V0) message of a session, all messages belonging to this session are deleted from $\mathcal{T}$ (since, once this happens, they become irrelevant to the rest of the simulation).

4.5.1 The Simulator Runs in Polynomial Time

Each invocation of the SOLVE procedure with parameter $\ell > 1$ involves four recursive invocations of the SOLVE procedure with parameter $\ell/2$. In addition, the work invested at the bottom of the recursion (i.e., when $\ell = 1$) is upper bounded by poly(n). Thus, the recursive work $W(m \cdot (k+1))$, that is invested by the SOLVE procedure in order to handle $m \cdot (k + 1)$ (first stage) verifier messages satisfies $W(m \cdot (k + 1)) \leq (m \cdot (k + 1))^2 \cdot \text{poly}(n) = \text{poly}(n)$ (see Sect. 5.2 for details).

4.5.2 The Simulator's Output is "Correctly" Distributed

Indistinguishability of the simulator's output from V^*'s view (of $m = \text{poly}(n)$ concurrent interactions with P) is shown assuming that the simulator does not get "stuck" during its execution (see below). Since the simulator S will get "stuck" only with negligible probability, indistinguishability will immediately follow. The key for proving the above lies in the following two properties:

- First stage messages output by S are (almost) *identically* distributed to first stage messages sent by P. This property is proved based on the definition of the simulator's actions. (We note that this property makes the analysis simpler than that of the RK protocol.)
- Second stage messages output by S are *computationally indistinguishable* from second stage messages sent by P. This property is proved based on the special zero-knowledge property of the underlying protocol (in our case, Blum's Hamiltonicity protocol).

4.5.3 The Simulator (Almost) Never Gets "Stuck"

This is the most challenging part of the proof. What is required is to show that whenever a session (out of $m = \text{poly}(|x|)$ sessions in the schedule) reaches the second stage in the protocol, the simulator has already managed to obtain the value of the "challenge" σ corresponding to this session (at least with overwhelming probability). We assume, for simplicity of presentation, that the concurrent scheduling applied by V^* is fixed in advance (where by "fixed schedule" we mean a schedule that does not vary "dynamically" as a function of the messages that V^* has seen so far). The ideas for coping with "dynamic" schedulings are presented in Chap. 5.

Partitioning the Schedule into Rewind Intervals. The execution of the SOLVE procedure induces a partitioning of the $2 \cdot m \cdot (k+1)$ (prover and verifier) messages in the schedule into *disjoint* rewind intervals. At the top level of the recursion there are two disjoint intervals of length $m \cdot (k+1)$ and at the bottom of the recursion there are $m \cdot (k+1)$ disjoint intervals of length 2. In general, at the wth level of the recursion (out of $d = \log_2(m \cdot (k+1))$ possible levels) there are 2^w disjoint intervals of $m(k + 1)/2^{w+1}$ messages each.

Notice that rewind intervals may contain messages from all sessions. Also notice that a rewind interval may be "visited" multiple times during the execution of the SOLVE procedure (a level-w interval is visited exactly 2^w times during the simulation). The fixed schedule assumption implies that each time an interval is "visited" it will contain the same scheduling of messages.

Minimal Rewind Intervals. We denote by $[a, b]$ an interval starting with prover message a and ending with verifier message b. Focusing on messages of a specific session, we note that for every pair of messages $(Pj), (Vj)$ in this session we can associate a level-w interval $[a_j, b_j]$ so that:

1. Both (Pj) and (Vj) are contained in $[a_j, b_j]$.
2. None of the level-$(w + 1)$ sub-intervals of $[a_j, b_j]$ contains both (Pj) and (Vj).

We call such a rewind interval a j-minimal interval. Notice that for every $j \in \{1, \ldots, k\}$ there is only one j-minimal interval $[a_j, b_j]$ (and that for every $j \neq j'$ the interval $[a_j, b_j]$ is different from $[a_{j'}, b_{j'}]$).

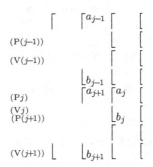

Fig. 4.2. Demonstrates the way in which minimal intervals are determined. Also demonstrates possible containments between minimal intervals of different iterations. In this example, the intervals $[a_{j-1}, b_{j-1}]$ and $[a_{j+1}, b_{j+1}]$ are disjoint (as well as the intervals $[a_{j-1}, b_{j-1}]$ and $[a_j, b_j]$), whereas the interval $[a_{j+1}, b_{j+1}]$ contains $[a_j, b_j]$.

In some sense j-minimal intervals correspond to the shortest interval in which the simulator can rewind message (Vj) (that is, while potentially changing the value of (Pj)). Intuitively, for such a rewinding to be useful, the interval should not contain message $(V0)$. Otherwise, the value that was revealed in some run of the interval becomes irrelevant once the rewinding is performed (since all the relevant values in the $\mathcal{T}$ table are deleted whenever we rewind past $(V0)$). Likewise, the interval should not contain message $(p1)$. Otherwise, the simulation faces the risk of getting "stuck" before it manages to reveal multiple $(Pj), (Vj)$ pairs of messages (by running the interval twice).

To rule out the above possibilities we focus on j-minimal intervals that contain neither (V0) nor (p1) (such intervals are called **good**). It can be seen that the number of minimal intervals that contain neither (V0) nor (p1) is at least $k - 2d$. This just follows from the fact that in every level the (V0) (resp. (p1)) message is contained in exactly one interval. In particular, the number of minimal intervals that are "spoiled" by (V0) (resp. (p1)) is at most d.

At this point, the simulator's task may seem easy to achieve. Indeed, if V^* acts according to the prescribed verifier strategy, then all that the simulator has to do is to run a good interval twice.[3] Since V^* is acting honestly, we are guaranteed that, with overwhelming probability, in each of the two runs the simulator obtains a "different" (Vj) message. In such a case, it will be sufficient to require that there *exists* a good interval. By the above discussion this is guaranteed whenever $k > 2d$ (and since $d = O(\log n)$, setting $k = w(\log n)$ will do).

Dealing with ABORT Messages: Unfortunately, the adversary verifier V^* may arbitrarily deviate from the prescribed strategy. In particular, it may be the case that throughout its interaction with the prover (simulator), V^* occasionally sends an ABORT message (in other words, V^* may potentially refuse to decommit to a previous commitment). Clearly, such an action on behalf of the verifier is considered illegal, and the interaction in the relevant session stops (i.e., there is no need to continue exchanging messages in this session). This may seem as good news (since, once this happens, the simulator does not really need to "invest" any more work in the corresponding session).

The problem is that V^* does not *always* refuse to decommit (but may refuse with some probability $0 \le p \le 1$, which is not known in advance by the simulator). Thus, if we focus on two consecutive runs of a specific interval, the simulator may find himself in a situation in which the first run is answered with ABORT whereas the second run of the interval is "properly answered". This means that the simulator has not managed to obtain the "challenge" from the two runs of this interval, and it thus faces the risk of getting "stuck" at a later stage of the interaction.

One naïve solution would be to let the simulator always output the run in which V^* has refused to decommit (that is, whenever it gets "stuck"). The problem with this solution is that it "skews" the distribution of transcripts outputted by the simulator towards transcripts that contain too many ill-formed messages. This may cause a too large deviation of the simulator's output distribution from the distribution of "real" interactions (between V^* and the honest prover P).

Another possible solution (which is the one used in the current analysis) would be to let the simulator always output the "most recently explored" run. This choice guarantees that the simulator indeed produces the "correct" distribution of first stage messages (in the sense discussed above). However

---

[3]Observe that whenever $[a_j, b_j]$ is reached during the simulation then it is run twice.

it makes him face the risk that V^* aborts in the first run of an interval and "properly answers" in the second run.

Achieving "Independent" Rewinds. Let p_j denote the probability that V^* sends a "proper" (Vj) message. Using this notation, the probability that V^* aborts in the first run of $[a_j, b_j]$ but "properly answers" in the second run is equal to $(1 - p_j) \cdot p_j \leq 1/4$ (we call this a "bad" event). Let $k' < k$ be the number of good intervals in the simulation. At first glance, it may seem that the probability of the above "bad" event to occur in *all* good intervals is upper bounded by $(1/4)^{k'}$ (which means that the probability of getting "stuck" is negligible whenever $k' = \omega(\log n)$).

However, this reasoning applies *only* when all runs of the good intervals are *independent*. Unfortunately, very strong dependencies may exist between different good intervals. This will happen whenever one good interval contains another good interval. In such a case, aborting in the first run of one interval may immediately imply abort in the first run of the other interval.

The solution is to focus on a set of *disjoint* intervals. Such intervals do not suffer from the dependencies described above, and can be shown to be "bad" independently from other (disjoint) intervals. The abundance of disjoint intervals can be easily guaranteed by taking k sufficiently large. Specifically, if $k = \omega(\log^2 n)$, then there must exist a level in the recursion (out of $d = \log(m \cdot (k+1)) = O(\log n)$ levels) that contains at least $k' = \omega(\log^2 n)/d = \omega(\log n)$ good intervals. Since same level intervals are all disjoint, then their runs are "independent." In particular, the probability that for all of them the "bad" event will occur is negligible. This yields the following theorem (due to Kilian and Petrank).

Theorem 4.2 ([82]) *Suppose that there exist statistically hiding commitment schemes, and let $\alpha : N \to N$ be any super-constant function. Then, there exists an $O(\alpha(n) \cdot \log^2 n)$-round black-box concurrent zero-knowledge proof system for every language $L \in \mathcal{NP}$.*

The above result yields a dramatic improvement over the Richardson–Kilian original analysis, but still falls short of obtaining optimal (namely logarithmic) round-complexity. In order to further reduce the number of rounds to $O(\alpha(n) \cdot \log n)$ several new ideas are required. These ideas were introduced by Prabhakharan, Rosen and Sahai [93], and are presented next.

Special Intervals. Unfortunately, the above argument (establishing the abundance of disjoint intervals) does not extend to the case when $k = \tilde{O}(\log n)$. Here we are not guaranteed that there exists a level with many good intervals. In fact, there may exist only few (i.e., $k' = o(\log n)$) disjoint intervals. To overcome this obstacle, we use a completely different approach. Rather than proving the existence of a *large* set of disjoint intervals (each being executed twice), we prove the existence of a (possibly small) set of disjoint intervals and guarantee that the *total* number of executions of these intervals is large. By doing so, we exploit the fact that, from the time that (V0) is visited until the time that (p1) is reached, the simulator *typically* visits each rewinding interval *many times* (and not just twice as we assumed before).

Specifically, for every scheduling applied by V^*, we define our set of intervals as the set of all minimal intervals that do not contain any other minimal interval (i.e., intervals $[a_j, b_j]$ that do not contain $[a_{j'}, b_{j'}]$ for any $j' \neq j$). We call such intervals **special** intervals. Notice that all special intervals are disjoint. We let $S \subseteq \{1, \ldots, k\}$ denote the set of all indices j for which $[a_j, b_j]$ is special. For simplicity, assume that $S = \{1, \ldots, |S|\}$.

Our goal will be to bound (from below) the total number of times that special intervals are visited. To do so, we introduce a notion of "distance" between consecutive special intervals. This "distance" is supposed to reflect the number of times that a certain special interval has been executed since the last time that the preceding special interval has been visited. For every $j \in S$, we let d_j denote the "distance" of $[a_j, b_j]$ from $[a_{j-1}, b_{j-1}]$.[4] Using this definition we show that, no matter what the scheduling strategy applied by V^* is, the following two conditions are always satisfied:

1. The number of "independent" runs of $[a_j, b_j]$ since $[a_{j-1}, b_{j-1}]$ has been last visited is 2^{d_j}.
2. $\sum_{j \in S} d_j \geq k - d$.

Loosely speaking, item 1 follows from the definition of d_j and from the fact that $[a_j, b_j]$ and $[a_{j-1}, b_{j-1}]$ are disjoint. As for item 2, this is a combinatorial statement on binary trees, which is proved by induction on the number of minimal intervals in the "recursion tree".

Bounding the Failure Probability. Recall that we are interested in the probability that the "bad" event occurs during the simulation. Whereas in the previous analysis, this happened only if for all intervals the first run was aborted and the second was "properly answered", in the current analysis the simulator will fail only if for *every* $j \in \{1, \ldots, |S|\}$, it holds that the first $2^{d_j} - 1$ runs of the interval $[a_j, b_j]$ are aborted and the last one is "properly answered" (since otherwise the simulator has managed to obtain two "different" answers to (Vj)).

Let $\mathcal{R}$ be the set of all random tapes used by the simulator. A specific $\rho \in \mathcal{R}$ is said to be "bad" if the "bad" event occurs during a simulation that uses ρ as random tape (if the "bad" event does not occur during the simulation then ρ is called "good"). We shall show that the fraction of "bad" tapes $\rho \in \mathcal{R}$ is negligible. To do this we will show that every "bad" random tape can be mapped into a set of *super-polynomially* many other "good" random tapes so that every two "bad" random tapes are mapped to two *disjoint* sets of "good" random tapes. This would imply that for every random tape that leads to the simulator's failure there exist super-polynomially many other tapes that do

---

[4] The value d_j is defined as the "recursive depth" of $[a_j, b_j]$ relative to the "common ancestor" of $[a_j, b_j]$ and $[a_{j-1}, b_{j-1}]$ (i.e., relative to the smallest rewind interval containing both $[a_j, b_j]$ and $[a_{j-1}, b_{j-1}]$).

not. Since the simulator picks a random tape uniformly amongst all possible random tapes, it follows that the simulator's failure probability is negligible.

Mapping a "Bad" Random Tape to Many "Good" Tapes. Let $u_1, \ldots, u_{|S|}$ (where for every $j \in \{1, \ldots, |S|\}$, the value of u_j is chosen in $\{1, \ldots, 2^{d_j}\}$). We map a random tape $\rho \in \mathcal{R}$ into another random tape $\rho' \in \mathcal{R}$ by swapping the portion of ρ used to produce prover messages in the u_j^{th} run of $[a_j, b_j]$ with the portion used in the $(2^{d_j})^{\text{th}}$ run (this is done for all $j \in S$). The swappings are made possible due to the following facts: (1) Prover messages in interval $[a_j, b_j]$ are produced using "fresh" randomness each time it is visited. (2) If two intervals $[a_j, b_j]$ and $[a_{j'}, b_{j'}]$ are disjoint then so is the randomness used to produce their corresponding prover messages (recall that all special intervals are disjoint).

We claim that if ρ is a "bad" random tape, then after the swappings have been applied, the resulting tape ρ' is "good". To see this, consider the smallest $j \in S$ for which $u_j \neq 2^{d_j}$ (i.e., for which the u_j^{th} run of $[a_j, b_j]$ and the $(2^{d_j})^{\text{th}}$ run have been actually swapped). The key observation is that, once the swappings have been applied to ρ, the last run of $[a_j, b_j]$ is aborted (and one of the first $2^{d_j} - 1$ runs is "properly answered").[5] In other words, there exists a $j \in S$ for which the "bad" event does not occur during the simulation (and so ρ' is "good").[6]

The above argument will apply as long as the sequence $u_1, \ldots, u_{|S|}$ causes the randomness of at least one special interval to be swapped. The number of possibilities to choose $u_1, \ldots, u_{|S|}$ so that this happens (i.e., the randomness of at least one special interval is swapped) is:

$$\prod_{j \in S} 2^{d_j} - 1 = 2^{\sum_{j \in S} d_j} - 1 \geq 2^{k-d} - 1$$

(the sequence $u_1, \ldots, u_{|S|} = 2^{d_1}, \ldots, 2^{d_{|S|}}$ being the only one that leaves the coin tosses intact). Overall, we get that a single "bad" random tape $\rho \in \mathcal{R}$ can be mapped to as many as $2^{k-d} - 1$ other "good" random tapes. As we show below, any two such "bad" tapes will be mapped to *disjoint* sets of "good" tapes and so the fraction of "bad" random tapes is at most $2^{k-d} = 2^{k-O(\log n)}$. Thus, whenever $k = \omega(\log n)$, the probability that the simulator gets "stuck" is negligible.

Defining an "Inverse" Mapping. To argue that any two "bad" random tapes are mapped to disjoint sets of "good" tapes we will define an "inverse"

---

[5] Here we rely on the fact that the simulator's coin tosses completely determine the outcome of an interval's run (that is, modulo the history of the interaction up to the starting point of the interval).

[6] To see that the simulator does not get "stuck" when using ρ' as its random tape, notice that when reaching the second stage of the corresponding session, the simulator will not have to do anything in order to successfully produce a second stage transcript (since all second stage messages should appear as being aborted anyway).

to the above mapping. To do this, we should be able, given a "good" random tape $\rho' \in \mathcal{R}$, to determine the value of u_j for every $j \in \{1, \ldots, |S|\}$ (that is, we should be able to determine with which run of $[a_j, b_j]$ the last run was swapped).

In order to determine the value of the u_j's we will run the simulation with ρ' as random tape and examine for which special intervals one of the first $2^{d_j} - 1$ runs is "properly answered" and the last run is aborted by V^*. Once u_j is determined for some interval, we will swap back its randomness and continue to inspect and swap the next special interval.

If we take care of inspecting the intervals and reversing the swapping of their randomness "inductively", we are guaranteed that for every interval that we are examining exactly one of the runs is "properly answered" and the others are aborted. Loosely speaking, this follows from the fact that the "good" tape that we are trying to invert originates from a "bad" tape in which every interval is aborted in the first $2^{d_j} - 1$ runs and "properly answered" in the last run.

The reason why the order of swapping is important is that V^*'s answer in a specific interval also depends on the randomness used to run the "most recent execution" of previous intervals (since, whenever we reach a specific interval, the outcome of these "recent" runs appears in the history of the interaction). In order to be able to say something meaningful about an interval's run we must make sure that, whenever we inspect the run of the simulator on this interval, the history of the interaction up to the starting point of the interval is consistent with the outcome of running the simulator with the "bad" tape that we are aiming to obtain.

As soon as we reach the last special interval we know that the resulting tape is the original "bad" random tape (since all along the way we preserve the "invariant" that the randomness used so far is consistent with the original "bad" random tape).

5

$c\mathcal{ZK}$ in Logarithmically Many Rounds

This chapter contains a full analysis of the PRS protocol. Specifically, assuming the existence of statistically hiding commitment schemes, it is shown that every language in $\mathcal{NP}$ can be proved in $c\mathcal{ZK}$ using (essentially) logarithmically many rounds of interaction. This is stated in the following theorem.

Theorem 5.1 ([93]) *Suppose that there exist statistically hiding commitment schemes, and let $\alpha : N \to N$ be any super-constant function.[1] Then, there exists an $O(\alpha(n) \cdot \log n)$-round black-box concurrent zero-knowledge proof system for every language $L \in \mathcal{NP}$.*

The proof of Theorem 5.1 is based on the work of Prabhakharan, Rosen and Sahai [93], which in turn builds on the protocol by Richardson and Kilian [94] and on the simulator by Kilian and Petrank [82]. The PRS analysis of the simulator's execution is more sophisticated than the KP one and thus yields a stronger result. It involves a novel counting argument that involves a direct analysis of the underlying probability space. This is in contrast to the previous approaches that involved subtle manipulations of conditional probabilities.

Our exposition of the proof follows the high-level analysis presented in Chap. 4. Due to the complexity of the material, it is advised to go over the high level analysis before actually delving into the details of the proof.

5.1 Detailed Description of the Simulator

In order to demonstrate the concurrent zero-knowledge property of Construction 4.3.1, we will show that for every polynomial $p(\cdot)$ there exists a "universal" black-box simulator, S_p, so that for every $G = (V, E) \in \mathrm{HC}$ and concurrent adversary verifier V^* (running at most $p(|V|)$ concurrent sessions), $S_p(G)$ runs in time $\mathrm{poly}(n)$ (where $n = |V|$), and so that the ensemble $\{\mathrm{view}_{V^*}^P(G)\}_{G \in HC}$ is computationally indistinguishable from the ensemble $\{S_p^{V^*}(G)\}_{G \in HC}$.

---

[1] $\alpha : N \to N$ is super-constant if for any $c > 0$ there exists $n_c \in N$ so that for all $n > n_c$ it holds that $\alpha(n) > c$.

5.1.1 The Main Procedure and Ideas

We assume that the number of sessions that are run by the concurrent adversary verifier V^* is fixed in advance and known to everybody. We denote it by m ($= \text{poly}(n)$). The simulator S_m starts by selecting and fixing a random tape r for V^*. It then proceeds by exploring various prefixes of possible interactions between P and V^*. This is done while having only "black-box" access to V^*'s strategy (as described in Sect. 3.7). For simplicity of presentation, we partition the description of the simulator's strategy into two disjoint (but not independent) procedures. The first procedure handles the messages that are exchanged in the first stage of the protocol. This is done while completely ignoring the messages of the second stage. The second procedure handles the messages in the second stage while using auxiliary information produced by the first procedure. This information is located in some "global" data structure that is dynamically updated (by the first procedure) as the simulation proceeds. To complete the simulator's description we describe how the two procedures can be merged into one super-procedure that with overwhelming probability outputs a "legal" transcript (representing a concurrent interaction between P and V^*). The analysis of the simulator's running time and output distribution are then presented in Sects. 5.2, 5.3 and 5.4.

Handling First-Stage Messages

First-stage messages are handled by the SOLVE procedure. The goal of this procedure is to supply the simulator with the values of V^*'s "challenges" before it reaches the second stage in the protocol (where by "challenges" we refer to messages σ that correspond to Step (v1) of Construction 4.3.1). To this end, the SOLVE procedure tries to make sure that for every session (out of m concurrent sessions) there exists $i, j \in \{1, \ldots, k\} \times \{1, \ldots, k\}$ for which the verifier V^* has properly revealed the values of both $\sigma_{i,j}^0$ and $\sigma_{i,j}^1$ (during the simulation process). This should always take place prior to reaching the second stage of the corresponding session (or otherwise, the simulator will get "stuck"). Once both $\sigma_{i,j}^0$ and $\sigma_{i,j}^1$ are revealed, the value of V^*'s challenge (which should be equal to $\sigma_{i,j}^0 \oplus \sigma_{i,j}^1$) can be easily determined, and the required goal is indeed achieved.

In order to receive both $\sigma_{i,j}^0$ and $\sigma_{i,j}^1$ (i.e., in some (Vj) message of a specific session), the simulator must explore at least two different interaction prefixes in which the corresponding (Pj) message is different. The way this is done is by means of "rewinding" the interaction with V^* to a point in the schedule that precedes the (Pj) message (while hoping that the (Pj) message is indeed modified in the process).[2]

---

[2] Note that great care should be taken in planning the rewinding strategy. As we have previously mentioned, rewinding a specific session in the concurrent setting may result in loss of work done for other sessions, and cause the simulator to do

The rewinding strategy of the SOLVE procedure is recursive and is essentially identical to the simulation strategy suggested by Kilian–Petrank [82]. The key idea underlying this simulation strategy is that the order and timing of the simulator's rewinds are determined *obliviously* of the concurrent scheduling (which is determined "on the fly" by the adversary verifier V^*). Specifically, the order and timing of the rewinds depend only on m, the number of concurrent sessions (which, by definition, is determined prior to the simulation process), and on the length of the execution prefix explored so far.[3]

The "Global" Data Structure. To store the values it has discovered about the verifier's "challenge" in session $s \in \{1, \ldots, m\}$, the SOLVE procedure will write information into a table denoted $\mathcal{T}$. This table will contain the (first stage) verifier messages that have been revealed so far (such messages may consist of the opened values of some $\{\sigma_{i,j}^{r_j}\}_{i=1}^k$'s or, alternatively, of an ABORT message). As we have already mentioned, "rewinds" that take place during the simulation process may render part of the data stored in the $\mathcal{T}$ table irrelevant. In particular, whenever the interaction is rewound to a point that precedes the verifier's preliminary commitment in session s (i.e., a (V0) message), all the values corresponding to session s in the $\mathcal{T}$ table are not relevant any more. In such cases, these values should be deleted from the table and the accumulation of information for session s should restart from scratch.

The Input of the SOLVE Procedure. The SOLVE procedure is given three arguments as input. The first argument, denoted ℓ, is a parameter determining the total number of verifier messages that the SOLVE procedure should handle. At the top level of the recursion, the argument ℓ equals $m \cdot (k+1)$, which is the total number of (first stage) verifier messages in a schedule of m sessions (that is, including the verifier's preliminary step, (V0)). For simplicity of exposition, we assume that $m \cdot (k+1)$ is a power of 2 (without any loss of generality). At the bottom level of the recursion, the SOLVE procedure should handle a single (first stage) verifier message (that is, ℓ equals 1).

The second argument given to the SOLVE procedure, denoted hist, is a sequence of alternating prover and verifier messages which corresponds to the "most recently visited" history of the interaction (as induced by the simulator's queries). In accordance with our conventions, all queries made by the relevant invocation of the SOLVE procedure will have hist as their prefix. At

---

the same amount of work again. In particular, all simulation work done for sessions starting after the point to which to rewind may be lost (since the revealed values of $\sigma_{i,j}^0$ and $\sigma_{i,j}^1$ become irrelevant once we rewind to a point preceding the verifier's preliminary commitment in Step (V0)). Conducting a "wasteful" rewinding strategy may cause the work done by the simulator to accumulate to too much (thus causing the simulator to run in super-polynomial time).

[3]This is in contrast to the rewinding strategy of the Richardson–Kilian simulator [94] which heavily depends on the schedule as it is being revealed (remember that the scheduling is dynamically determined by the adversary verifier and is not necessarily known to the simulator in advance).

the top level of the recursion, the hist argument is initialized as an empty
list and becomes increasingly longer as the simulation proceeds (its eventual
length being $2m \cdot (k + 1)$). In intermediate stages of the recursion the hist
argument may initially be of arbitrary length and is eventually augmented
with a suffix containing a total of 2ℓ (prover and verifier) messages.

The third argument of the SOLVE procedure is the table $\mathcal{T}$. As mentioned
above, this argument is used in order to store the first stage messages revealed
so far. In order to keep these messages relevant, the SOLVE procedure will
inspect the hist argument to see for which sessions the (V0) message does not
appear in the history of the interaction. Since for such sessions, any value that
is possibly stored in the $\mathcal{T}$ table is not relevant for the rest of the simulation
(see above discussion about the "global" data structure), the SOLVE procedure
will delete this value from the $\mathcal{T}$ table and will restart the accumulation of
information for these sessions from scratch.

The SOLVE Procedure. We are now ready to proceed with the description
of the SOLVE procedure. Given ℓ, hist and $\mathcal{T}$ as inputs, the SOLVE procedure
acts as follows (see also Fig. 4.1):

If $\ell = 1$ (i.e., we are at the bottom level of the recursion):
1. If (V0) message of session s does not appear in hist, delete all session
   s messages from $\mathcal{T}$.
2. Uniformly choose a first stage prover message p, and feed V^* with
   $\overline{q} = (\text{hist}, \text{p})$.
3. Store V^*'s answer v, in $\mathcal{T}$.[4]
4. Output (p, v), $\mathcal{T}$.

If $\ell > 1$ (i.e., we are at some intermediate level of the recursion):
1. Invoke the SOLVE procedure recursively with parameters $\ell/2$, hist and
   $\mathcal{T}$. The recursive invocation outputs a table $\mathcal{T}_1$, as well as a transcript
   of ℓ (first stage) messages denoted $(\tilde{\text{p}}_1, \tilde{\text{v}}_1, \ldots, \tilde{\text{p}}_{\ell/2}, \tilde{\text{v}}_{\ell/2})$.
2. "Rewind" the interaction and perform Step 1 again. That is, invoke
   the SOLVE procedure recursively with parameters $\ell/2$, hist and $\mathcal{T}_1$.
   The recursive invocation outputs a table $\mathcal{T}_2$, as well as a transcript of
   ℓ (first stage) messages denoted $(\text{p}_1, \text{v}_1, \ldots, \text{p}_{\ell/2}, \text{v}_{\ell/2})$.[5]
3. Augment the hist argument with the "most recently visited" transcript
   (that is, the transcript $(\text{p}_1, \text{v}_1, \ldots, \text{p}_{\ell/2}, \text{v}_{\ell/2})$ computed in Step 2)
   and invoke recursively the SOLVE procedure with parameters $\ell/2$,

---

[4]The message $\text{v} = V^*(\overline{q})$ consists of a first stage verifier message in some session
$s' \in \{1, \ldots, m\}$. It is either of the form (V0) or (Vj) for some $j \in \{1, \ldots, k\}$
(supposedly containing the "legal" openings of $\sigma_{1,j}^{r_{1,j}}, \ldots, \sigma_{k,j}^{r_{k,j}}$).

[5]We stress that corresponding messages in the $(\tilde{\text{p}}_1, \tilde{\text{v}}_1, \ldots, \tilde{\text{p}}_{\ell/2}, \tilde{\text{v}}_{\ell/2})$ and the
$(\text{p}_1, \text{v}_1, \ldots, \text{p}_{\ell/2}, \text{v}_{\ell/2})$ sequences do not necessarily belong to the same sessions
$s \in \{1, \ldots, m\}$. This is because the concurrent schedule may be "dynamically"
determined by V^* as a function of the history of the interaction (in particular, dif-
ferent values of $\tilde{\text{p}}_1, \ldots, \tilde{\text{p}}_{\ell/2}$ and $\text{p}_1, \ldots, \text{p}_{\ell/2}$ may cause the corresponding answers
of V^* to belong to different sessions).

(hist, $p_1, v_1, \ldots, p_{\ell/2}, v_{\ell/2}$) and $\mathcal{T}_2$. The recursive invocation outputs a table $\mathcal{T}_3$, as well as a transcript of the ℓ subsequent (first stage) messages denoted $(\tilde{p}_{\ell/2+1}, \tilde{v}_{\ell/2+1}, \ldots, \tilde{p}_\ell, \tilde{v}_\ell)$.

4. "Rewind" the interaction and perform Step 3 again. That is, invoke the SOLVE procedure recursively with parameters $\ell/2$, (hist, $p_1, v_1, \ldots,$ $p_{\ell/2}, v_{\ell/2}$) and $\mathcal{T}_2$. The recursive invocation outputs a table $\mathcal{T}_4$, as well as a transcript of the ℓ subsequent (first stage) messages denoted $(p_{\ell/2+1}, v_{\ell/2+1}, \ldots, p_\ell, v_\ell).$[6]

5. Output $\mathcal{T}_4$ and the "most recently visited" transcript, which consists of the messages $(p_1, v_1, \ldots, p_\ell, v_\ell)$.

Some Comments. Notice that the order and timing of the "rewinds" performed by the SOLVE procedure are determined obliviously of the concurrent schedule (whereas the order in which the $\mathcal{T}$ table is updated *does* depend on the scheduling of the various messages in the various sessions). Also note that, as opposed to the [94, 82] simulation strategies, the values of the (first stage) prover messages (i.e., of (Pj) messages) do not depend on the values revealed by the verifier in the corresponding answers (i.e., in the (Vj) messages), but are rather chosen uniformly and independently each time. Since the transcript output by the simulator consists of the prover/verifier messages that were "most recently visited" by the SOLVE procedure, the first stage messages that eventually appear in the simulator's output are *identically* distributed to "real" first stage messages (i.e., messages that are actually exchanged between an honest prover P and the verifier V^*).

Updating the $\mathcal{T}$ Table. The $\mathcal{T}$ table is updated only when visiting the bottom level of the recursion. Given a first stage verifier message v, the SOLVE procedure determines the session number, $s \in \{1, \ldots, m\}$, of the corresponding (Vj) message (according to the session identifiers that appear in v) and stores (Vj) in $\mathcal{T}$. The (Vj) message may either contain a sequence $\sigma_{1,j}^{r_{1,j}}, \ldots, \sigma_{1,j}^{r_{1,j}}$ of n-bit strings or an ABORT message. Since the (Pj) message to which (Vj) is given as answer may occur in the schedule much earlier than (Vj) does, the simulator may perform rewinds that do not reach (Pj) (and so do not change its value), but repeatedly obtain different (Vj)'s as answer. In such cases, the SOLVE procedure will always store the "recently obtained" (Vj) message instead of previous ones (that were given as answer to the same (Pj)).

Note that since the schedule may vary "dynamically" as a function of the history of the interaction, it may be the case that not all messages in a specific session $s \in \{1, \ldots, m\}$ are "visited" the same number of times by the SOLVE procedure. In particular, the number of verifier messages that appear in $\mathcal{T}$ may differ from session to session and from iteration to iteration (within a specific session). A detailed analysis of the contents of the $\mathcal{T}$ table whenever the simulator reaches the second stage in session s appears in Section 5.4.

---

[6] Again, corresponding messages in the $(\tilde{p}_{\ell/2+1}, \tilde{v}_{\ell/2+1}, \ldots, \tilde{p}_\ell, \tilde{v}_\ell)$ and the $(p_{\ell/2+1}, v_{\ell/2+1}, \ldots, p_\ell, v_\ell)$ sequences do not necessarily belong to the same session.

Handling Second Stage Messages

Second-stage messages are handled by the PROVE procedure. The goal of this procedure is to produce a second-stage transcript that is indistinguishable from actual second stage transcripts (that is, between P and V^*). This should be done while avoiding a situation in which the basic Hamiltonicity proof system that is conducted in the second-stage of the protocol is rejected by the verifier V^* (since in such cases the simulator may get "stuck"). The key for the success of the PROVE procedure lies in the success of the SOLVE procedure to discover the "challenge" sent by V^* already during the first stage of the protocol. Given that the SOLVE procedure has indeed succeeded in discovering the "challenge", the task of the PROVE procedure is trivial (whereas if the SOLVE procedure did not succeed to discover the "challenge" then the PROVE procedure is bound to fail). One other case in which the task of the PROVE procedure is trivial is when the "current history" of the interaction contains an ABORT message on behalf of the verifier V^* (that is, in the relevant session). In such cases the interaction in the relevant session stops and the PROVE procedure does not need to do anything in order to produce a "legal" second stage transcript.

The PROVE Procedure. The PROVE procedure is invoked either when the concurrent schedule reaches the first prover message in the second stage of session $s \in \{1, \ldots, m\}$ (that is, a (p1) message) or when it reaches the second prover message in the second stage (that is, a (p2) message). Note that this may happen many times during the simulation process (as induced by the adversary verifier's scheduling strategy and the "rewinds" of the SOLVE procedure). On input $s \in \{1, \ldots, m\}$ and a partial execution transcript (denoted hist), the PROVE procedure acts as follows:

1. Start by checking whether the hist argument contains an ABORT message on behalf of the verifier (in session s). Specifically, for every $j \in \{1, \ldots, k\}$, check whether the (Vj) message of session s (as it appears in hist) consists of an ABORT message. If it does (for some j), abort session s (just as an honest prover P would have done in such a case).

2. Otherwise (i.e., the hist argument does not contain an ABORT message in session s), search the $\mathcal{T}$ table for a pair $\sigma_{i,j}^0, \sigma_{i,j}^1$ belonging to session s:

   a) If the $\mathcal{T}$ table does not contain such a pair (that is, if for every i, j the $\mathcal{T}$ table contains only $\sigma_{i,j}^b$ for some fixed $b \in \{0, 1\}$, and possibly some additional ABORT messages), output $\perp$ (indicating failure of simulation).

   b) If the $\mathcal{T}$ table indeed contains a pair $\sigma_{i,j}^0$ and $\sigma_{i,j}^1$ belonging to session s, compute the value of V^*'s "challenge", $\sigma = \sigma_{i,j}^0 \oplus \sigma_{i,j}^1$ and invoke the CONVINCE subroutine with input (σ, hist). The CONVINCE subroutine handles the execution of second-stage messages in the protocol (and is described below).

c) Let p denote the output of the CONVINCE subroutine (where p is either of the form (p1) or (p2), depending on our location in the schedule). Output p.

The CONVINCE Subroutine. Given the value of $\sigma = \sigma_1 \sigma_2 \ldots \sigma_n$, the pair i, j, and hist, the CONVINCE subroutine handles the ℓth (parallel) execution in the second stage of session s in the following way:

Prover's first step (p1): *If $\sigma_\ell = 0$, act according to Step $(\widehat{p1})$ in Construction 4.1.1. Specifically, select a random permutation, π, of the vertices V, and commit (using a statistically-binding commitment scheme) to the entries of the adjacency matrix of the resulting permuted graph. That is, output an n-by-n matrix of commitments so that the $(\pi(u), \pi(v))^{\text{th}}$ entry is a commitment to 1 if $(u, v) \in E$, and is a commitment to 0 otherwise.*
Otherwise (i.e., if $\sigma_\ell = 1$), commit to the entries of the adjacency matrix of the full graph K_n. That is, output an n-by-n matrix of commitments so that for every $(u, v) \in \{1, \ldots, n\}$, the $(u, v)^{\text{th}}$ entry is a commitment to 1.

Prover's second step (p2): *Check (in hist) that V^* has properly decommitted to all relevant values (just as the honest prover in Construction 4.3.1 would have done). In addition, check that the ℓth bit of $\sigma_{i,j}^0 \oplus \sigma_{i,j}^1$ indeed equals σ_ℓ for the given i, j. In case that the ℓth bit of $\sigma_{i,j}^0 \oplus \sigma_{i,j}^1$ is NOT equal to σ_ℓ for some ℓ, but all the decommitments are proper, output $\perp$.[7]*
If $\sigma_\ell = 0$, output π along with the revealing of all commitments.
Otherwise (i.e., if $\sigma_\ell = 1$), output only the openings of commitments to entries $(\pi(u), \pi(v))$ with $(u, v) \in C$ where C is an arbitrary Hamiltonian cycle in K_n. In both cases also supply the corresponding decommitments.

Some Comments. Note that the CONVINCE subroutine never causes the verifier V^* to reject in the second stage (that is, unless V^* manages to break the computational binding property of the commitment used in (V0)). The reason for this is that it is always invoked with the correct value of σ (which was previously revealed by the SOLVE procedure). In particular, once the PROVE procedure has "safely" reached Step 2b the success of the PROVE procedure is guaranteed (at least with overwhelming probability).

The actions taken by the CONVINCE subroutine are identical to the actions taken by the simulator of Blum's basic Hamiltonicity protocol (again, conditioning on V^* not breaking the commitment in (V0)). As a consequence, the distribution of the simulated second stages in our protocol are (almost) identical to the distribution produced by Blum's simulator. This fact will be used later in order to reduce the indistinguishability property of our simulator's output to the indistinguishability property of Blum's simulator's output.

---

[7]Notice that the latter will occur only in case that V^* has violated the computational binding property of the commitment used in message (V0) (and hence happens only with negligible probability).

5.1.2 The Actual Simulator

The SIM procedure which merges the SOLVE and PROVE procedures together handles all messages sent by V^* during the simulation process (that is, both first-stage and second-stage messages). In general, the SIM procedure is obtained by incorporating the PROVE procedure into the SOLVE procedure in a way that enables the SOLVE procedure to handle also second-stage messages (see Fig. 5.1 for a "pseudocode" description of the SIM procedure).

Procedure $\text{SIM}(\ell, \text{hist}, \mathcal{T})$:

1. If $\ell = 1$,
   a) If session s does not appear in hist, delete all session s messages in $\mathcal{T}$.
   b) As long as no first-stage verifier message has been reached, do:
      i. If next scheduled message, $\mathbf{p}_u$, is a first-stage prover message:
         Uniformly choose $\mathbf{p}_u$, and set $\mathbf{v}_u \leftarrow V^*(\text{hist}, \mathbf{p}_1, \mathbf{v}_1, \ldots, \mathbf{p}_{u-1}, \mathbf{v}_{u-1}, \mathbf{p}_u)$.
      ii. If next scheduled message, $\mathbf{p}_u$, is a second-stage prover message:
         Set $\mathbf{p}_u \leftarrow \text{PROVE}(i, (\text{hist}, \mathbf{p}_1, \mathbf{v}_1, \ldots, \mathbf{p}_{u-1}, \mathbf{v}_{u-1}))$,
         and $\mathbf{v}_u \leftarrow V^*(\text{hist}, \mathbf{p}_1, \mathbf{v}_1, \ldots, \mathbf{v}_{u-1}, \mathbf{p}_u)$.
   c) As soon as a first-stage message $\mathbf{v}_\alpha$ has been reached store $\mathbf{v}_\alpha$ in $\mathcal{T}$.
   d) Output $\mathcal{T}$ and $(\mathbf{p}_1, \mathbf{v}_1, \ldots, \mathbf{p}_\alpha, \mathbf{v}_\alpha)$.
   Remark: $\mathbf{v}_\alpha$ is the only first-stage verifier message in $(\mathbf{p}_1, \mathbf{v}_1, \ldots, \mathbf{p}_\alpha, \mathbf{v}_\alpha)$.
2. Otherwise (i.e., if $\ell > 1$),
   a) Set $\mathcal{T}_1, (\tilde{\mathbf{p}}_1, \tilde{\mathbf{v}}_1, \ldots, \tilde{\mathbf{p}}_{\tilde{\alpha}}, \tilde{\mathbf{v}}_{\tilde{\alpha}}) \leftarrow \text{SIM}(\ell/2, \text{hist}, \mathcal{T})$.
   b) Set $\mathcal{T}_2, (\mathbf{p}_1, \mathbf{v}_1, \ldots, \mathbf{p}_\alpha, \mathbf{v}_\alpha) \leftarrow \text{SIM}(\ell/2, \text{hist}, \mathcal{T}_1)$.
   c) Set $\mathcal{T}_3, (\tilde{\mathbf{p}}_{\alpha+1}, \tilde{\mathbf{v}}_{\alpha+1}, \ldots, \tilde{\mathbf{p}}_{\alpha+\tilde{\beta}}, \tilde{\mathbf{v}}_{\alpha+\tilde{\beta}}) \leftarrow \text{SIM}(\ell/2, (\text{hist}, \mathbf{p}_1, \mathbf{v}_1, \ldots, \mathbf{p}_\alpha, \mathbf{v}_\alpha), \mathcal{T}_2)$.
   d) Set $\mathcal{T}_4, (\mathbf{p}_{\alpha+1}, \mathbf{v}_{\alpha+1}, \ldots, \mathbf{p}_{\alpha+\beta}, \mathbf{v}_{\alpha+\beta}) \leftarrow \text{SIM}(\ell/2, (\text{hist}, \mathbf{p}_1, \mathbf{v}_1, \ldots, \mathbf{p}_\alpha, \mathbf{v}_\alpha), \mathcal{T}_3)$.
   e) Output $\mathcal{T}_4$ and $(\mathbf{p}_1, \mathbf{v}_1, \ldots, \mathbf{p}_{\alpha+\beta}, \mathbf{v}_{\alpha+\beta})$.
   Remark: (1) The value of $\tilde{\alpha}$ (resp. $\tilde{\beta}$) is not necessarily equal to the value of α (resp. β). (2) The sequence $(\mathbf{p}_1, \mathbf{v}_1, \ldots, \mathbf{p}_{\alpha+\beta}, \mathbf{v}_{\alpha+\beta})$ contains exactly 2ℓ first-stage prover and verifier messages (as well as arbitrarily many second-stage messages). In particular, $\alpha + \beta \geq \ell$.

Fig. 5.1. The SIM procedure. Handles both first and second stage messages. It is obtained by merging the SOLVE and PROVE procedures (while using the table $\mathcal{T}$).

The two main modifications applied to the SOLVE procedure (in order to obtain the SIM procedure) are the following: (1) If $\ell = 1$ (that is, at the bottom level of the recursion), the SIM procedure will keep exchanging messages until it reaches a first-stage verifier message. This is done while augmenting the hist argument with the corresponding outcomes of the PROVE procedure (according to the schedule that is being revealed by V^*). Once a first-stage message is reached, the SIM procedure acts exactly as the SOLVE procedure. (2) Similarly to the SOLVE procedure, the output of the SIM procedure is a partial execution transcript. However, unlike the SOLVE procedure, the output length of the SIM procedure is greater than 2ℓ (since, besides 2ℓ first-stage messages, it will also contain second-stage messages).

5.2 The Simulator's Running Time

We start by showing that the simulator's running time is polynomial both in m and in $n = |V|$. Since $m = \text{poly}(n)$ it will follow that the simulator runs in polynomial-time in n.

Using the fact that the total number of sessions run by the adversary verifier V^* is at most m, we infer that the number of invocations of the PROVE procedure at the bottom level of the recursion (i.e., when $\ell = 1$) is upper bounded by m. In particular, the work invested by the SIM procedure at the bottom level of the recursion is upper bounded by $\text{poly}(n) \cdot m = \text{poly}(n)$ (where the $\text{poly}(n)$ factor in the $\text{poly}(n) \cdot m$ term results from the polynomial amount of work invested in each invocation of the PROVE procedure). Since each invocation of the SIM procedure with parameter $\ell > 1$ involves four recursive invocations of the SIM procedure with parameter $\ell/2$, we have that the work $W(\ell)$ that is invested by the SIM procedure in order to handle ℓ (first stage) verifier messages satisfies:

$$W(\ell) \leq \begin{cases} \text{poly}(n) & \text{If } \ell = 1 \\ 4 \cdot W(\ell/2) & \text{If } \ell > 1. \end{cases} \tag{5.1}$$

Since the total number of first stage verifier messages in the m sessions of the concurrent schedule equals $m \cdot (k + 1)$, the total running time of the simulation process (which consists of a single invocation of the SIM procedure with parameter $m \cdot (k+1)$) equals $W(m \cdot (k+1))$. A straightforward solution of the recursive formula in (5.1) establishes that $W(m \cdot (k+1))$ is upper bounded by:

$$4^{\log_2(m \cdot (k+1))} \cdot \text{poly}(n) = (m \cdot (k+1))^2 \cdot \text{poly}(n) = \text{poly}(n).$$

Hence, we have:

Proposition 5.2.1 *For every* $m = \text{poly}(n)$, *the simulator* S_m *runs in (strict) polynomial-time in* n.

5.3 The Simulator's Output Distribution

We now turn to show that for every $G \in HC$, the simulator's output distribution is computationally indistinguishable from V^*'s view of interactions with the honest prover P. Specifically,

Proposition 5.3.1 *The ensemble* $\{S_m^{V^*}(G)\}_{G \in HC}$ *is computationally indistinguishable from the ensemble* $\{\text{view}_{V^*}^P(G)\}_{G \in HC}$.

Proof As a hybrid experiment, consider what happens to the output distribution of the simulator S_m if we (slightly) modify its simulation strategy in the following way. Suppose that on input $G = (V, E) \in HC$, the simulator S_m obtains a directed Hamiltonian cycle $C \subset E$ in G (as auxiliary input) and uses it in order to produce real prover messages whenever it reaches the second stage of the protocol. Specifically, whenever it reaches the second stage of session $s \in \{1, \ldots, m\}$, the hybrid simulator inspects the $\mathcal{T}$ table and checks whether the PROVE procedure should output $\perp$.

If the PROVE procedure has to output $\perp$, the hybrid simulator outputs $\perp$ and halts (this could happen both in Step 2.a of the PROVE procedure or in Step (p2) of the CONVINCE subroutine). Otherwise, the hybrid simulator follows the prescribed prover strategy and generates prover messages for the corresponding second stage (by using the cycle it possesses rather than invoking the PROVE procedure). We claim that the ensemble consisting of the resulting output (which we denote by $\widehat{S}_m^{V^*}(G, C)$) is computationally indistinguishable from $\{S_m^{V^*}(G)\}_{G \in HC}$. Namely,

Claim 5.3.2 *The ensemble $\{S_m^{V^*}(G)\}_{G \in HC}$ is computationally indistinguishable from the ensemble $\{\widehat{S}_m^{V^*}(G, C)\}_{G \in HC}$.*

Proof Sketch The claim is proved using a standard hybrid argument. It reduces the indistinguishability of two neighboring hybrids to the indistinguishability of Blum's simulator's output (that is, if the output of Blum's simulator [18] is computationally indistinguishable from the view of real executions of the basic Hamiltonicity proof system, then so are neighboring hybrids). The latter is proved to hold based on the computational-secrecy property of the commitment scheme that is used by the prover in Step $(\widehat{p1})$ of Construction 4.1.1 (see [18, 57] for further details).

We consider $m + 1$ hybrid distributions that are induced by the output of the following hybrid simulation procedure. For $s \in \{0, \ldots, m\}$, given $G \in HC$, a Hamiltonian cycle C in G and black-box access to V^*, the sth hybrid simulation procedure (which we denote by H_s), handles first-stage messages exactly as the "original" simulator S_m would have handled. For every session index $s' \leq s$, the hybrid simulator H_s handles also second-stage messages exactly as S_m does (that is, by invoking the PROVE procedure), whereas for every session index $s' > s$, the hybrid simulator H_s handles the relevant second-stage messages exactly as the "modified" simulator $\widehat{S}_m$ does (that is, by using the cycle it possesses in order to produce real prover messages). Note that the output of $H_m^{V^*}$ is identically distributed to the output of $S_m^{V^*}$, whereas the output of $H_0^{V^*}$ is identically distributed to the output of $\widehat{S}_m^{V^*}$. Also note that for every $s \in \{0, \ldots, m\}$, the distribution $H_s^{V^*}(G, C)$ is efficiently constructible (specifically, given a Hamiltonian cycle C in G, it is easy to follow $S_m^{V^*}(G)$'s strategy, while producing real prover messages whenever necessary). Thus, indistinguishability of the ensemble $\{S_m^{V^*}(G)\}_{G \in HC}$ from the ensemble $\{\widehat{S}_m^{V^*}(G)\}_{G \in HC}$ follows from indistinguishability of $\{H_{s-1}(G, C)\}_{G \in HC}$ and $\{H_s(G, C)\}_{G \in HC}$.

Claim 5.3.3 *For all $s \in \{1, \ldots, m\}$, the ensembles $\{H_{s-1}(G, C)\}_{G \in HC}$ and $\{H_s(G, C)\}_{G \in HC}$ are computationally indistinguishable.*

Proof Sketch Follows from indistinguishability of Blum's simulator's output (by applying an additional hybrid argument). We use the extra property that the output is indistinguishable even if the distinguisher has a priori knowledge of a Hamiltonian cycle C in G (this follows from the auxiliary input $\mathcal{ZK}$ property of Blum's protocol). ∎

This completes the proof of Claim 5.3.2. ∎

We next consider what happens to the output distribution of the hybrid simulator $\widehat{S}_m$ if we assume that it does not output $\perp$ (i.e., does not get "stuck"). It turns out that in such a case, the resulting output distribution is *identical* to the distribution of $\{\text{view}_{V^*}^P(G)\}_{G \in HC}$. Namely,

Claim 5.3.4 *The ensemble $\{\widehat{S}_m^{V^*}(G, C)\}_{G \in HC}$ conditioned on it not being $\perp$, is identically distributed to the ensemble $\{\text{view}_{V^*}^P(G)\}_{G \in HC}$.*

Proof Notice that the first-stage messages that appear in the output of the "original" simulator (that is, S_m) are identically distributed to the first-stage messages that are produced by an honest prover P (since they are uniformly and independently chosen). Since the first-stage messages that appear in the output of the "modified" simulator (that is, $\widehat{S}_m$) are identical to the ones appearing in the output of S_m, we infer that they are identically distributed to the first-stage messages that are produced by an honest prover P. Using the fact that the second-stage messages that appear in the output of the "modified" simulator are (by definition) identically distributed to the second-stage messages that are produced by an honest prover P, we infer that the ensembles $\{\widehat{S}_m^{V^*}(G, C)\}_{G \in HC}$ and $\{\text{view}_{V^*}^P(G)\}_{G \in HC}$ are identically distributed. We stress that the first-stage prover messages that appear in the output of $\widehat{S}_m$ are distributed uniformly and randomly *regardless* of whether $\widehat{S}_m$ outputs $\perp$. (In particular, every outcome of these messages could potentially occur, independently of whether the output of $\widehat{S}_m$ equals $\perp$.) ∎

As we show in Proposition 5.4.1 (see next section), $\widehat{S}_m$ outputs $\perp$ only with negligible probability. In particular, the ensemble $\{\widehat{S}_m^{V^*}(G, C)\}_{G \in HC}$ is computationally indistinguishable from (and in fact statistically close to) the ensemble $\{\widehat{S}_m^{V^*}(G, C)\}_{G \in HC}$, conditioned on it not being $\perp$. Namely,

Claim 5.3.5 *The ensemble $\{\widehat{S}_m^{V^*}(G, C)\}_{G \in HC}$ is computationally indistinguishable from the ensemble $\{\widehat{S}_m^{V^*}(G, C)\}_{G \in HC}$ conditioned on it not being $\perp$.*

It can be seen that Claims 5.3.2, 5.3.4 and 5.3.5 imply the correctness of Proposition 5.3.1. ∎

5.4 The Probability of Getting "Stuck"

We next analyze the probability that the SIM procedure gets "stuck" during its execution. We are particularly interested in the probability that any specific invocation of the PROVE procedure returns $\bot$ during the simulation process (note that this is the only reason for which the simulator may get "stuck"). As will turn out from our analysis, any specific invocation of the PROVE procedure will return $\bot$ with probability at most $1/2^{\Omega(k)}$. Since the number of invocations of the PROVE procedure is polynomial in n, it follows that the SIM procedure outputs $\bot$ with probability $\text{poly}(n) \cdot 1/2^{\Omega(k)}$. By setting the number of rounds in the protocol to be $k(n) = \alpha(n) \cdot \log n$, where $\alpha(\cdot)$ is any super-constant function (e.g., $\alpha(n) = \log\log n$), we are guaranteed that the SIM procedure outputs $\bot$ with negligible probability. Specifically:

Proposition 5.4.1 *Let $\alpha : N \to N$ be any super-constant function, let $k(n) = \alpha(n) \cdot \log n$, and consider any instantiation of Construction 4.3.1 with parameter $k = k(n)$. Then the probability of getting "stuck" during the simulation is negligible. Specifically, for every sufficiently large $G = (V, E) \in HC$:*

$$\Pr\left[\widehat{S}_m^{V^*}(G) = \bot\right] < \frac{1}{n^{\alpha(n)/8}}$$

where $n = |V|$ and the probability is taken over the simulator's coin tosses.

Proof We consider executions of the hybrid simulator $\widehat{S}_m$, given input $G = (V, E)$, random coins ρ, and black-box access to V^* (we let $\widehat{S}_{m,\rho}^{V^*}(G)$ denote the resulting output).

Let $q_S(n)$ be a (polynomial) bound on the total number of invocations of the PROVE procedure during an execution of the simulator (note that $q_S(n)$ is upper bounded by the simulator's running time). As we have mentioned before, the (hybrid) simulator $\widehat{S}_m$ gets "stuck" (i.e., outputs $\bot$) if and only if there exists a session $s \in \{1, \ldots, m\}$ and an index $\ell \in \{1, \ldots, q_S(n)\}$ so that the ℓth invocation of the PROVE procedure (for session s) outputs $\bot$. Let $\text{hist}_{s,\ell} = \text{hist}_{s,\ell}(\rho)$ be a random variable describing the contents of the hist argument at the moment that the PROVE procedure is invoked for the ℓth time (with s as its first argument). Using the union-bound we have:

$$\Pr_\rho\left[\widehat{S}_{m,\rho}^{V^*}(G) = \bot\right] \leq \sum_{i=1}^{m} \sum_{\ell=1}^{q_S(n)} \Pr_\rho\left[\text{PROVE}(s, \text{hist}_{s,\ell}(\rho)) = \bot\right]. \quad (5.2)$$

Equation (5.2) will be bounded using the following lemma. This lemma, which in some sense is the crux of the proof (of the zero-knowledge property), establishes an upper bound on the probability that a specific invocation of the PROVE procedure outputs $\bot$.[8]

---

[8]Note that if some invocation of the PROVE procedure has been reached during the execution of $\widehat{S}$, then it must be the case that all previous invocations of the PROVE procedure did not output $\bot$ (since otherwise the the execution of $\widehat{S}$ would have halted at an earlier stage).

Lemma 5.4.2 *For every* $(s, \ell) \in \{1, \ldots, m\} \times \{1, \ldots, q_S(n)\}$ *and all sufficiently large* $G \in HC$:

$$\Pr_\rho\left[\text{PROVE}(s, \text{hist}_{s,\ell}(\rho)) = \bot\right] < \frac{1}{n^{\alpha(n)/4}}$$

where $n = |V|$.

Combining Lemma 5.4.2, (5.2) and the hypothesis of Proposition 5.4.1 we infer that for all sufficiently large $n = |V|$:

$$\begin{aligned}
\Pr_\rho\left[\widehat{S}_{m,\rho}^{V^*}(G) = \bot\right] &\leq m \cdot q_S(n) \cdot \frac{1}{n^{\alpha(n)/4}} \\
&= \frac{m \cdot q_S(n)}{n^{\alpha(n)/8}} \cdot \frac{1}{n^{\alpha(n)/8}} \\
&< \frac{1}{n^{\alpha(n)/8}}
\end{aligned} \tag{5.3}$$

Where (5.3) holds whenever $m \cdot q_S(n) < n^{\alpha(n)/8}$ (which is satisfied for sufficiently large $n = |V|$). ∎

Proof of Lemma 5.4.2 Let $s \in \{1, \ldots, m\}$ and $\ell \in \{1, \ldots, q_S(n)\}$. We next show that the probability that the ℓth invocation of the PROVE procedure outputs $\bot$ is upper bounded by $1/n^{\alpha(n)/4}$.

Throughout the analysis we will assume that the simulator never uses the same prover message twice during its execution. Such an assumption is justified by the following claim.

Claim 5.4.3 *There exists a constant* $c > 0$, *so that the probability that the same prover message occurs twice during the simulation is at most* $n^c/2^k$.

Proof The proof relies on the fact that prover messages in the protocol are k-bits long. In particular, the probability that any two uniformly chosen (Pj) messages are equal is at most $1/2^k$. Since for every session, the number of prover messages sent is at most $\text{poly}(n)$, then the overall probability of sending the same prover message twice is at most $\text{poly}(n)/2^k$. ∎

We will also assume that the PROVE procedure never outputs $\bot$ in Step (p2) of the CONVINCE subroutine. This assumption is justified by the following claim.

Claim 5.4.4 *The probability that the PROVE procedure outputs* $\bot$ *in Step* (p2) *of the CONVINCE subroutine is at most* $1/2^k$.

Proof Sketch The proof relies on the computational binding property of the commitment used by the verifier in message (V0). The key point is that the PROVE procedure outputs $\bot$ in Step (p2) of the CONVINCE subroutine only if the ℓth bit of $\sigma_{i,j}^0 \oplus \sigma_{i,j}^1$ is NOT equal to σ_ℓ for some ℓ, but all the decommitments sent by V^* in the corresponding message (v1) are proper.

Notice that this event could have occurred only in case that V^* has sent valid decommitments to two different values for the ℓth bit of $\sigma_{i,j}^{1-r_{i,j}}$ (where $r_j = r_{1,j}, \ldots, r_{k,j}$ is the k-bit string sent in the (Pj) message appearing in $\text{hist}_{s,\ell}(\rho)$). One of these decommitments was sent during the execution of the SOLVE procedure (while obtaining the corresponding $\sigma_{i,j}^0, \sigma_{i,j}^1$ values in Stage 1), whereas the second one was sent in message (v1). So if the PROVE procedure outputs $\perp$ in Step (p2) of the CONVINCE subroutine then it must be the case that the computational binding property of the commitment used in message (V0) has been broken. This can only happen with probability smaller than $1/2^k$ (or otherwise the execution of $\widehat{S}$ along with V^* could have been used to break the computational binding property of the commitment with the same probability of success). ∎

We thus set our goal to bound the probability that the PROVE procedure outputs $\perp$ assuming that:

1. The simulator never sends the same prover message twice.
2. The PROVE procedure never outputs $\perp$ in Step (p2) of the CONVINCE subroutine.

By the above discussion, it will be sufficient to bound this probability by $1/2^{k/2}$. Taking n to be sufficiently large, the probability that the PROVE procedure outputs $\perp$ would be then upper bounded by

$$n^c/2^k + 1/2^k + 1/2^{k/2} < (n^c + 2)/2^{k/2}$$
$$= (n^c + 2)/n^{\alpha(n)/2}$$
$$< 1/n^{\alpha(n)/4}. \tag{5.4}$$

From now on, we focus on messages that belong to session s and ignore messages from other sessions (unless otherwise specified). For every choice ρ of the simulator's randomness we focus on an invocation of the PROVE procedure with input $(s, \text{hist}_{s,\ell}) = (s, \text{hist}_{s,\ell}(\rho))$. We associate the invocation of the PROVE procedure with the value of the (V0) message that appears in the $\text{hist}_{s,\ell}(\rho)$ argument. We will analyze the execution of the simulator from the time (V0) has been last visited until the time that PROVE$(s, \text{hist}_{s,\ell})$ is invoked.

The Contents of the $\mathcal{T}$ Table. For every $j \in \{1, \ldots, k\}$, we consider the sequence of (first stage) verifier messages, (Vj), that appear in the $\mathcal{T}$ table at the moment that PROVE$(s, \text{hist}_{s,\ell})$ is invoked. Let α_j denote the length of this sequence. The value α_j actually corresponds to the number of times that the (Vj) message has been visited since all session s messages have been last deleted from $\mathcal{T}$. (Recall that this happens whenever a (V0) message is visited by the SIM procedure.) Note that α_j is not necessarily equal for all $j \in \{1, \ldots, k\}$.

For $u \in \{1, \ldots, \alpha_j\}$, let $(\text{P}j)_u, (\text{V}j)_u$ denote the uth pair of (Pj), (Vj) messages that was visited by the SIM procedure since (V0) has been last visited.[9] (Using this notation, the jth above sequence can be written as $(\mathrm{V}j)_1, (\mathrm{V}j)_2, \ldots, (\mathrm{V}j)_{\alpha_j}$.) We now have the following claim.

Claim 5.4.5 *Suppose that* PROVE$(s, \mathrm{hist}_{s,\ell}) = \perp$. *Then for all* $j \in \{1, \ldots, k\}$:

1. $(\mathrm{V}j)_u = $ ABORT *for all* $u < \alpha_j$.
2. $(\mathrm{V}j)_{\alpha_j} \neq $ ABORT.

Proof Going back to the description of the PROVE procedure, and based on our assumption that the PROVE never outputs $\perp$ in step (p2) of the CONVINCE subroutine (following Claim 5.4.4), we observe that the only reason for which it outputs $\perp$ is that it has reached Step (2a). Put in other words, the PROVE procedure will output $\perp$ if and only if:

1. The $\mathrm{hist}_{s,\ell}$ argument does not contain an ABORT message in session s.
2. The $\mathcal{T}$ table does not contain a pair $\sigma_{i,j}^0, \sigma_{i,j}^1$ belonging to session s.

We start by showing that for all $j \in \{1, \ldots, k\}$, it holds that $(\mathrm{V}j)_{\alpha_j} \neq $ ABORT. Consider the sequence of first stage verifier messages that appear in $\mathrm{hist}_{s,\ell}$ and belong to session s. Notice that this sequence contains all $k+1$ first stage messages in session s (since PROVE$(s, \mathrm{hist}_{s,\ell})$ is always invoked only after the first stage of session s has been completed). Using the fact that the $\mathrm{hist}_{s,\ell}$ argument consists of the "most recently visited" execution transcript in the simulation, we have that the sequence of first-stage verifier messages that appear in $\mathrm{hist}_{s,\ell}$ and belong to session s can be written as $(\mathrm{V}0), (\mathrm{V}1)_{\alpha_1}, (\mathrm{V}2)_{\alpha_2}, \ldots, (\mathrm{V}k)_{\alpha_k}$. Since, by Condition (1) above, the $\mathrm{hist}_{s,\ell}$ argument does not contain an ABORT message in session s it immediately follows that for all $j \in \{1, \ldots, k\}$, it holds that $(\mathrm{V}j)_{\alpha_j} \neq $ ABORT.

Suppose now for contradiction that there exists a $j \in \{1, \ldots, k\}$ and a $u \in \{1, \ldots, \alpha_j - 1\}$ so that $(\mathrm{V}j)_u \neq $ ABORT. Since we are assuming that all $(\mathrm{P}j)$'s in the simulation are different, then so are $(\mathrm{P}j)_u$ and $(\mathrm{P}j)_{\alpha_j}$. Since both $(\mathrm{V}j)_u$ and $(\mathrm{V}j)_{\alpha_j}$ are not equal to ABORT it immediately follows that the table contains a pair $\sigma_{i,j}^0, \sigma_{i,j}^1$ belonging to session s.[10] This is in contradiction to Condition (2) above and thus to our hypothesis that the PROVE procedure outputs $\perp$. ∎

---

[9]Note that the $(\mathrm{P}j)$ message may occur in the schedule much earlier than $(\mathrm{V}j)$ does. In particular, the simulator may perform rewinds that do not reach $(\mathrm{P}j)$ (and so do not change its value), but repeatedly obtain different $(\mathrm{V}j)$'s as answer. In such cases, the $(\mathrm{V}j)_u$ message stored in $\mathcal{T}$ as answer to $(\mathrm{P}j)_u$ will always correspond to the "most recently obtained" $(\mathrm{V}j)$ message that was given as answer to $(\mathrm{P}j)_u$ (see discussion on Page 71).

[10]To see this notice that, if $(\mathrm{P}j)_u = r_{1,j}, \ldots, r_{k,j}$ and $(\mathrm{P}j)_{\alpha_j} = s_{1,j}, \ldots, s_{k,j}$ are different, then there must exist $i \in \{1, \ldots, k\}$ so that $r_{i,j} \neq s_{i,j}$. Since both $(\mathrm{V}j)_u$ and $(\mathrm{V}j)_{\alpha_j}$ are not equal to ABORT, then the values of both $\sigma_{i,j}^{r_{i,j}}$ and $\sigma_{i,j}^{s_{i,j}}$ must have been revealed by V^*.

Definition 5.4.6 (Bad random tapes) *Let $\mathcal{R}$ be the set of all random tapes used by the simulator and let $\rho \in \mathcal{R}$. For any $j \in \{1, \ldots, k\}$ define a Boolean indicator $\mathsf{bad}_j(\rho) = \mathsf{bad}_{s,\ell,j}(\rho)$ to be true if and only if when S uses ρ as random tape it holds that:*

1. $(Vj)_u = \mathtt{ABORT}$ *for all $u < \alpha_j$.*
2. $(Vj)_{\alpha_j} \neq \mathtt{ABORT}$.

By Claim 5.4.5, we have:

$$\Pr_\rho \left[\mathrm{PROVE}(s, \mathsf{hist}_{s,\ell}(\rho)) = \bot \right] \leq \Pr_\rho \left[\bigwedge_{j=1}^{k} \mathsf{bad}_j(\rho) \right]. \qquad (5.5)$$

We shall show that for all sufficiently large n, the fraction of "bad" tapes $\rho \in \mathcal{R}$ for which $\bigwedge_{j=1}^{k} \mathsf{bad}_j(\rho)$ holds is at most $1/2^{k-3d}$ where d $(= \log_2(m \cdot (k+1)))$ is the depth of the simulator's recursion. To do this we will show that every "bad" random tape can be mapped into a set of $2^{k-3d} - 1$ random tapes for which $\mathsf{bad}_j(\rho)$ does not hold for some j. Moreover, this will be done so that every two "bad" random tapes are mapped to two *disjoint* sets of "good" random tapes. Put in other words, for every random tape that causes $\bigwedge_{j=1}^{k} \mathsf{bad}_j(\rho)$ to hold, there exist $2^{k-3d} - 1$ other tapes that do not. Since the simulator picks a random tape uniformly amongst all possible random tapes, it will then follow that the probability that $\bigwedge_{j=1}^{k} \mathsf{bad}_j(\rho)$ holds is at most $1/2^{k-3d}$.

Lemma 5.4.7 (Counting bad random tapes) *Let $\mathcal{B} \subseteq \mathcal{R}$ be the set of all $\rho \in \mathcal{R}$ for which $\bigwedge_{j=1}^{k} \mathsf{bad}_j(\rho)$ holds. Then, there exists a mapping $f : \mathcal{R} \longrightarrow 2^{\mathcal{R}}$ such that for every $\rho \in \mathcal{B}$:*

1. $|f(\rho)| \geq 2^{k-3d}$.
2. *For all $\rho' \in \mathcal{B} \setminus \{\rho\}$, the sets $f(\rho)$ and $f(\rho')$ are disjoint.*
3. *The sets $f(\rho) \setminus \{\rho\}$ and $\mathcal{B}$ are disjoint.*

The proof of Lemma 5.4.7 is the most involved part in the simulator's analysis. Before we prove it (in Sect. 5.4.1), we show how it can be used in order to complete the proof of Lemma 5.4.2. We start with the following corollary of Lemma 5.4.7.

Corollary 5.4.8 *Let $\mathcal{B} \subseteq \mathcal{R}$ be as above. Then $|\mathcal{B}|/|\mathcal{R}| \leq \frac{1}{2^{k-3d}}$.*

Proof Consider the set:

$$\mathcal{G} \overset{\mathrm{def}}{=} \bigcup_{\rho \in \mathcal{B}} \left(f(\rho) \setminus \{\rho\} \right).$$

By Condition (3) in Lemma 5.4.7 it holds that $\mathcal{G} \subseteq \mathcal{R} \setminus \mathcal{B}$. We thus have:

$$|\mathcal{R}| - |\mathcal{B}| = |\mathcal{R} \setminus \mathcal{B}|$$

$$\geq |\mathcal{G}|$$

$$= \sum_{\rho \in \mathcal{B}} |f(\rho) \setminus \{\rho\}| \tag{5.6}$$

$$\geq |\mathcal{B}| \cdot \left(2^{k-3d} - 1\right) \tag{5.7}$$

where (5.6) follows from Condition (2) in Lemma 5.4.7 and (5.7) follows from Condition (1) in Lemma 5.4.7. ∎

Using Corollary 5.4.8 we are now able to complete the proof of Lemma 5.4.2:

$$\mathrm{Pr}_\rho \left[\bigwedge_{j=1}^{k} \mathsf{bad}_j(\rho) \right] = \mathrm{Pr}_\rho \left[\rho \in \mathcal{B} \right]$$

$$= \frac{|\mathcal{B}|}{|\mathcal{R}|}$$

$$\leq \frac{1}{2^{k-3d}}. \tag{5.8}$$

Since $k = \omega(\log n)$ and $d = \log m \cdot (k+1) = O(\log n)$ then for all sufficiently large n's it holds that $1/2^{k-3d} < 1/2^{k/2}$. By combining (5.8) with (5.5) we infer that for all sufficiently large n's:

$$\mathrm{Pr}_\rho \left[\mathrm{PROVE}(s, \mathsf{hist}_{s,\ell}(\rho)) = \bot \right] < \frac{1}{2^{k/2}}.$$

This completes the proof of Lemma 5.4.2. ∎

5.4.1 Counting Bad Random Tapes

We now turn to prove Lemma 5.4.7. We will start by defining the notion of rewind intervals. Loosely speaking, these are segments of the concurrent schedule that are induced by the various rewindings of the simulator and are executed multiple times during the simulation. We will then focus on a subset of "special" intervals. These intervals satisfy some useful properties that enable us to use them in order to define the desired mapping $f : \mathcal{R} \to 2^{\mathcal{R}}$. Using the properties of the "special" intervals we will then be able to argue that the mapping f indeed satisfies the required properties.

Throughout the proof of Lemma 5.4.7, we consider the actions taken during the execution of the SOLVE procedure (rather than considering the full execution of the SIM procedure). This renders our analysis much "cleaner" since we only have to refer only to first-stage messages (namely, (P0), (V0), (P1), (V1), ..., (Pk), (Vk)), and can ignore second-stage messages (namely, (p1), (v1), (p2)). Extension of the analysis to the SIM procedure case can be then achieved in a straightforward way (the reason this is possible is that the timing of the simulator's "rewinds" depends only on the number of first-stage messages exchanged so far).

Partitioning the Schedule into Rewind Intervals. The execution of the SOLVE procedure induces a partitioning of the $2 \cdot m \cdot (k+1)$ (prover and verifier) messages in the schedule into *disjoint* rewind intervals. At the top level of the recursion there are two disjoint intervals of length $m \cdot (k+1)$ and at the bottom of the recursion there are $m \cdot (k+1)$ disjoint intervals of length 2. In general, at the wth level of the recursion (out of $d = \log_2(m \cdot (k+1))$ possible levels) there are 2^w disjoint intervals of $m(k+1)/2^{w+1}$ messages each.

Notice that rewind intervals may contain messages from all sessions. Also notice, that a rewind interval may be "visited" multiple times during the execution of the SOLVE procedure (in particular, a level-w interval is visited exactly 2^w times during the simulation). Since the scheduling of messages may vary "dynamically" with the history of the interaction, a specific interval may contain a different scheduling of messages each time it is visited.

Minimal Rewind Intervals. We denote by $[a, b]$ an interval starting with prover message a and ending with verifier message b. Consider the scheduling of messages as they appear in the $\text{hist}_{s,\ell}$ argument (i.e., at the moment that PROVE(s, $\text{hist}_{s,\ell}$) is invoked). Focusing on messages of session s, we note that for every pair of messages (Pj), (Vj) in this session we can associate a level-w interval $[a_j, b_j]$ so that:

1. Both (Pj) and (Vj) are contained in $[a_j, b_j]$.
2. None of the level-$(w+1)$ subintervals of $[a_j, b_j]$ contains both (Pj) and (Vj).

We call such a rewind interval a *j-minimal interval*. Notice that for every $j \in \{1, \ldots, k\}$ there is only one j-minimal interval $[a_j, b_j]$ and that for every $j \neq j'$ the interval $[a_j, b_j]$ is different from $[a_{j'}, b_{j'}]$.

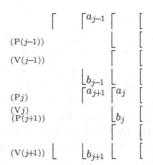

Fig. 5.2. Demonstrates how minimal intervals are determined. Also demonstrates possible containments between minimal intervals of different iterations. In this example, the intervals $[a_{j-1}, b_{j-1}]$ and $[a_{j+1}, b_{j+1}]$ are disjoint (as well as the intervals $[a_{j-1}, b_{j-1}]$ and $[a_j, b_j]$), whereas the interval $[a_{j+1}, b_{j+1}]$ contains $[a_j, b_j]$.

In some sense j-minimal intervals correspond to the shortest interval in which the simulator can rewind message (Vj) (that is, while potentially changing the value of (Pj)). Intuitively, for such a rewinding to be useful, the interval should not contain message $(V0)$. Otherwise, the values that were revealed in some run of the interval become irrelevant once rewinds are performed (since all the relevant values in the $\mathcal{T}$ table are deleted whenever we rewind past $(V0)$). Likewise, the interval should not contain message $(p1)$. Otherwise, the simulation faces the risk of getting "stuck" before it manages to reveal multiple $(Pj), (Vj)$ pairs of messages (by running the interval multiple times).

It can be seen that the number of minimal intervals that do not contain neither $(V0)$ or $(p1)$ is at least $k' = k - 2d$ (for simplicity, these intervals will be indexed by $\{1, \ldots, k'\}$). The reason for this is that in every level of the recursion the $(V0)$ (resp. $(p1)$) message is contained in exactly one interval. In particular, the number of minimal intervals that are "spoiled" by $(V0)$ (resp. $(p1)$) is at most d. This guarantees that $(V0)$ and $(p1)$ are not visited during single invocations of $[a_j, b_j]$. For the sake of our analysis, however, we will want to make sure that $(V0)$ and $(p1)$ are not visited also during *multiple* invocations of $[a_j, b_j]$. In such a case, requiring that $[a_j, b_j]$ contains neither $(V0)$ nor $(p1)$ may not be sufficient.[11] Jumping ahead, we remark that what we will have to require is that for some intervals, even intervals containing them contain neither $(V0)$ nor $(p1)$.

Special Rewind Intervals. In order to define the mapping $f : \mathcal{R} \to 2^{\mathcal{R}}$, we will need to focus on a specific set of *disjoint* minimal intervals (called special intervals). An important fact that we will extensively use is that if two intervals are disjoint then so is the portion of the random tape that used to run them (i.e., in order to produce uniformly chosen (Pj) messages for the corresponding interval). Another important fact is that in each run of the interval, the SOLVE procedure makes use of "fresh" randomness (i.e., randomness used in one run is never used in a later run).

Definition 5.4.9 (Special intervals) *A minimal interval $[a_j, b_j]$ is said to be special if it does not contain any other minimal interval (i.e., if $[a_j, b_j]$ does not contain $[a_{j'}, b_{j'}]$ for any $j' \neq j$).*

Notice that all special intervals are disjoint. We let $S \subseteq \{1, \ldots, k'\}$ denote the set of all indices j for which $[a_j, b_j]$ is special. For simplicity, assume that $S = \{1, \ldots, |S|\}$.

For $j \in S$, let δ_j be the number of times $[a_j, b_j]$ is run since $[a_{j-1}, b_{j-1}]$ is "last" visited (where by "last" we mean during the time $(V0)$ is visited until $(p1)$ is reached). A trivial upper bound on δ_j is 2^w, where w is the recursive depth of interval $[a_j, b_j]$. However, since we restrict ourselves to the time between $(V0)$ is visited until $(p1)$ is reached, the value of δ_j is typically

---

[11]For example, if the interval containing $[a_j, b_j]$ contains either $(V0)$ or $(p1)$, then, in some cases, the number of "safe" invocations of $[a_j, b_j]$ is not more than two (even though $[a_j, b_j]$ itself does not contain $(V0)$ or $(p1)$).

smaller than 2^w and is in fact upper bounded by α_j (recall that α_j denotes the number of times $(\mathrm{V}j)$ has been visited since the $\mathcal{T}$ table was initialized). Notice that δ_j may be actually smaller than α_j since we are counting only the runs of $[a_j, b_j]$ that have occurred after $[a_{j-1}, b_{j-1}]$ was "last" visited.

The Mapping f. We are finally ready to define the mapping $f : \mathcal{R} \to 2^{\mathcal{R}}$ (Fig. 5.4). This mapping makes use of another mapping $h_s : \mathcal{R} \times [\delta_1] \times \dots \times [\delta_{|S|}] \to \mathcal{R}$ (Fig. 5.3) that depends on the set S (as determined by the schedule at the moment that PROVE(s, hist$_{s,\ell}$) is invoked).

At a high level, given input ρ and $u_1, \dots, u_{|S|}$, the mapping h_s takes the portion of the random tape ρ that corresponds to the u_j^{th} run of interval $[a_j, b_j]$ and swaps it with the portion that corresponds to the "last" (i.e., δ_j^{th}) run of this interval (in case $u_j = \delta_j$ then h_s leaves the runs of $[a_j, b_j]$ intact). This is done for all $j \in S$. As we have observed above, different runs of a specific interval use disjoint portions of the random tape. In particular, swapping the randomness of two runs of $[a_j, b_j]$ is an operation that makes sense. Moreover, since disjoint intervals use disjoint portions of the random tape, for every $j \neq j'$ swapping two runs of $[a_j, b_j]$ will not interfere with swapping two runs of $[a_{j'}, b_{j'}]$.

Mapping $h_S : \mathcal{R} \times [\delta_1] \times \dots \times [\delta_{|S|}] \longrightarrow \mathcal{R}$

Input: A random tape $\rho \in \mathcal{R}$ and a sequence $\bar{u} = u_1, \dots, u_{|S|} \in [\delta_1] \times \dots \times [\delta_{|S|}]$
Output: A random tape $\rho_{u_1, \dots, u_{|S|}} \in \mathcal{R}$

1. Set $\rho_{u_0} \leftarrow \rho$.
2. For $j = 1, \dots, |S|$:
   a) Let ρ_w denote the portion of $\rho_{u_1, \dots, u_{j-1}}$ that is used in wth run of $[a_j, b_j]$.
   b) Swap the locations of ρ_{u_j} and ρ_{δ_j} within $\rho_{u_1, \dots, u_{j-1}}$.
   c) Denote by $\rho_{u_1, \dots, u_j}$ the resulting string.
3. Output $\rho_{u_1, \dots, u_{|S|}}$.

Fig. 5.3. Mapping a "bad" random tape to a "good" random tape.

The mapping f is obtained by invoking $h_S(\rho, u_1, \dots, u_{|S|})$ with all possible values of $u_1, \dots, u_{|S|} \in [\delta_1] \times \dots \times [\delta_{|S|}]$ as input. The set S and the values $\delta_1, \dots, \delta_{|S|}$ used in order to define the mapping h_S are determined by the mapping f. This is done by running and monitoring the simulation with random tape ρ and black-box access to V^*. Once PROVE(s, hist$_{s,\ell}$) is reached, f can inspect the scheduling of messages as it appears in hist$_{s,\ell}$ and determine S.[12]

---

[12] Here we implicitly assume that all invocations of the PROVE procedure prior to the ℓth invocation did not return $\perp$. This assumption is valid, since otherwise the simulator $\widehat{S}_m$ would have never reached the ℓth invocation of the PROVE procedure (as it would have halted before reaching the ℓth invocation, cf. Footnote 8).

Notice that the mapping f can be computed efficiently. However, this fact is immaterial for the correctness of the analysis since all we have to do is to establish the *existence* of such a mapping (regardless of its efficiency).

Mapping $f : \mathcal{R} \longrightarrow 2^{\mathcal{R}}$

Input: A random tape $\rho \in \mathcal{R}$
Output: A set of random tapes $\mathcal{G} \subseteq 2^{\mathcal{R}}$

1. Determine the set of special indices $S \subseteq \{1, \ldots, k'\}$:
   a) Run the simulator given random tape ρ and access to V^*.
   b) Check for which j, interval $[a_j, b_j]$ is special (as induced by V^*'s scheduling).
2. For $j \in S$, let δ_j be the number of times $[a_j, b_j]$ is run since $[a_{j-1}, b_{j-1}]$ is "last" visited.
3. Let $\bar{u} = u_1, \ldots, u_{|S|}$ denote a sequence in $\Delta \stackrel{\text{def}}{=} [\delta_1] \times \ldots \times [\delta_{|S|}]$. Set

$$\mathcal{G} = \bigcup_{\bar{u} \in \Delta} \{ h_S(\rho, \bar{u}) \}.$$

4. Output $\mathcal{G}$.

Fig. 5.4. Mapping a single "bad" random tape to a set of "good" random tapes.

The following claim will establish item (3) of Lemma 5.4.7.

Claim 5.4.10 *Let $\rho \in \mathcal{B}$ be a bad random tape. Then the sets $f(\rho) \setminus \{\rho\}$ and $\mathcal{B}$ are disjoint.*

Proof It will be sufficient to show that for every $u_1, \ldots, u_{|S|} \neq \delta_1, \ldots, \delta_{|S|}$, the random tape $\rho_{u_1, \ldots, u_{|S|}} = h_S(\rho, u_1, \ldots, u_{|S|})$ does not belong to $\mathcal{B}$ (notice that $h_S(\rho, \delta_1, \ldots, \delta_{|S|}) = \rho$).

Consider the smallest $j \in S$ for which $u_j \neq \delta_j$. We start by observing that, up to the point in which $[a_j, b_j]$ is run for the first time (after the "last" run of interval $[a_{j-1}, b_{j-1}]$), the randomness used by the simulator when running with $\rho_{u_1, \ldots, u_{|S|}}$ is equal to the randomness used by the simulator when running with ρ. This means that all runs of $[a_j, b_j]$ that occur after $[a_{j-1}, b_{j-1}]$ has been "last" visited will have the same "history" of interaction regardless of whether $\rho_{u_1, \ldots, u_{|S|}}$ or ρ is used.

The key observation for proving the claim is that, modulo the history of the interaction at the starting point of an interval, the randomness used in a specific run of an interval completely determines its outcome (remember that V^*'s random tape is fixed in advance). Since the last occurrence of (Vj) in T corresponds to the "last" time $[a_j, b_j]$ is visited, then the portion of the random tape used for the δ_j^{th} run of $[a_j, b_j]$ completely determines the value of $(Vj)_{\alpha_j}$ (which is the last occurrence of (Vj) in T).

Notice that, when using $\rho_{u_1,\ldots,u_{|S|}}$ as random tape, the randomness used in ρ in order to perform the δ_j^{th} run of $[a_j, b_j]$ is instead used for the u_j^{th} run of interval $[a_j, b_j]$. Since the randomness used in a specific run of an interval completely determines its outcome, the value of (Vj) in the u_j^{th} run of $[a_j, b_j]$ is now equal to $(Vj)_{\alpha_j}$. Recall that $\rho \in \mathcal{B}$. This in particular means that, when using ρ as random tape, it holds that $(Vj)_{\alpha_j} \neq$ ABORT (by Condition (2) in Definition 5.4.6). Denoting the (Vj) message that appears in the u_j^{th} run of interval $[a_j, b_j]$ by $(Vj)_u$ we then have that, when the simulator uses $\rho_{u_1,\ldots,u_{|S|}}$ as random tape, $(Vj)_u = (Vj)_{\alpha_j} \neq$ ABORT.

Since $u_j < \delta_j$, then $(Vj)_u$ does not appear in $\text{hist}_{s,\ell}$ (since it appears in the outcome of the u_j^{th} run of $[a_j, b_j]$ and the "most recently visited" run when $\text{PROVE}(s, \text{hist}_{s,\ell})$ is invoked is the δ_j^{th} run). In addition since whenever $\text{PROVE}(s, \text{hist}_{s,\ell})$ is invoked, some (Vj) message must appear in $\text{hist}_{s,\ell}$, we infer that there exists a (Vj) that occurs after $(Vj)_u$ does. This message corresponds to $(Vj)_{\alpha_j'}$ where α_j' is the number of occurrences of (Vj) in $\mathcal{T}$ when using $\rho_{u_1,\ldots,u_{|S|}}$ as random tape.

We thus have that, when using $\rho_{u_1,\ldots,u_{|S|}}$ as random tape, there must exist a $u < \alpha_j'$ for which $(Vj)_u \neq$ ABORT. By Condition (1) in Definition 5.4.6 this implies that $\rho_{u_1,\ldots,u_{|S|}} \notin \mathcal{B}$. ∎

We now turn to establish Item (2) of Lemma 5.4.7. Let $g : \mathcal{B} \times \{0,1\}^k \times [\delta_1] \times \ldots \times [\delta_{|S|}] \to \mathcal{R}$ be a mapping defined as:

$$g(\rho, S, \overline{u}) \stackrel{\text{def}}{=} h_s(\rho, \overline{u})$$

where $\rho \in \mathcal{B}$. To show that for all $\rho \neq \rho' \in \mathcal{B}$, the sets $f(\rho)$ and $f(\rho')$ are disjoint it will be sufficient to show that g is one-to-one. In such a case we would have that for any two $S \neq S' \subseteq \{1, \ldots, k'\}$, it holds that $h_s(\rho, \overline{u}) \neq h_{s'}(\rho', \overline{u}')$ (regardless of the values of $\rho, \overline{u}$ and $\rho', \overline{u}'$) and so the sets $f(\rho) = \bigcup_{\overline{u}} \{h_s(\rho, \overline{u})\}$ and $f(\rho') = \bigcup_{\overline{u}} \{h_{s'}(\rho', \overline{u})\}$ are disjoint.

Claim 5.4.11 *Let $g : \mathcal{B} \times \{0,1\}^k \times [\delta_1] \times \ldots \times [\delta_{|S|}] \to \mathcal{R}$ be as above. Then, g is one-to-one.*

Proof To argue that g is one-to-one we will define an inverse mapping g^{-1} so that for every random tape $\rho' \in \text{range}(g)$, the value of $g^{-1}(\rho') = (\rho, S, \overline{u})$ satisfies $g(\rho, S, \overline{u}) = \rho'$.

Given $\rho' \in \text{range}(g)$, the basic idea for defining g^{-1} is to recognize the subset of intervals whose randomness was swapped by f (while "producing" ρ' from some $\rho \in \mathcal{B}$) and to reverse the swapping (i.e. to swap back the randomness of these intervals). The main difficulty in doing so lies in the task of recognizing which are these intervals whose randomness is to be swapped (i.e., to recognize what is the set S that corresponds to a run of the simulator with $\rho \in \mathcal{B}$ as random tape).

The solution to this problem will be to inspect the intervals and reverse the swapping of their randomness "inductively". The reason for which the order of swapping is important is that V^*'s answer in a specific interval also depends on the randomness used to run the "most recent execution" of previous intervals (since, whenever we reach a specific interval, the outcome of these "recent" runs appears in the history of the interaction). In order to be able to say something meaningful about an interval's run we must make sure that, whenever we inspect the run of the simulator on this interval, the history of the interaction up to the starting point of the interval is consistent with the outcome of running the simulator with the bad tape $\rho \in \mathcal{B}$ that ρ' "originates" from. The process describing the mapping g^{-1} is depicted in Fig. 5.5.

Mapping $g^{-1} : \mathcal{R} \longrightarrow \mathcal{B} \times \{0,1\}^k \times [\delta_1] \times \ldots \times [\delta_{|S|}]$

Input: A random tape $\rho \in \text{range}(g) \subseteq \mathcal{R}$.
Output: A random tape $\rho' \in \mathcal{B}$, a set $S \subseteq \{1, \ldots, k'\}$ and a sequence $\bar{u} \in [\delta_1] \times \ldots \times [\delta_{|S|}]$.

1. Set $\rho_{u_0} \leftarrow \rho$ and $S = \phi$.
2. For $j = 1, \ldots, k'$:
   a) Run the simulator given random tape $\rho_{u_1, \ldots, u_{j-1}}$ and access to V^*.
   b) Find *unique* u_j so that u_j^{th} run of $[a_j, b_j]$ is "properly answered".
   c) If $u_j < \delta_j$:
      i. Set $S \leftarrow S \cup \{j\}$.
      ii. Let ρ_w denote the portion of $\rho_{u_1, \ldots, u_{j-1}}$ that is used in wth run of $[a_j, b_j]$.
      iii. Swap the locations of ρ_{u_j} and ρ_{δ_j} within $\rho_{u_1, \ldots, u_{j-1}}$.
      iv. Denote by $\rho_{u_1, \ldots, u_j}$ the resulting string.
   d) Otherwise, continue to next $j \in \{1, \ldots, k'\}$.
3. Output $\rho' = \rho_{u_1, \ldots, u_{|S|}}$, S and $\bar{u} = u_1, \ldots, u_{|S|}$.

Fig. 5.5. Mapping a "good" tape back to the original "bad" tape.

Since the tape $\rho' \in \text{range}(g)$ that we are trying to invert originates from a bad tape $\rho \in \mathcal{B}$ then for every $j \in \{1, \ldots, k'\}$, when using ρ as random tape, the interval $[a_j, b_j]$ is aborted in all but the last runs of $[a_j, b_j]$, where by last run we mean the last time $[a_j, b_j]$ is executed prior to the invocation of PROVE$(s, \text{hist}_{s,\ell})$. Notice that, once PROVE$(s, \text{hist}_{s,\ell})$ is invoked, we can determine the value of δ_j by counting the number of times $[a_j, b_j]$ has been visited from the time (V0) was visited until (p1) is reached. If it happens to be the case that when using ρ' as random tape the last (i.e., δ_j^{th}) run of the currently inspected interval $[a_j, b_j]$ is not properly answered, then we know that the randomness of $[a_j, b_j]$ has been swapped by f and should be swapped back.

If along the way we preserve the "invariant" that the randomness used so far is consistent with the original bad random tape $\rho \in \mathcal{B}$ then it must be the case that, for the above interval, there exists a *unique* $u_j < \delta_j$ so that the u_j^{th} run of $[a_j, b_j]$ is properly answered. We can thus swap the randomness used for the u_j^{th} run with the randomness used for the δ_j^{th} run. As soon as we reach the last special interval we know that the resulting tape is the original "bad" random tape (since all along the way we have preserved the "invariant" that the randomness used so far is consistent with the original $\rho \in \mathcal{B}$).   ∎

All that remains in order to complete the proof, is to establish Item (1) of Lemma 5.4.7. To do so, we will need to argue that for all $\rho \in \mathcal{B}$ it holds that $|f(\rho)| \geq 2^{k-3d}$. This will be achieved by proving the following lemma.

Lemma 5.4.12 *Let $d = log_2(m \cdot (k+1))$. Then, there exist values $d_1, \ldots, d_{|S|} \in \{1, \ldots, d\}$ so that:*

1. *For all $j \in S$, it holds that $\delta_j = 2^{d_j}$.*
2. *$\sum_{j \in S} d_j \geq k' - d$.*

Corollary 5.4.13 *Let $\rho \in \mathcal{B}$ be a bad random tape. Then $|f(\rho)| \geq 2^{k-3d}$.*

Proof By the definition of $f : \mathcal{R} \longrightarrow 2^{\mathcal{R}}$ and by Claim 5.4.11, we have:

$$|f(\rho)| = \left| \bigcup_{\overline{u} \in \Delta} \{h_s(\rho, \overline{u})\} \right| = \sum_{\overline{u} \in \Delta} |\{h_s(\rho, \overline{u})\}|$$

Since $|\{h_s(\rho, \overline{u})\}| = 1$, then the size of $f(\rho)$ is in fact equal to the number of $\overline{u}$'s in Δ. The size of $\Delta \stackrel{\text{def}}{=} [\delta_1] \times \ldots \times [\delta_{|S|}]$ is precisely $\prod_{j \in S} \delta_j$, and so:

$$|f(\rho)| = \prod_{j \in S} \delta_j$$

$$= \prod_{j \in S} 2^{d_j} \tag{5.9}$$

$$= 2^{\sum_{j \in S} d_j}$$

$$\geq 2^{k' - d} \tag{5.10}$$

where (5.9) and (5.10) follow from items (1) and (2) of Lemma 5.4.12 respectively. Since $k' = k - 2d$, we get that $|f(\rho)| \geq 2^{k-3d}$, as required.   ∎

5.4.2 Special Intervals Are Visited Many Times

We now turn to prove Lemma 5.4.12. A central tool in the proof will be the notion of the recursion tree. This is a full binary tree whose nodes correspond to the rewind intervals as induced by the recursive calls of the SOLVE procedure. Every node $[a, b]$ in the recursion tree has two descendants. Each one of the descendants corresponds to one of the recursive calls made during some visit to $[a, b]$. The root of the tree corresponds to a rewind interval of size $m \cdot (k+1)$. At the bottom level of the recursion tree there are $m \cdot (k+1)$ nodes each corresponding to distinct interval of length 2. In general, at the wth level of the tree (out of $d = log_2(m \cdot (k+1))$ possible levels) there are 2^w nodes, each corresponding to a distinct interval of length $m(k+1)/2^{w+1}$.

It can be seen that, for any two nodes labelled $[a, b]$ and $[a', b']$ in the recursion tree, $[a, b]$ is a descendant of $[a', b']$ if and only if interval $[a, b]$ is contained in $[a', b']$. The distance of $[a, b]$ from $[a', b']$ is determined in the straightforward manner by considering the distance between these nodes in the binary tree. Recall that we are focusing on the scheduling as it appears in $\text{hist}_{s,\ell}$ (i.e., at the moment that PROVE($s, \text{hist}_{s,\ell}$) is invoked). This scheduling induces a specific labelling of the tree's nodes according to the messages that appear at each one of the rewind intervals at that time. It also determines the identity of the nodes that correspond to minimal intervals, as well as the nodes that correspond to special intervals. By Definition 5.4.9, nodes that correspond to a special interval do not have any descendant that corresponds to a minimal interval.

Let $S \subseteq \{1, \ldots, k'\}$ be the set of all indices j for which interval $[a_j, b_j]$ is special. Let $j \in S$ and let $[\mathsf{A}_j, \mathsf{B}_j]$ be the common ancestor of $[a_{j-1}, b_{j-1}]$ and $[a_j, b_j]$ in the recursion tree. That is, $[\mathsf{A}_j, \mathsf{B}_j]$ is the "deepest" node in the tree that has both $[a_{j-1}, b_{j-1}]$ and $[a_j, b_j]$ as descendants (this corresponds to the smallest rewind interval that contains both $[a_{j-1}, b_{j-1}]$ and $[a_j, b_j]$).

Defining the d_j's – First Step. We are now ready to define the value of the d_j's. This will proceed in two steps. We first define a sequence of values $c_1, \ldots, c_{|S|}$. For any $j \in S$, the value of c_j will reflect the overall number of times that interval $[a_j, b_j]$ is visited after $[a_{j'}, b_{j'}]$ is last visited. We then turn to show how to "correct" the values of the c_j's so as to take into consideration only those visits that have occurred *before* (**p1**) has been reached. The resulting sequence of values $d_1, \ldots, d_{|S|}$ will then faithfully reflect the number of times that $[a_j, b_j]$ is visited after $[a_{j'}, b_{j'}]$ is last visited (as required by the definition of the δ_j's). The values $c_1, \ldots, c_{|S|}$ are defined as follows:

- If $j = 1$, then $c_j = 1$.
- If $j > 1$, then c_j equals to the distance of $[a_j, b_j]$ from $[\mathsf{A}_j, \mathsf{B}_j]$.

Notice that for all $j \in S$, it holds that $c_j \geq 1$. Figure 5.6 demonstrates the way in which $c_1, \ldots, c_{|S|}$ are defined.

Claim 5.4.14 *Let $j \in S$. Then, for every invocation of the common ancestor of $[a_{j-1}, b_{j-1}]$ and $[a_j, b_j]$, the number of times that $[a_j, b_j]$ is visited after $[a_{j-1}, b_{j-1}]$ is last visited is precisely 2^{c_j}.*

Proof Let $j \in S$ and let $[\mathsf{A}_j, \mathsf{B}_j]$ be the common ancestor of $[a_{j-1}, b_{j-1}]$ and $[a_j, b_j]$. By definition, the value of c_j equals the recursive depth of $[a_j, b_j]$ relative to $[\mathsf{A}_j, \mathsf{B}_j]$. We thus know that for every invocation of interval $[\mathsf{A}_j, \mathsf{B}_j]$, the interval $[a_j, b_j]$ is invoked precisely 2^{c_j} times. To see that all 2^{c_j} invocations of $[a_j, b_j]$ occur after the last invocation of $[a_{j-1}, b_{j-1}]$, we recall that $[a_{j-1}, b_{j-1}]$ and $[a_j, b_j]$ are contained in different halves of the common ancestor $[\mathsf{A}_j, \mathsf{B}_j]$. By definition of the SOLVE procedure, the two invocations of the second half of an interval occur only after the two invocations of the first half have occured. Thus all 2^{c_j} invocations of $[a_j, b_j]$ (which occur as a result of the two

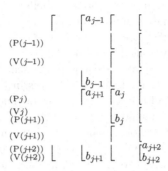

Fig. 5.6. Diagram to demonstrate the definition of the c_j's. In this example the special intervals are $[a_{j-1}, b_{j-1}]$, $[a_j, b_j]$ and $[a_{j+2}, b_{j+2}]$ (and $j+1 \notin S$). Notice that the distance of $[a_{j+2}, b_{j+2}]$ from its common ancestor with $[a_j, b_j]$ is 2, and so $c_{j+2} = 2$ (the common ancestor being $[a_{j+1}, b_{j+1}]$). Similarly, the distance of $[a_j, b_j]$ from its common ancestor with $[a_{j-1}, b_{j-1}]$ is also 2 and so $c_j = 2$.

recursive invocations of the second half of $[A_j, B_j]$) occur after all invocations of $[a_{j-1}, b_{j-1}]$ (which occur as a result of the two recursive invocations of the first half of $[A_j, B_j]$).   ∎

Interfering Intervals. Consider any run of the simulator from the time that message (V0) was visited until message (p1) is reached. Since this run involves the exchange of messages (P0), (V0), (P1), (V1), ..., (Pk), (Vk), then it must have been caused by some invocation of an interval $[A, B]$ that contains $[a_j, b_j]$ for all $j \in \{1, \ldots, k'\}$. Notice that for all $j \in S$ the interval $[A, B]$ contains $[A_j, B_j]$. In particular, for every $j \in S$, by the time that (p1) is reached, the interval $[A_j, B_j]$ is invoked at least once. By, Claim 5.4.14, this implies that for all $j \in S$, the number of times that $[a_j, b_j]$ is visited after the last visit of $[a_{j-1}, b_{j-1}]$ is precisely 2^{c_j}.

At first glance this seems to establish that $\delta_j = 2^{c_j}$. However, this is not necessarily true. The reason for this is that, by definition, the value of δ_j reflects only the number of visits to $[a_j, b_j]$ *before* (p1) is reached. It might very well be the case that not all of the 2^{c_j} runs of $[a_j, b_j]$ have occurred before (p1) is reached.

Specifically, whenever the second half of the common ancestor $[A_j, B_j]$ contains the message (p1), only one of its invocations will occur prior to reaching (p1). This already cuts the number of visits to $[a_j, b_j]$ by a factor of two. The situation is made even worse by the fact that *every* interval that lies "in between" $[A_j, B_j]$ and $[a_j, b_j]$ and that contains (p1) can be invoked at most once before reaching (p1) (such intervals are said to be **interfering** to $[a_j, b_j]$). Thus, the number of invocations of $[a_j, b_j]$ before (p1) is reached decreases exponentially with the number of interfering intervals. For every $j \in S$, let e_j denote the number of intervals interfering with $[a_j, b_j]$. Notice that for all $j \in S$, it holds that $c_j > e_j$ (since for all $j \in \{1, \ldots, k'\}$ interval $[a_j, b_j]$ does not contain (p1)).

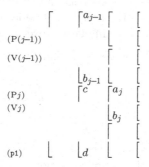

Fig. 5.7. Diagram to demonstrate the definition of interfering intervals. In this example the special intervals are $[a_{j-1}, b_{j-1}]$ and $[a_j, b_j]$. Notice that $[c, d]$ lies "in between" $[a_j, b_j]$ and its common ancestor with $[a_{j-1}, b_{j-1}]$. Since the interval $[c, d]$ contains (p1), then it is interfering with $[a_j, b_j]$. This means that e_j equals 1 (whereas $c_j = 2$), and that the number of invocations of $[a_j, b_j]$ prior to reaching (p1) (and after visiting $[a_{j-1}, b_{j-1}]$ for the last time) is equal to $2^{c_j - e_j} = 2$ (whereas, without taking interference into account, it would have been $2^{c_j} = 4$).

Claim 5.4.15 *Let $j \in S$. Then, for every invocation of the common ancestor of $[a_{j-1}, b_{j-1}]$ and $[a_j, b_j]$, the number of times that $[a_j, b_j]$ is visited after $[a_{j-1}, b_{j-1}]$ is last visited and before (p1) is reached is precisely $2^{c_j - e_j}$.*

Proof Sketch   Let $j \in S$ and let $[A_j, B_j]$ be the common ancestor of $[a_{j-1}, b_{j-1}]$ and $[a_j, b_j]$. By definition, the number of "non-interfering" intervals that: (1) are contained in $[A_j, B_j]$, (2) contain $[a_j, b_j]$ but, (3) do not contain (p1), is exactly $c_j - e_j$. The key observation is that no such "non-interfering" interval contains an interfering interval (since otherwise it would have contained (p1) as well). Thus, prior to reaching (p1), all these intervals are invoked at least twice by the interval containing them. This means that the total number of invocations of $[a_j, b_j]$ (which is contained in all of these intervals) is exactly $2^{c_j - e_j}$. ∎

We are finally ready to define $d_1, \ldots, d_{|S|}$. For any $j \in S$, let

$$d_j \overset{\text{def}}{=} c_j - e_j$$

To complete the proof of Lemma 5.4.12 we need to prove the following claim.

Claim 5.4.16 *Let $d_1, \ldots, d_{|S|}$ be defined as above. Then,*

$$\sum_{j \in S} d_j \geq k' - d.$$

Proof   The proof is by induction on k'. For any choice of k', let $S \subseteq \{1, \ldots, k'\}$, $\{(c_j, d_j, e_j)\}_{j \in S}$ be as above. We will show that for every $k' \geq d$, it holds that $\sum_{j \in S}(c_j - e_j) \geq k' - d$. We stress that throughout the proof, we do not make use of any property of the schedule (besides using the "binary-tree structure" and the depth, d, of the simulator's execution).

Base Case ($k' = d + 1$). Since $|S| \geq 1$, and for all $j \in S$, it holds that $c_j - e_j > 0$, we have:

$$\sum_{j \in S}(c_j - e_j) \geq 1 = k' - d.$$

Induction Step ($k' > d$). Consider the $k' - 1$ intervals that are obtained by removing the index $|S|$ (i.e., the index corresponding to the "latest" special interval $[a_{|S|}, b_{|S|}]$). Let $S' \subseteq \{1, \ldots, k'\} \setminus \{|S|\}$ denote the set of special intervals after the removal of the index $|S|$. Notice that $S \subseteq S'$. This is because any interval that was special before the removal of $|S|$ will remain special after the removal. Moreover, for all $j \in S \cap S'$, the value of $c_j - e_j$ has not been changed by the removal of $|S|$ (since it is always defined relative to the "preceding" element in $|S|$). We now have two cases.

Case 1: There exists $J \in S' \setminus S$ so that the interval $[a_J, b_J]$ is special. That is, by removing $[a_{|S|}, b_{|S|}]$ we have caused $[a_J, b_J]$ to be special (even though it was not special before). This could have happened only if the *unique* interval previously contained by $[a_J, b_J]$ was $[a_{|S|}, b_{|S|}]$ (otherwise, $[a_J, b_J]$ would have not become special after removing $[a_{|S|}, b_{|S|}]$). In particular, $[a_J, b_J]$ does not contain the intervals $[a_{|S|-1}, b_{|S|-1}]$ (i.e., the special interval preceding $[a_{|S|}, b_{|S|}]$) and $[A_{|S|}, B_{|S|}]$ (i.e., the common ancestor of $[a_{|S|-1}, b_{|S|-1}]$ and $[a_{|S|}, b_{|S|}]$). This means that both $[a_J, b_J]$ and $[a_{|S|}, b_{|S|}]$ have the same common ancestor with $[a_{|S|-1}, b_{|S|-1}]$. Since $[a_J, b_J]$ contains $[a_{|S|}, b_{|S|}]$ then $c_{|S|} > c_J$. In addition, since the set of intervals interfering to $[a_J, b_J]$ is equal to the set of intervals interfering to $[a_{|S|}, b_{|S|}]$ then $e_{|S|} = e_J$. As a consequence, $c_{|S|} - e_{|S|} > c_J - e_J$. Using the induction hypothesis (for $k' - 1$), we get:

$$\begin{aligned}
\sum_{j \in S}(c_j - e_j) &= \sum_{j \in S' \setminus \{J\}}(c_j - e_j) + (c_{|S|} - e_{|S|}) \\
&\geq \sum_{j \in S' \setminus \{J\}}(c_j - e_j) + (c_J - e_J + 1) \\
&\geq \sum_{j \in S'}(c_j - e_j) + 1 \\
&\geq (k' - 1) - d + 1 \\
&= k' - d.
\end{aligned}$$

Case 2: $S' = S$. Using the induction hypothesis, and the fact that $c_{|S|} - e_{|S|} > 0$, we get:

$$\sum_{j \in S}(c_j - e_j) = \sum_{j \in S'}(c_j - e_j) + (c_{|S|} - e_{|S|})$$

$$\geq \sum_{j \in S'}(c_j - e_j) + 1$$

$$\geq (k' - 1) - d + 1$$

$$= k' - d.$$

In both cases, we obtain the desired result. This completes the proof of Claim 5.4.16. ∎

Using, Claims 5.4.15 and 5.4.16, we have:

1. For all $j \in S$, it holds that $\delta_j = 2^{d_j}$.
2. $\sum_{j \in S} d_j \geq k' - d$.

This completes the proof of Lemma 5.4.12.

5.5 Extensions

5.5.1 Applicability to Other Protocols

Theorem 5.1 is proved by adding an $O(\alpha(n) \cdot \log n)$-round "preamble" to the well-known three-round protocol for Hamiltonicity by Blum [18]. The crucial property of Blum's protocol that we need in order to prove concurrent zero-knowledge is that it is a "challenge–response" type of protocol so that the simulation task becomes trivial if the verifier's "challenge" is known in advance. Using the Prabhakharan–Rosen–Sahai preamble, it is possible to transform *any* such protocol into concurrent zero-knowledge, while paying only a logarithmic cost in the round complexity.

Denote by $\mathcal{CRZK}(r(\cdot))$ the class of all languages $L \subseteq \{0,1\}^*$ having an $r(\cdot)$-round "challenge–response" interactive proof (resp. argument) system, so that the simulation task becomes "trivial" if the verifier's "challenges" are known in advance. We now have the following theorem.

Theorem 5.2 (A generic transformation for $\mathcal{CRZK}$) *Let* $\alpha : N \to N$ *be any super-constant integer function, and let* $r : N \to N$ *be any integer function. Then, assuming the existence of statistically hiding commitment schemes (resp. one-way functions), every language* $L \in \mathcal{CRZK}(r(\cdot))$ *has an* $(r(n) + O(\alpha(n) \cdot \log n))$*-round concurrent zero-knowledge proof (resp. argument) system.*

In light of Theorem 5.2, Construction 4.3.1 may be viewed as a generic transformation that enhances such protocols and makes them secure in the concurrent setting with only a logarithmic increase in the round complexity. Examples for protocols satisfying the above property are the well known protocols for graph 3-coloring [65], for proving the knowledge of a square root modulo a composite [47], as well as the protocol for proving knowledge of discrete logarithms modulo a prime [98].

5.5.2 c𝒵𝒦 Arguments Based on Any One-Way Function

Using Construction 4.1.1 as a building block, it is possible to obtain a $c\mathcal{ZK}$ argument system for Hamiltonicity, while assuming only the existence of one-way functions. Since Hamiltonicity is $\mathcal{NP}$-complete, it will follow that every language in $\mathcal{NP}$ can be argued in $c\mathcal{ZK}$.

Construction 5.5.1 (A $c\mathcal{ZK}$ argument system for HC)

Common input: *a directed graph* $G = (V, E)$ *with* $n \stackrel{\text{def}}{=} |V|$, *and a parameter* $k = k(n)$ *(determining the number of rounds).*

Auxiliary input to prover: *a directed Hamiltonian cycle,* $C \subset E$, *in* G.

First stage: *This stage involves* $2k + 2$ *rounds and is independent of the common input* G.

1. Prover's preliminary step (P0): *Uniformly select a first message for a (two-round) statistically binding commitment scheme and send it to the verifier.*

2. Verifier's preliminary step (V0): *Uniformly select* $\sigma \in \{0, 1\}^n$, *and two sequences,* $\{\sigma_{i,j}^0\}_{i,j=1}^k$, $\{\sigma_{i,j}^1\}_{i,j=1}^k$, *each consisting of* k^2 *random* n-*bit strings. The sequences are chosen under the constraint that for every* i, j *the value of* $\sigma_{i,j}^0 \oplus \sigma_{i,j}^1$ *equals* σ. *Commit (using the statistically binding commitment scheme) to all* $2k^2 + 1$ *selected strings. The commitments are denoted* $\beta, \{\beta_{i,j}^0\}_{i,j=1}^k, \{\beta_{i,j}^1\}_{i,j=1}^k$.

3. *For* $j = 1, \ldots, k$:
   a) Prover's j^{th} step (Pj): *Uniformly select a* k-*bit string* $r_j = r_{1,j}, \ldots, r_{k,j} \in \{0, 1\}^k$ *and send it to the verifier.*
   b) Verifier's j^{th} step (Vj): *Reveal the values (preimages) of* $\beta_{1,j}^{r_{1,j}}, \ldots, \beta_{k,j}^{r_{k,j}}$.

4. *The prover proceeds with the execution if and only if for every* $j \in \{1, \ldots, k\}$, *the verifier has properly decommitted to the values of* $\sigma_{1,j}^{r_{1,j}}, \ldots, \sigma_{k,j}^{r_{k,j}}$ *(i.e., that for every* $i \in \{1, \ldots, k\}$, $\sigma_{i,j}^{r_{i,j}}$ *is a valid decommittment of* $\beta_{i,j}^{r_{i,j}}$).

Second stage: *The prover and verifier engage in* n *(parallel) executions of a slightly modified version of the basic Hamiltonicity protocol (described in Construction 4.1.1):*

1. Prover's first step (p1): *Send the first message in the Hamiltonicity proof system (i.e.,* n *parallel copies of Step* ($\widehat{\text{p1}}$) *in Construction 4.1.1).*

2. Verifier's first step (v1): *Send the value of* σ, *as well as the value of all* k^2 *commitments that have not been revealed in the first stage (i.e.,* $\{\sigma_{i,j}^{1-r_{i,j}}\}_{i,j=1}^k$). *In addition prove (using an ordinary zero-knowledge argument of knowledge) the knowledge of* $k + 1$ *strings,* $s, s_1, \ldots, s_k$, *so that* $C_s(\sigma) = \beta$ *and* $C_{s_j}(\sigma_j^{1-r_j}) = \beta_j^{1-r_j}$ *for all* j.

3. Prover's second step (p2): *Check that the zero-knowledge arguments given by the verifier are accepting, and that the values of* σ *and* $\{\sigma_{i,j}^{1-r_{i,j}}\}_{i,j=1}^k$ *sent by the verifier satisfy* $\sigma_{i,j}^0 \oplus \sigma_{i,j}^1 = \sigma$ *for all* j. *If so, send the third message in the basic Hamiltonicity proof system (i.e.,* n *parallel copies of Step* ($\widehat{\text{p2}}$) *in Construction 4.1.1).*

4. Verifier's second step (v2): *Conduct the verification of the prover's proofs (i.e., as described in Step* ($\widehat{\text{v2}}$) *of Construction 4.1.1), and accept if and only if all corresponding conditions hold.*

Completeness and soundness of Construction 5.5.1 are proved in a similar way to Construction 4.3.1. The main difference is in the proof of soundness. This time, rather than using the statistical secrecy of the commitments used in Step (V0) of Construction 4.3.1, we use the zero-knowledge property of the argument used in Step (v1), as well as the computational secrecy of the commitments used in Step (V0) of Construction 5.5.1. Details follow.

Claim 5.5.2 (Soundness) *Suppose that the commitment used in Step (V0) is computationally hiding. Further suppose that the interactive argument used in Step (v1) is zero-knowledge. Then, Construction 5.5.1 is computationally sound.*

Proof Let $G \in \{0,1\}^n \setminus \mathrm{HC}$, and let P^* be a cheating prover for Construction 5.5.1. Suppose that P^* succeeds in convincing the honest verifier V that G is Hamiltonian with probability greater than $1/p(n)$ (for some polynomial $p(\cdot)$). Using P^* we construct a (polynomial time) cheating prover, P^{**}, for the basic Hamiltonicity proof system. P^{**} will succeed in convincing the honest verifier V_{HC} (i.e., the verifier strategy from Construction 4.1.1) with probability greater than $1/(2 \cdot p(n))$. This will be in contradiction to the soundness property of Construction 4.1.1.

The cheating prover P^{**} starts by uniformly selecting $\sigma \in \{0,1\}^n$ and two sequences, $\{\sigma_{i,j}^0\}_{i,j=1}^k$, $\{\sigma_{i,j}^1\}_{i,j=1}^k$, each consisting of k^2 random n-bit strings. The prover next emulates an interaction between P^* and the verifier V of Construction 5.5.1, while interacting with V_{HC} in the following way. Playing the role of V, the cheating prover P^{**} feeds P^* with (statistically-binding) commitments to the $2k^2 + 1$ strings it has previously selected (i.e., as in Step (V0) of Construction 5.5.1). These are denoted $\beta, \{\beta_{i,j}^0\}_{i,j=1}^k, \{\beta_{i,j}^1\}_{i,j=1}^k$. The cheating prover then engages in an execution of the first stage of Construction 5.5.1 together with P^*. That is, for $j = 1, \ldots, k$, given a string $r_j = r_{1,j}, \ldots, r_{k,j}$, the cheating prover opens the commitments $\beta_{1,j}^{r_{1,j}}, \ldots, \beta_{k,j}^{r_{k,j}}$ to the values $\sigma_{1,j}^{r_{1,j}}, \ldots, \sigma_{k,j}^{r_{k,j}}$ (just as the honest verifier of Construction 5.5.1 would have done). Notice that up to this point the execution of P^{**} does not involve any interaction with V_{HC}.

Upon finishing the execution of the first stage, the cheating prover P^{**} initiates an execution of the basic Hamiltonicity proof system by forwarding the first Stage 2 message it receives from P^* (i.e., a (p1) message) to V_{HC}. Given V_{HC}'s answer, denoted σ' (i.e., a $\widehat{(v1)}$ message), the cheating prover P^{**} sends over the value of σ' along with with "consistent" values that correspond to the opening of all commitments which were not opened during the execution of the first stage with P^* (specifically, P^{**} sends the values $\sigma' \oplus \sigma_{i,j}^{1-r_{i,j}}$). Using the simulator for the $\mathcal{ZK}$ argument of Step (v1), P^{**} proves that the values σ' and $\sigma' \oplus \sigma_{i,j}^{1-r_{i,j}}$ are indeed consistent with $\beta, \beta_{i,j}^{1-r_{i,j}}$. By doing so P^{**} is guaranteed that the generated Step (v2) is computationally indistinguishable from a "real" Step 2. This follows from the computational hiding of the commitments used in Step (V0) as well as from the computational indistinguishability of the simulator's output from real interactions between P^*

(playing the role of the verifier) and V (playing the role of the prover). As a consequence, the transcript of the interaction between P^* and P^{**} (emulating the role of V) is computationally indistinguishable from the transcript of a "real" interaction between P^* and V.

Since in such transcripts P^* makes V accept with probability greater than $1/p(n)$ (by our contradiction assumption), and since V accepts the second stage if and only if V_{HC} would have accepted the corresponding basic Hamiltonicity proof system (i.e., as described in Construction 4.1.1), we conclude that P^{**} makes V_{HC} accept with probability greater than $1/p(n) - \mathrm{neg}(n) > 1/(2 \cdot p(n))$. This is in contradiction to the soundness property of Construction 4.1.1. ∎

Combining the completeness and soundness properties, we get

Proposition 5.5.3 *Suppose there exist one-way functions. Then Construction 5.5.1 constitutes an interactive argument system for Hamiltonicity.*

Using the same simulator as the one used for Construction 4.3.1 and with some more work on the analysis of its success probability and output distribution (building on the soundness of the $\mathcal{ZK}$ argument used in Step (v1)), we obtain.

Theorem 5.3 ($c\mathcal{ZK}$ argument) *Suppose there exist one-way functions. Let $\alpha : N \to N$ be any super-constant function, and let $k(n) = \alpha(n) \cdot \log n$. Then, any instantiation of Construction 5.5.1 with parameter $k = k(n)$ is concurrent zero-knowledge.*

5.5.3 Applicability to Resettable Zero-Knowledge

The results of this chapter also enable improvement in the round complexity of *resettable* zero-knowledge [28]. Specifically, using a general transformation of (certain) concurrent zero-knowledge protocols into resettable zero-knowledge [28], we obtain:

Theorem 5.4 (Resettable $\mathcal{ZK}$) *Suppose there exist statistically hiding commitment schemes. (resp. one-way functions). Then, there exists an $\tilde{O}(\log n)$-round resettable zero-knowledge proof (resp. argument) system for every language $L \in \mathcal{NP}$.*

Proof Sketch Theorem 5.4 is proved by employing a general transformation (by Canetti et al. [28]) that applies to a subclass of $c\mathcal{ZK}$ protocols. When applied to the $c\mathcal{ZK}$ proof system presented in Construction 4.3.1 (as well as Construction 5.5.1), the transformation yields a resettable $\mathcal{ZK}$ proof (resp. argument) system. The class of protocols to which the [28] transformation applies is the class of admissible protocols. Loosely speaking, the class of admissible protocols consists of all $c\mathcal{ZK}$ protocols in which the first verifier message "essentially determines" all its subsequent messages. What we mean by "essentially determines" is that the only freedom retained by the verifier is either to abort (or act so that the prover aborts) or to send a practically predetermined message. Recall that, in our case, the first verifier message is a sequence of commitments that are revealed (i.e., decommitted) in subsequent verifier steps. In such a case, the verifier's freedom in subsequent steps is confined to either send an illegal decommitment (which is viewed as aborting and actually causes the prover to abort) or properly decommit to the predetermined value. It follows that our $c\mathcal{ZK}$ protocol satisfies the "admissibility" property required by [28], and can be thus transformed into resettable $\mathcal{ZK}$. For more details, see [28]. ∎

5.5.4 $c\mathcal{ZK}$ Arguments with Poly-Logarithmic Efficiency

Another application is the existence of concurrent zero-knowledge arguments with *poly-logarithmic efficiency*. Denote by $c\mathcal{ZK}(r(\cdot), m(\cdot))$ the class of all languages $L \subseteq \{0,1\}^*$ having a zero-knowledge argument system, so that on common input $x \in \{0,1\}^*$, the number of messages exchanged is at most $r(|x|)$, and the total length of the messages exchanged is at most $m(|x|)$. In case that $m(n) = \text{polylog}(n)$, the argument system is said to have poly-logarithmic efficiency. Zero-knowledge arguments with poly-logarithmic efficiency have been constructed by Kilian [80], while assuming the existence of strong collision-resistant hash functions (i.e., so that for some $\epsilon > 0$ forming collisions with probability greater than 2^{-k^ϵ} requires at least 2^{k^ϵ} time). We now have the following theorem.

Theorem 5.5 ($c\mathcal{ZK}$ with poly-logarithmic efficiency) *Suppose there exist strong collision-resistant hash functions. Then, $\mathcal{NP}$ is contained in the class $c\mathcal{ZK}(\tilde{O}(\log), \text{polylog})$. That is, for every language $L \in \mathcal{NP}$, there exists an $\tilde{O}(\log n)$-round black-box concurrent zero-knowledge argument system with poly-logarithmic efficiency.*

Proof Sketch Theorem 5.5 is proved by applying the transformation referred to in Sect. 5.5.1 to the protocol of Kilian [80] while using the techniques of Construction 5.5.1. The theorem will follow by noting that the preamble of Construction 5.5.1 can be constructed with polylogarithmic efficiency, and that Kilian's arguments satisfy the property required by Theorem 5.2. The commitments used in Step (V0) of the preamble will be statistically binding and will have polylogarithmic length (this is made possible by the fact that the "challenges" in Kilian's protocol are of polylogarithmic length). We note that such commitments can be constructed assuming the existence of one-way functions (whose existence is implied by the existence of strong collision-resistant hash functions). The proof of soundness is essentially identical to the proof of Claim 5.5.2. The key observation that enables the adaptation of the proof to the current setting is the fact that the prover P^{**} runs in polynomial-time (and thus yields contradiction to the computational soundness of Kilian's arguments). ∎

6

A Simple Lower Bound

As far as black-box simulation is concerned, the protocol presented in Chap. 5 is close to being optimal (at least in terms of round-complexity). In this chapter we make a preliminary step towards demonstrating this fact. We will show that the $c\mathcal{ZK}$ property of "non-trivial" four-message protocols cannot be demonstrated via black-box simulation.

The proof presented in this chapter and the proof establishing the impossibility of black-box $c\mathcal{ZK}$ protocol with significantly less than $\log n$ rounds (presented in Chap. 7) have a lot in common. In particular, they share the same high level structure. Thus, the current chapter can serve as a "gentle" introduction to the considerably more complex result presented in Chap. 7.

Theorem 6.1 ([83]) *Suppose that (P, V) is a 4-message proof system for a language L, and that concurrent executions of P can be simulated in polynomial-time using black-box simulation. Then $L \in \mathcal{BPP}$. This holds even if the proof system is only computationally sound (with negligible soundness error) and the simulation is only computationally indistinguishable (from the actual executions).*

The proof of Theorem 6.1 was originally established by Kilian, Petrank and Rackoff [83], extending work of Goldreich and Krawczyk [63] on the impossibility of "non-trivial" three-message black-box $\mathcal{ZK}$ (i.e., negligible error protocols for languages outside $\mathcal{BPP}$). The proof utilizes a fixed scheduling of the concurrent executions, originally proposed by Dwork, Naor and Sahai [39]. The actual presentation of the proof follows the one given by Rosen [97] (in a work demonstrating the impossibility of non-trivial seven-message black-box $c\mathcal{ZK}$).

6.1 Proof of Theorem 6.1

At a high level, the proof proceeds by constructing a concurrent schedule of sessions, and demonstrating that a black-box simulator cannot successfully generate a simulated accepting transcript for this schedule unless it "rewinds" the verifier *many times*. The work spent on these rewinds will be super-polynomial (actually exponential) unless the number of rounds used by the protocol obeys the bound, or $L \in \mathcal{BPP}$.

6.1.1 Schedule, Adversary Verifiers and Decision Procedure

For each $x \in \{0,1\}^n$, we consider the following concurrent scheduling of n sessions all run on common input x. The scheduling is defined recursively, where the scheduling of m sessions (denoted $\mathcal{R}_m$) proceeds in three phases:

First phase: The first session exchanges two messages (i.e., v_1, p_1).
Second phase: The schedule is applied recursively on the next $m{-}1$ sessions.
Third phase: The first session exchanges two messages (i.e., v_2, p_2).

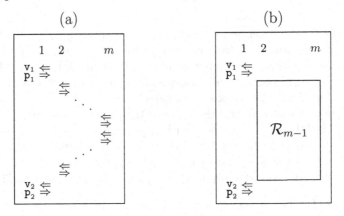

Fig. 6.1. The schedule. Columns correspond to n individual sessions and rows correspond to the time progression. (a) Depicts the schedule explicitly. (b) Depicts the schedule in a recursive manner ($\mathcal{R}_m$ denotes the recursive schedule for m sessions).

Definition 6.1.1 (Identifiers of next message) *The fixed schedule defines a mapping from partial execution transcripts ending with a prover message to the identifiers of the next verifier message; that is, the session and round number to which the next verifier message belongs.* (Recall that such partial execution transcripts correspond to queries of a black-box simulator and so the mapping defines the identifier of the answer.) *For such a query* $\bar{q} = (a_1, b_1, ..., a_t, b_t, a_{t+1})$, *we let* $\pi_{sn}(\bar{q}) \in \{1, ..., n\}$ *denote the session to which the next verifier message belongs, and by* $\pi_{msg}(\bar{q}) \in \{1, 2\}$ *its index within the verifier's messages in this session.*

Definition 6.1.2 (Initiation prefix) *The* initiation prefix $\overline{ip}$ *of a query* $\bar{q}$ *is the prefix of* $\bar{q}$ *ending with the prover's initiation message of session* $\pi_{sn}(\bar{q})$. *More formally,* $\overline{ip} = a_1, b_1, ..., a_\ell, b_\ell, a_{\ell+1}$, *is the initiation prefix of* $\bar{q} = (a_1, b_1, ..., a_t, b_t, a_{t+1})$ *if* $a_{\ell+1}$ *is of the form* $p_1^{(i)}$ *for* $i = \pi_{sn}(\bar{q})$. *(Note that* $\pi_{msg}(\bar{q})$ *may be any index in* $\{1, 2\}$, *and that* a_{t+1} *need not belong to session* i.)

Definition 6.1.3 (Prover sequence) *The* prover sequence *of a query $\overline{q}$ is the sequence of all prover messages in session $\pi_{sn}(\overline{q})$ that appear in the query $\overline{q}$. The length of such a sequence is $\pi_{msg}(\overline{q}) \in \{1, 2\}$.*

We consider what happens when a black-box simulator (for the above schedule) is given oracle access to a verifier strategy V_h defined as follows (depending on a hash function h and the input x).

The Verifier Strategy V_h

On query $\overline{q} = (a_1, b_1, ..., a_t, b_t, a_{t+1})$, where the a's are prover messages (and x is implicit in V_h), the verifier answers as follows:

1. First, V_h checks if the execution transcript given by the query is legal (i.e., consistent with V_h's prior answers), and answers with an error message if the query is not legal. (In fact this is not necessary since by our convention the simulator only makes legal queries. From now on we ignore this case.)
2. More importantly, V_h checks whether the query contains the transcript of a session in which the last verifier message indicates rejecting the input. In case such a session exists, V_h refuses to answer (i.e., answers with some special "refuse" symbol).
3. Next, V_h determines the initiation prefix, denoted $a_1, b_1, ..., a_\ell, b_\ell, a_{\ell+1}$, of query $\overline{q}$. It also determines $i = \pi_{sn}(\overline{q})$, $j = \pi_{msg}(\overline{q})$, and the prover sequence of query $\overline{q}$, denoted $p_1^{(i)}, ..., p_j^{(i)}$.
4. Finally, V_h determines $r_i = h(a_1, b_1, ..., a_\ell, b_\ell, a_{\ell+1})$ (as coins to be used by V), and answers with the message $V(x, r_i; p_1^{(i)}, ..., p_j^{(i)})$ that would have been sent by the honest verifier on common input x, random-pad r_i, and prover's messages $p_1^{(i)}, ..., p_j^{(i)}$.

Assuming towards the contradiction that a black-box simulator, denoted S, contradicting Theorem 6.1 exists, we now describe a probabilistic polynomial-time decision procedure for L, based on S. Recall that we may assume that S runs in strict polynomial time: we denote such time bound by $t_S(\cdot)$. On input $x \in L \cap \{0,1\}^n$ and oracle access to any (probabilistic polynomial-time) V^*, the simulator S must output transcipts with distribution having computational deviation of at most $1/6$ from the distribution of transcripts in the actual concurrent executions of V^* with P.

A Slight Modification of the Simulator. Before presenting the procedure, we slightly modify the simulator so that it never makes a query that is refused by a verifier V_h. Note that this condition can be easily checked by the simulator, and that the modification does not affect the simulator's output. From this point on, when we talk of the simulator (which we continue to denote by S) we mean the modified one.

The Decision Procedure for L

On input $x \in \{0,1\}^n$, proceed as follows:

1. Uniformly select a function h out of a small family of $t_S(n)$-wise independent hash functions mapping poly(n)-bit long sequences to $\rho_V(n)$-bit sequences, where $\rho_V(n)$ is the number of random bits used by V on an input $x \in \{0,1\}^n$.
2. Invoke S on input x providing it black-box access to V_h (as defined above). That is, the procedure emulates the execution of the oracle machine S on input x along with emulating the answers of V_h.
3. Accept iff all sessions in the transcript output by S are accepting.

By our hypothesis, the above procedure runs in probabilistic polynomial-time. We next analyze its performance.

Lemma 6.1.4 (Performance on YES-instances) *For all but finitely many $x \in L$, the above procedure accepts x with probability at least $2/3$.*

Proof Sketch The key observation is that for uniformly selected h, the behavior of V_h in actual (concurrent) interactions with P is identical to the behavior of V in such interactions. The reason is that, in such actual interactions, a randomly selected h determines uniformly and independently distributed random-pads for all n sessions. Since with high probability (say at least $5/6$), V accepts in all n concurrent sessions, the same must be true for V_h, when h is uniformly selected. Since the simulation deviation of S is at most $1/6$, it follows that for every h the probability that $S^{V_h}(x)$ is a transcript in which all sessions accept is lower bounded by $p_h - 1/6$, where p_h denotes the probability that V_h accepts x (in all sessions) when interacting with P. Taking expectation over all possible h's, the lemma follows. ∎

Lemma 6.1.5 (Performance on NO-instances) *For all but finitely many $x \notin L$, the above procedure rejects x with probability at least $2/3$.*

We can actually prove that for every polynomial p and all but finitely many $x \notin L$, the above procedure accepts x with probability at most $1/p(|x|)$. Assuming towards the contradiction that this is not the case, we will construct a (probabilistic polynomial-time) strategy for a cheating prover that fools the honest verifier V with success probability at least $1/\text{poly}(n)$ (in contradiction to the computational-soundness of the proof system). Loosely speaking, the argument capitalizes on the fact that rewinding of a session requires the simulator to work on a new simulation subproblem (one level down in the recursive construction). New work is required since each different message for the rewinded session forms an unrelated instance of the simulation subproblem (by virtue of definition of V_h). The schedule causes work involved in such rewinding to accumulate to too much, and so it must be the case that the simulator does not rewind some (full instance of some) session. In this case the cheating prover may use such a session in order to fool the verifier.

6.1.2 Proof of Lemma 6.1.5

Let us fix an $x \in \{0,1\}^n \setminus L$ as above.[1] Define by $\mathsf{AC} = \mathsf{AC}_x$ the set of pairs (σ, h) so that on input x, coins σ and oracle access to V_h, the simulator outputs a transcript, denoted $S_\sigma^{V_h}(x)$, in which all n sessions accept. Recall that our contradiction assumption is that $\Pr_{\sigma,h}[(\sigma, h) \in \mathsf{AC}] > 1/p(n)$, for some fixed polynomial $p(\cdot)$.

The Cheating Prover

The cheating prover starts by uniformly selecting a pair (σ, h) and hoping that (σ, h) is in AC. It next selects uniformly an element ℓ in $\{1, ..., q_S(n)\}$, where $q_S(n) < t_S(n)$ is a bound on the number of queries made by S on input $x \in \{0,1\}^n$. The prover next emulates an execution of $S_\sigma^{V_{h'}}(x)$ (where h', which is essentially equivalent to h, will be defined below), while interacting with the honest verifier V. The prover handles the simulator's queries as well as the communication with the verifier as follows: Suppose that the simulator makes query $\bar{q} = (a_1, b_1, ..., a_t, b_t, a_{t+1})$, where the a's are prover messages.

1. Operating as V_h, the cheating prover first determines the initiation prefix, $\overline{ip}$ corresponding to the current query $\bar{q}$. Let $\overline{ip} = a_1, b_1, ..., a_\ell, b_\ell, a_{\ell+1}$, (Note that by our convention and the modification of the simulator there is no need to perform Steps 1 and 2 of V_h.)
2. If $\overline{ip}$ is the ℓth distinct initiation prefix resulting from the simulator's queries so far then the cheating prover operates as follows:
   a) The cheating prover determines $i = \pi_{\text{sn}}(\bar{q})$, $j = \pi_{\text{msg}}(\bar{q})$, and the prover sequence of $\bar{q}$, denoted $\mathbf{p}_1^{(i)}, ..., \mathbf{p}_j^{(i)}$ (as done by V_h in Step 3).
   b) If the cheating prover has only sent $j-1$ messages to the actual verifier then it forwards $\mathbf{p}_j^{(i)}$ to the verifier, and feeds the simulator with the verifier's response (i.e., which is of the form $\mathbf{v}_j^{(i)}$).[2]
   c) If the cheating prover has already sent j messages to the actual verifier, the prover retrieves the jth message it has received and feeds it to the simulator.[3]

---

[1] In a formal proof we need to consider infinitely many such x's.

[2] We comment that by our conventions regarding the simulator, it cannot be the case that the cheating prover has sent less than $j-1$ messages to the actual verifier: The prefixes of the current query dictate $j-1$ such messages.

[3] We comment that the cheating prover may fail to conduct Step 2c. This will happen whenever the simulator makes two queries with the same initiation prefix and the same number of prover messages in the corresponding session, but with a different sequence of such messages. Whereas this will never happen when $j = 1$ (as once the initiation prefix is fixed then so is the value of $\mathbf{p}_1^{(i)}$), it may very well be the case that for $j \in \{2, 3\}$ a previous query regarding initiation prefix $\overline{ip}$ had a different $\mathbf{p}_j^{(i)}$ message. In such a case the cheating prover will indeed fail. The punchline of the analysis is that with noticeable probability this will not happen.

3. If $\overline{ip}$ is NOT the ℓth distinct initiation prefix resulting from the queries so far then the prover emulates V_h in the obvious manner (i.e., as in Step 4 of V_h): it first determines $r_i = h(a_1, b_1, ..., a_\ell, b_\ell, a_{\ell+1})$, and then answers with $V(x, r_i; \mathrm{p}_1^{(i)}, ..., \mathrm{p}_j^{(i)})$, where all notations are as above.

Defining h' (Mentioned Above): Let (σ, h) and ℓ be the initial choices made by the cheating prover, and suppose that the honest verifier uses coins r. Then, the function h' is defined to be uniformly distributed among the functions h'' which satisfy the following conditions. The value of h'' on the ℓth initiation prefix equals r, whereas for every $\ell' \neq \ell$, the value of h'' on the ℓ'^{th} initiation prefix equals the value of h on this prefix. (Here we use the hypothesis that the functions are selected in a family of $t_S(n)$-wise independent hash functions. We note that replacing h by h' does not effect Step 3 of the cheating prover, and that the prover does not know h'.)

The probability that the cheating prover makes the honest verifier accept is lower bounded by the probability that both $(\sigma, h') \in \mathsf{AC}$ and the messages forwarded by the cheating prover in Step 2 are consistent with an accepting conversation with $V_{h'}$. For the latter event to occur, it is necessary that the ℓth distinct initiation prefix will be useful (in the sense hinted above and defined now). It is also necessary that ζ was "successfully" chosen (i.e., that the ℓth initiation prefix is accepted by $V_{h'}$).

Definition 6.1.6 (Accepting query) *A query $\overline{q} = (a_1, b_1, ..., a_t, b_t, a_{t+1})$ is said to be* accepting *if $V_{h'}(a_1, b_1, ..., a_t, b_t, a_{t+1})$ equals 1 (i.e., session $\pi_{\text{sn}}(\overline{q})$ is accepted by $V_{h'}$). (Note that this implicitly implies that $\pi_{\text{msg}}(\overline{q}) = 2$.)*

Definition 6.1.7 (Useful initiation prefix) *A specific initiation prefix $\overline{ip}$ in an execution of $S_\sigma^{V_{h'}}(x)$ is called* useful *if the following conditions hold:*

1. *During its execution, $S_\sigma^{V_{h'}}(x)$ made at least one accepting query that corresponds to the initiation prefix $\overline{ip}$.*
2. *The number of different prover sequences that correspond to $\overline{ip}$ that were made during the execution of $S_\sigma^{V_{h'}}(x)$ is at most 2, and these prover sequences are prefixes of one another.*

Otherwise, the prefix is called unuseful.

The Success Probability

Define a Boolean indicator $\chi(\sigma, h', \ell)$ to be true if and only if the ℓth distinct initiation prefix in an execution of $S_\sigma^{V_{h'}}(x)$ is useful. It follows that if the cheating prover happens to select (σ, h, ℓ) so that $\chi(\sigma, h', \ell)$ holds then it convinces $V(x, r)$; the first reason being that there exists a query with the ℓth initiation prefix is answered by an accept message[4], and the second reason

---

[4] We use the fact that $V(x, r)$ behaves exactly as $V_{h'}(x)$ behaves on queries for the ℓth distinct initiation prefix.

being that the emulation does not get into trouble (in Step 2c). To see this, notice that all the queries having the ℓth distinct initiation prefix have prover sequences that are prefixes of one another (which implies that the cheating prover never has to forward such queries to the verifier twice). Thus, the probability that when selecting (σ, h, ℓ) the cheating prover convinces $V(x, r)$ is at least:

$$\Pr\left[\chi(\sigma, h', \ell)\right] \geq \Pr\left[(\sigma, h') \in \mathsf{AC} \ \& \ \chi(\sigma, h', \ell)\right] \tag{6.1}$$

Using the fact that, for every value of ℓ and σ, when h and r are uniformly selected the function h' is uniformly distributed, we infer that ℓ is distributed independently of (σ, h'). Thus, (6.1) is lower bounded by

$$\Pr[(\sigma, h') \in \mathsf{AC}] \cdot \frac{\Pr[\exists i \ \text{s.t.} \ \chi(\sigma, h', i) \mid (\sigma, h') \in \mathsf{AC}]}{q_S(n)} \tag{6.2}$$

where $q_S(n) = \text{poly}(n)$ is the bound used by the cheating prover (for the number of distinct queries/initiation prefixes in the execution). Thus, (6.2) is noticeable (i.e., at least $1/\text{poly}(n)$) provided that so is the value of

$$\Pr[\exists i \ \text{s.t.} \ \chi(\sigma, h', i) \mid (\sigma, h') \in \mathsf{AC}]$$

The rest of the proof is devoted to establishing the last hypothesis. In fact we prove a much stronger statement:

Lemma 6.1.8 *For every* $(\sigma, h') \in \mathsf{AC}$, *the execution of* $S_\sigma^{V_{h'}}(x)$ *contains a useful initiation prefix (that is, there exists an i s.t. $\chi(\sigma, h', i)$ holds).*

6.1.3 Existence of Useful Initiation Prefixes

The proof of Lemma 6.1.8 is by contradiction. We assume the existence of a pair $(\sigma, h') \in \mathsf{AC}$ so that all initiation prefixes in the execution of $S_\sigma^{V_{h'}}(x)$ are unuseful and show that this implies that $S_\sigma^{V_{h'}}(x)$ made at least $2^n \gg \text{poly}(n)$ queries which contradicts the assumption that it runs in polynomial time.

The Query-and-Answer Tree

Throughout the rest of the proof, we fix an arbitrary $(\sigma, h') \in \mathsf{AC}$ so that all initiation prefixes in the execution of $S_\sigma^{V_{h'}}(x)$ are unuseful, and study this execution. A key vehicle in this study is the notion of a query-and-answer tree. This is a rooted tree in which vertices are labelled with verifier messages and edges are labelled by prover's messages. The root is labelled by the empty string, and it has outgoing edges corresponding to the possible prover's messages initializing the first session. In general, paths down the tree (i.e., from the root to some vertices) correspond to queries. The query associated with such a path is obtained by concatenating the labelling of the vertices and edges

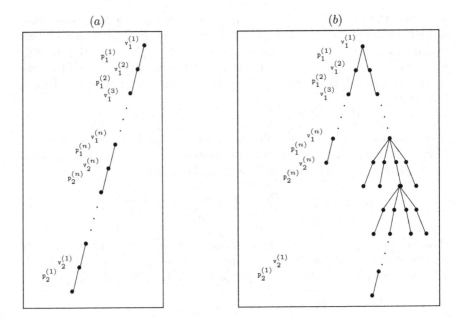

Fig. 6.2. The query-and-answer tree. (a) Interaction with P. (b) Simulation.

in the order traversed. We stress that each vertex in the tree corresponds to a query actually made by the simulator.

Satisfied Subpath. A subpath from one node in the tree to some of its descendants is said to satisfy session i if the subpath contains edges (resp., vertices) for each of the messages sent by the prover (resp., verifier) in session i, and if the last such message (i.e., $v_2^{(i)}$) indicates that the verifier accepts session i. A subpath is called satisfied if it satisfies all sessions for which the first prover's message appears on the subpath.

Forking Subtree. For any i, we say that a subtree i-forks if it contains two subpaths, $\bar{p}$ and $\bar{r}$, having the same initiation prefix, so that

1. $\bar{p}$ and $\bar{r}$ differ in the edge representing the $p_1^{(i)}$ message for session i.
2. Each of $\bar{p}$ and $\bar{r}$ reaches a vertex representing the $v_2^{(i)}$ message.

In such a case, we may also say that the subtree i-forks on $\bar{p}$ (or on $\bar{r}$).

Good Subtree. Consider an arbitrary subtree rooted at a vertex corresponding to the first message in some session so that this session is the first at some level of the recursive construction of the schedule. The full tree is indeed such a tree, but we will need to consider subtrees which correspond to m sessions in the recursive schedule construction. We call such a subtree m-good if it contains a subpath satisfying all m sessions for which the prover's first message appears in the subtree (all these first messages are in particular contained in the subpath). Since $(\sigma, h') \in$ AC it follows that the full tree contains a path from the root to a leaf representing an accepting transcript. The path from the root to this leaf thus satisfies all sessions (i.e., 1 through n) which implies that the full tree is n-good.

The Structure of Good Subtrees. The crux of the entire proof is given in the following lemma.

Lemma 6.1.9 *Let T be an m-good subtree. Then, T contains at least two different $(m-1)$-good subtrees.*

Denote by $W(m)$ the size of an m-good subtree (where $W(m)$ stands for the work actually performed by the simulator on m concurrent sessions in our fixed scheduling). It follows (from Lemma 6.1.9) that any m-good subtree must satisfy

$$W(m) \geq \begin{cases} 2 & \text{if } m = 1 \\ 2 \cdot W(m-1) & \text{if } m > 1. \end{cases} \tag{6.3}$$

Since 6.3 solves to $W(n) = 2^n$ (proof omitted), and since every vertex in the query-and-answer tree corresponds to a query actually made by the simulator, then the assumption that the simulator runs in poly(n)-time (and hence the tree is of poly(n) size) is contradicted. Thus, Lemma 6.1.8 follows from Lemma 6.1.9.

6.1.4 The Structure of Good Subtrees

We now prove Lemma 6.1.9. Considering the m sessions corresponding to an m-good subtree, we focus on the single session dealt explicitly at this level of the recursive construction.

Claim 6.1.10 *Let T be an m-good subtree, and let $i \in [n]$ be the index of the first session in the corresponding subschedule. Then, the subtree i-forks.*

Proof Let $\bar{p}_i$ be the first subpath reached during the execution of $S_\sigma^{V_{h'}}(x)$ which satisfies session i (since the subtree is m-good such a subpath must exist, and since session i belongs to the corresponding subschedule every such subpath must be contained in the subtree). Recall that by the contradiction assumption for the proof of Lemma 6.1.8, all initiation prefixes in the execution of $S_\sigma^{V_{h'}}(x)$ are unuseful. In particular, the initiation prefix corresponding to subpath $\bar{p}_i$ is unuseful. Still, path $\bar{p}_i$ contains vertices for each prover message in session i and contains an accepting message by the verifier. So the only thing which may prevent the above initiation prefix from being useful is having two (non-terminating) queries with the very same initiation prefix $\overline{ip_i}$ so that these queries have different (non-terminating) prover sequences of the same length. Note that these sequences must differ at their second element (i.e., a $p_2^{(i)}$ message). This is because the prover sequences are non-terminating and the first prover message, $p_1^{(i)}$, is constant once the initiation prefix is fixed. Also note that the two (non-terminating) queries were answered by the verifier (rather than refused), since the (modified) simulator avoids queries which will be refused. By associating a subpath to each one of the above queries we obtain two different subpaths (having the same initiation prefix), that differ in their $p_2^{(i)}$ edge and eventually reach a $v_2^{(i)}$ vertex.   ∎

Claim 6.1.11 *If the subtree i-forks, then the subtree contains at least two different $(m-1)$-good subtrees.*

Proof Suppose that the subtree i-forks. Then, there exist two subpaths, $\bar{p}_i$ and $\bar{r}_i$, that differ in the edge representing a $p_1^{(i)}$ message, and that eventually reach some $v_2^{(i)}$ vertex. In particular, paths $\bar{p}_i$ and $\bar{r}_i$ split from each other before the edge which corresponds to the $p_1^{(i)}$ message occurs along these paths (as otherwise the $p_1^{(i)}$ edge would have been identical in both paths). By nature of the fixed scheduling, the vertex in which the above splitting occurs precedes the first message of all (nested) sessions in the recursive construction (that is, sessions $i+1, \dots, n$). It follows that both $\bar{p}_i$ and $\bar{r}_i$ contain the first and last messages of each of these (nested) sessions (as they both reach a $v_2^{(i)}$ vertex). Therefore, by definition of V_h, all these sessions must be satisfied by both these paths (or else V_h would have not answered with a $v_2^{(i)}$ message but rather with a "refuse" symbol). Consider now the corresponding subpaths of $\bar{p}_i$ and $\bar{r}_i$ which begin at edge $p_1^{(i+1)}$ (i.e., with the edge that corresponds to the first message of the first session in the second recursive construction). Each of these new subpaths is contained in a disjoint subtree corresponding to the recursive construction, and satisfies all of its $m-1$ sessions. It follows that the (original) subtree contains two different $(m-1)$-good subtrees.   ∎

By combining Claims 6.1.10 and 6.1.11 we infer that if T is m-good then it contains at least two distinct $(m-1)$-good subtrees. This completes the proof of Lemma 6.1.9 which in turn implies Lemmata 6.1.8 and 6.1.5. The proof of Theorem 6.1 is complete.

Black-Box $c\mathcal{ZK}$ Requires Logarithmically Many Rounds

In this chapter we show that the analysis of the PRS protocol from Chap. 5 is essentially optimal with respect to black-box simulation. Specifically, we present an $\Omega(\log n/\log\log n)$ lower bound on the round-complexity of black-box $c\mathcal{ZK}$. This almost matches the round-complexity obtained in Chap. 5.

Theorem 7.1 ([30]) *Let $r : N \rightarrow N$ be a function so that $r(n) = o(\frac{\log n}{\log\log n})$. Suppose that $\langle P, V\rangle$ is an $r(\cdot)$-round black-box concurrent zero-knowledge proof system for L. Then $L \in \mathcal{BPP}$. The theorem holds even if $\langle P, V\rangle$ is only computationally sound (with negligible soundness error) and the simulation is only computationally indistinguishable (from the actual executions).*

The proof of Theorem 7.1 is based on the work of Canetti, Kilian, Petrank and Rosen [30], which in turn builds on the works of Goldreich and Krawczyk [63], Kilian, Petrank and Rackoff [83], and Rosen [97]. On a high level, the proof proceeds by constructing a specific concurrent schedule of sessions, and demonstrating that a black-box simulator cannot successfully generate an accepting transcript for this schedule unless it "rewinds" the verifier *many times*. The work spent on these rewindings will be super-polynomial unless the number of rounds used by the protocol obeys the bound, or $L \in \mathcal{BPP}$.

While the general outline of the proof remains roughly the same as the proof presented in Chap. 6, the actual schedule of sessions, and its analysis, are different. One main idea that, together with other ideas, enables the proof of the bound is to have the verifier *abort* sessions depending on the history of the interaction. A more detailed outline, presenting both the general structure and the new ideas in the proof, appears in the next section.

Remark. Theorem 7.1 is actually stronger than stated. It will hold even if the simulator knows the scheduling of messages in advance (in particular, it knows the number of concurrent sessions), and even if the schedule of the messages does not change dynamically (as a function of the history of the interaction). Moreover, the actual scheduling and the number of sessions are known even before the protocol itself is determined.

7.1 Proof Outline

This section contains an outline of the proof of Theorem 7.1. The actual proof will be given in Sects. 7.2 and 7.3. To facilitate reading, we partition the outline into two parts: The first part reviews the general framework. (This part mainly follows previous works, namely [63, 83, 97].) The second part concentrates on the actual schedule and the specifics of our lower bound argument.

7.1.1 The High-Level Framework

Consider a k-round concurrent zero-knowledge proof system $\langle P, V \rangle$ for language L, and let S be a black-box simulator for $\langle P, V \rangle$. We use S to construct a $\mathcal{B}\mathcal{P}\mathcal{P}$ decision procedure for L. For this purpose, we construct a family $\{V_h\}$ of "cheating verifiers". To decide on an input x, run S with a cheating verifier V_h that was chosen at random from the constructed family, and decide that $x \in L$ iff S outputs an accepting transcript of V_h.

The general structure of the family $\{V_h\}$ is roughly as follows. A member V_h in the family is identified via a hash function h taken from a hash-function family H having "much randomness" (or high independence). Specifically, the independence of H will be larger than the running time of S. This guarantees that, for our purposes, a function drawn randomly from H behaves like a random function. We define some fixed concurrent schedule of a number of sessions between V_h and the prover. In each session, V_h runs the code of the honest verifier V on input x and random input $h(a)$, where a is the current history of the (*multisession*) interaction at the point where the session starts. V_h accepts if all the copies of V accept.

The proof of validity of the decision procedure is structured as follows. Say that S *succeeds* if it outputs an accepting transcript of V_h. It is first claimed that if $x \in L$ then a valid simulator S must succeed with high probability. Roughly speaking, this is so because each session behaves like the original proof system $\langle P, V \rangle$, and $\langle P, V \rangle$ accepts x with high probability. Demonstrating that the simulator almost never succeeds when $x \notin L$ is much more involved. Given S we construct a "cheating prover" P^* that makes the honest verifier V accept x with probability that is polynomially related to the success probability of S. The soundness of $\langle P, V \rangle$ now implies that in this case S succeeds only with negligible probability. See details below.

Session Prefixes and Useful Session Prefixes. In order to complete the high-level description of the proof, we must first define the following notions that play a central role in the analysis. Consider the conversation between V_h and a prover. A session prefix a is a prefix of this conversation that ends at the point where some new session starts (including the first verifier message in that session). (Recall that V's random input for that new session is set to $h(a)$.) Next, consider the conversation between S and V_h in some run of S. (Such a conversation may contain many interleaved and incomplete conversations of

V_h with a prover.) Roughly speaking, a message sent by S to the simulated V_h is said to have session prefix a if it relates to the session where the verifier randomness is $h(a)$. A session prefix a is called useful in a run of S if:

1. It was accepted (i.e., V_h sent an ACCEPT message for session prefix a).
2. V_h has sent exactly $k + 1$ messages for session prefix a.

Loosely speaking, Condition 2 implies that S did not rewind the relevant session prefix, where rewind session prefix a is an informal term meaning that S rewinds V_h to a point where V_h provides a second continuation for session prefix a. By rewinding session prefix a, the simulator is able to obtain more than $k + 1$ verifier messages for session prefix a. This is contrast to an actual execution of the protocol $\langle P, V \rangle$ in which V sends exactly $k + 1$ messages.

The Construction of the Cheating Prover. Using the above terms, we sketch the construction of the cheating prover P^*. It first randomly chooses a function $h \xleftarrow{R} H$ and an index (of a session prefix) i. It then emulates an interaction between S and V_h, with the exception that P^* uses the messages sent by S that have the ith session prefix as the messages that P^* sends to the actual verifier it interacts with; similarly, it uses the messages received from the actual verifier V instead of V_h's messages in the ith session prefix. The strategy of the cheating prover is depicted in Fig. 7.1.

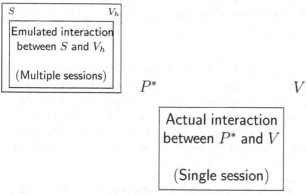

Fig. 7.1. Describes the strategy of the cheating prover P^*. The box on the left-hand side represents the (multiple session) emulation of the interaction between S and V_h (executed "internally" by P^*). The box on the right-hand side represents the actual execution of a single session between P^* and V. (Recall that P^* relays some of the actual interaction messages to its internal emulation.)

The Success Probability of the Cheating Prover. We next claim that if the session prefix chosen by P^* is useful, then $\langle P^*, V \rangle (x)$ accepts. The key point is that whenever P^* chooses a useful session prefix, the following two conditions (corresponding to the two conditions in the definition of a useful session prefix) are satisfied:

1. The session corresponding to the ith session prefix is accepted by V_h (and so by V).
2. P^* manages to reach the end of the $\langle P^*, V \rangle$ interaction without "getting into trouble".[1]

Loosely speaking Item (1) is implied by Condition (1) in the definition of a useful session prefix. As for Item (2), this just follows from the fact that S does not rewind the ith session prefix (as implied by Condition (2) in the definition of a useful session prefix). In particular, P^* (playing the role of V_h) will not have to send the jth verifier message with the ith session prefix more than once to S (since the number of messages sent by V_h for that session prefix is exactly $k + 1$).

Since the number of session prefixes in an execution of S is bounded by a polynomial, it follows that if the conversation between S and V_h contains a useful session prefix with non-negligible probability, then $\langle P^*, V \rangle(x)$ accepts with non-negligible probability.

7.1.2 The Schedule and Additional Ideas

Using the above framework, the crux of the lower bound is to come up with a schedule and V_h's that allow demonstrating that whenever S succeeds, the conversation between S and V_h contains a useful session prefix (as we have argued above, it is in fact sufficient that the conversation between S and V_h contains a useful session prefix with non-negligible probability). This is done next.

The Two-Round Case. Our starting point is the schedule used in [83] to demonstrate the impossibility of black-box concurrent zero-knowledge with protocols in which four messages are exchanged (i.e., v_1, p_1, v_2, p_2). The schedule is recursive and consists of n concurrent sessions (n is polynomially related to the security parameter). Given parameter $m \leq n$, the scheduling on m sessions (denoted $\mathcal{R}_m$) proceeds as follows (see Fig. 7.2 for a graphical description):

1. If $m = 1$, the relevant session exchanges all of its messages (i.e., v_1, p_1, v_2, p_2).
2. Otherwise (i.e., if $m > 1$):
   Initial message exchange: The first session (out of m) exchanges 2 messages (i.e., v_1, p_1);
   Recursive call: The schedule is applied recursively on the remaining $m - 1$ sessions;
   Final message exchange: The first session (out of m) exchanges 2 messages (i.e., v_2, p_2).

---

[1] The problem is that P^* does not know V's random coins, and so it cannot compute the verifier's answers by himself. Thus, whenever P^* is required in the emulation to send the jth verifier message in the protocol more than once to S it might get into trouble (since it gets the jth verifier message only once from V).

At the end of each session V_h continues in the interaction if and only if the transcript of the session that has just terminated would have been accepted by the prescribed verifier V. This means that in order to proceed beyond the ending point of the ℓth session, the simulator must make the honest verifier accept the sth session for all $s > \ell$.

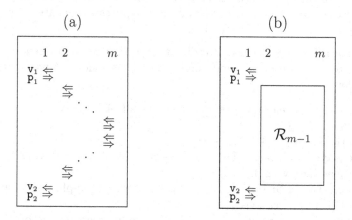

Fig. 7.2. The "telescopic" schedule used to demonstrate impossibility of black-box concurrent zero-knowledge in two rounds. Columns correspond to n individual sessions and rows correspond to the time progression. (a) Depicts the schedule explicitly. (b) Depicts the schedule in a recursive manner ($\mathcal{R}_m$ denotes the recursive schedule for m sessions).

Suppose now that S succeeds in simulating the above V_h but the conversation between S and V_h does not contain a useful session prefix. Since V_h proceeds beyond the ending point of a session only if this session is accepted, then the only reason for which the corresponding session prefix can be non-useful is because S has rewound that session prefix. Put in other words, a session prefix becomes non-useful if and only if S resends the first prover message in the protocol (i.e., p_1).[2] This should cause V_h to resend the second verifier message (i.e., v_2), thus violating Condition (2) in the definition of a useful session prefix.

The key observation is that whenever the first prover message in the ℓth session is modified, then so is the session prefix of the sth session for *all* $s > \ell$.

---

[2]Notice that the first prover message in the protocol (i.e., p_1) is the only place in which rewinding the interaction may cause a session prefix to be non-useful. The reason for this is that the first verifier message in the protocol (i.e., v_1) is part of the session prefix. Rewinding past this message (i.e., v_1) would modify the session prefix itself. As for p_2, it is clear that rewinding this message would not cause any change in verifier messages that correspond to the relevant session prefix (since, v_1 and v_2 occur after p_2 anyway).

Thus, whenever S resends the first prover message in the ℓth session, it must do so also in the sth session for all $s > \ell$ (since otherwise the "fresh" session prefix of the sth session, that is induced by resending the above message, will be useful). But this means that the work $W(m)$, invested in the simulation of a schedule with m levels, must satisfy $W(m) \geq 2 \cdot W(m-1)$ for all m. Thus, either the conversation between V_h and S contains a useful session prefix (in which case we are done), or the simulation requires exponential-time (since $W(m) \geq 2 \cdot W(m-1)$ solves to $W(n) \geq 2^{n-1}$).

The k-round Case – First Attempt. A first attempt to generalize this schedule to the case of k rounds may proceed as follows. Given parameter $m \leq n$ do:

1. If $m = 1$, the relevant session exchanges all of its messages (i.e., $\mathsf{v}_1, \mathsf{p}_1$, $\ldots, \mathsf{v}_{k+1}, \mathsf{p}_{k+1}$).
2. Otherwise, for $j = 1, \ldots, k+1$:
   Message exchange: The first session (out of m) exchanges two messages (i.e., $\mathsf{v}_j, \mathsf{p}_j$);
   Recursive call: If $j < k+1$, the scheduling is applied recursively on $\lfloor \frac{m-1}{k} \rfloor$ new sessions;
   (This is done using the next $\lfloor \frac{m-1}{k} \rfloor$ remaining sessions out of $2, \ldots, m$.)

As before, at the end of each session V_h continues in the interaction if and only if the transcript of the session that has just terminated would have been accepted by the prescribed verifier V. The schedule is depicted in Fig. 7.3.

The crucial problem of the above schedule is that one can come up with a k-round protocol and a corresponding simulator that manages to succesfully simulate V_h *and* cause all session prefixes in its conversation with V_h to be non-useful. Specifically, there exist protocols (cf. [94]) in which the simulator is required to successfully rewind an honestly behaving verifier exactly once for every session. Whereas in the case of two-rounds this could have had devastating consequences (since, in the case of the previous schedule, it would have implied $W(m) \geq (k+1) \cdot W(m-1) = 2 \cdot W(m-1)$, which solves to $W(n) \geq 2^{n-1}$), in the general case (i.e., when $k+1 > 2$) any rewinding of the schedule that we have suggested would have forced the simulator to re-invest simulation "work" only for $\frac{m-1}{k}$ sessions. Note that such a simulator satisfies $W(m) = (k+1) \cdot W(\frac{m-1}{k})$, which solves to $k^{O(\log_k n)} = n^{O(1)}$. In particular, by investing polynomial amount of work the simulator is able to make all session prefixes not useful while succesfully simulating all sessions.

The k-round Case – Second Attempt. One method to circumvent this difficulty was used in [97]. However, that method extends the lower bound only up to three rounds (more precisely, seven messages). Here we use a different method. What we do is let the cheating verifier abort (i.e., refuse to answer) every message in the schedule with some predetermined probability (independently of other messages). To do this, we first add another, binary hash function, g, to the specification of V_h. This hash function is taken from

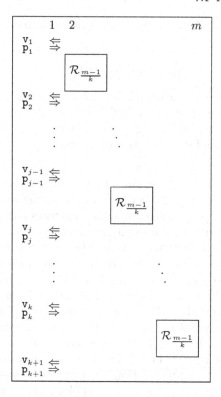

Fig. 7.3. First attempt to generalize the recursive schedule for k-round protocols.

a family G with sufficient independence, so that it looks like a random binary function. Now, before generating the next message in some session, $V_{g,h}$ first applies g to some predetermined part of the conversation so far. If g returns 0 then $V_{g,h}$ aborts the session by sending an ABORT message. If g returns 1 then $V_{g,h}$ is run as usual.

The rationale behind the use of aborts can be explained as follows. Recall that a session prefix a stops being useful only when $V_{g,h}$ sends more than k messages whose session prefix is a. This means that a stops being useful only if S rewinds the session prefix a *and in addition* g returns 1 in at least two of the continuations of a. This means that S is expected to rewind session prefix a several times before it stops being useful. Since each rewinding of a involves extra work of S on higher-level sessions, this may force S to invest considerably more work before a session stops being useful.

A bit more specifically, let p denote the probability, taken over the choice of g, that g returns 1 on a given input. In each attempt, the session is not aborted with probability p. Thus S is expected to rewind a session prefix $1/p$ times before it becomes non-useful. This gives hope that, in order to make sure that no session prefix is useful, S must do work that satisfies a condition of the sort:

$$W(m) \geq \Omega(1/p) \cdot W\left(\tfrac{m-1}{k}\right). \tag{7.1}$$

This would mean that the work required to successfully simulate n sessions *and* make all session prefixes non-useful is at least $\Omega(p^{-\log_k n})$. Consequently, when the expression $p^{-\log_k n}$ is super-polynomial there is hope that the conversation between S and V_h contains a useful session prefix with non-negligible probability.

The k-round Case – Final Version. However, demonstrating 7.1 brings up the following difficulty. Once the verifier starts aborting sessions, the probability that a session is ever completed may become too small. As a consequence, it is not clear anymore that the simulator must invest simulation "work" for all sessions in the schedule. It may very well be the case that the simulator will go about the simulation task while "avoiding" part of the simulation "work" in some recursive invocations (as some of these invocations may be aborted anyway during the simulation). In other words, there is no guarantee that the recursive "work" invested by the simulator behaves like 7.1.

To overcome this problem, we replace each session in the above schedule (for k rounds) with a "block" of, say, n sessions (see Fig. 7.4 in page 121). We now have n^2 sessions in a schedule. (This choice of parameters is arbitrary, and is made for convenience of presentation.) $V_{g,h}$ accepts a block of n sessions if at least $1/2$ of the non-aborted sessions in this block were accepted and not too many of the sessions in this block were aborted. Once a block is rejected, $V_{g,h}$ halts. At the end of the execution, $V_{g,h}$ accepts if all blocks were accepted. The above modification guarantees that, with a careful setting of the parameters, the simulator's recursive "work" must satisfy 7.1, at least with overwhelming probability.

Setting the Value of p. It now remains to set the value of p so that 7.1 is established. Clearly, the smaller p is chosen to be, the larger $p^{-\log_k n}$ is. However, p cannot be too small, or else the probability of a session to be ever completed will be too small, and Condition (1) in the definition of a useful session prefix (see page 112) will not be satisfied. Specifically, a k-round protocol is completed with probability p^k. We thus have to make sure that p^k is not negligible (and furthermore that $p^k \cdot n \gg 1$).

In the proof we set $p = n^{-1/2k}$. This will guarantee that a session is completed with probability $p^k = n^{-1/2}$ (thus Condition (1) has hope to be satisfied). Furthermore, since $p^{-\log_k n}$ is super-polynomial whenever $k = o(\log n / \log \log n)$, there is hope that Condition (2) in the definition of a useful session prefix (see page 112) will be satisfied for $k = o(\log n / \log \log n)$.

7.1.3 The Actual Analysis

Demonstrating that there exist many accepted session prefixes is straight-forward. Demonstrating that one of these session prefixes is useful requires arguing on the dependency between the expected work done by the simulator and its success probability. This is a tricky business, since the choices made by the simulator (and in particular the amount of effort spent on making each session non-useful) may depend on past events.

We go about this task by pinpointing a special (combinatorial) property that holds for *any* successful run of the simulator, unless the simulator runs in super-polynomial time (Lemma 7.3.9). Essentially, this property states that there exists a block of sessions such that none of the session prefixes in this block were rewound too many times. Using this property, we show (in Lemma 7.3.7) that the probability (over the choices of $V_{g,h}$ and the simulator) that a run of the simulator contains no useful session prefix is negligible.

7.2 The Actual Proof

Assuming towards the contradiction that a black-box simulator, denoted S, contradicting Theorem 7.1 exists, we will describe a probabilistic polynomial-time decision procedure for L, based on S. The first step towards describing the decision procedure for L involves the construction of an adversary verifier in the concurrent model. This is done next.

7.2.1 The Concurrent Adversarial Verifier

The description of the adversarial strategy proceeds in several steps. We start by describing the underlying fixed schedule of messages. Once the schedule is presented, we describe the adversary's strategy regarding the contents of the verifier messages.

The Schedule

For each $x \in \{0,1\}^n$, we consider the following concurrent scheduling of n^2 sessions, all run on common input x.[3] The scheduling is defined recursively, where the scheduling of $m \le n^2$ sessions (denoted $\mathcal{R}_m$) proceeds as follows:[4]

1. If $m \le n$, sessions $1, \ldots, m$ are executed sequentially until they are all completed;

---

[3] Recall that each session consists of $2k + 2$ messages, where $k \stackrel{\text{def}}{=} k(n) = o(\log n / \log \log n)$.

[4] In general, we may want to define a recursive scheduling for sessions $i_1, \ldots, i_m$ and denote it by $\mathcal{R}_{i_1,\ldots,i_m}$. We choose to simplify the exposition by renaming these sessions as $1, \ldots, m$ and denote the scheduling by $\mathcal{R}_m$.

2. Otherwise, for $j = 1, \ldots, k+1$:

   Message exchange: Each of the first n sessions exchanges two messages (i.e., $\mathsf{v}_j, \mathsf{p}_j$);
   (These first n sessions out of $\{1, \ldots, m\}$ will be referred to as the main sessions of $\mathcal{R}_m$.)
   Recursive call: If $j < k+1$, the scheduling is applied recursively on $\lfloor \frac{m-n}{k} \rfloor$ new sessions;
   (This is done using the next $\lfloor \frac{m-n}{k} \rfloor$ remaining sessions out of $1, \ldots, m$.)

The schedule is depicted in Fig. 7.4. We stress that the verifier typically postpones its answer (i.e., v_j) to the last prover's message (i.e., p_{j-1}) till after a recursive subschedule is executed, and that in the jth iteration of Step 2, $\lfloor \frac{m-n}{k} \rfloor$ new sessions are initiated (with the exception of the first iteration, in which the first n (main) sessions are initiated as well). The order in which the messages of various sessions are exchanged (in the first part of Step 2) is fixed but immaterial. Say that we let the first session proceed, then the second and so on. That is, we have the order $\mathsf{v}_j^{(1)}, \mathsf{p}_j^{(1)}, \ldots, \mathsf{v}_j^{(n)}, \mathsf{p}_j^{(n)}$, where $\mathsf{v}_j^{(i)}$ (resp., $\mathsf{p}_j^{(i)}$) denotes the verifier's (resp., prover's) j^{th} message in the ith session.

The set of n sessions that are explicitly executed during the message exchange phase of the recursive invocation (i.e., the main sessions) is called a recursive block. (Notice that each recursive block corresponds to exactly one recursive invocation of the schedule.) Taking a closer look at the schedule we observe that every session in the schedule is explicitly executed in exactly one recursive invocation (that is, belongs to exactly one recursive block). Since the total number of sessions in the schedule is n^2, and since the message exchange phase in each recursive invocation involves the explicit execution of n sessions (in other words, the size of each recursive block is n), we have that the total number of recursive blocks in the schedule equals n. Since each recursive invocation of the schedule involves the invocation of k additional subschedules, the recursion actually corresponds to a k-ary tree with n nodes. The depth of the recursion is thus $\lfloor \log_k((k-1)n+1) \rfloor$, and the number of "leaves" in the recursion (i.e., subschedules of size at most n) is at least $\lfloor \frac{(k-1)n+1}{k} \rfloor$.

Identifying Sessions According to their Recursive Block. To simplify the exposition of the proof, it will be convenient to associate every session appearing in the schedule with a pair of indices $(\ell, i) \in \{1, \ldots, n\} \times \{1, \ldots, n\}$, rather than with a single index $s \in \{1, \ldots, n^2\}$. The value of $\ell = \ell(s) \in \{1, \ldots, n\}$ will represent the index of the recursive block to which session s belongs (according to some canonical enumeration of the n invocations in the recursive schedule, say according to the order in which they are invoked), whereas the value of $i = i(s) \in \{1, \ldots, n\}$ will represent the index of session s within the n sessions that belong to the ℓth recursive block (in other words, session (ℓ, i) is the ith main session of the ℓth recursive invocation in the schedule). Typically, when we explicitly refer to messages of session (ℓ, i), the index of the corresponding recursive block (i.e., ℓ) is easily deducible from the context. In such cases, we will sometimes omit the index ℓ from the "natural" notation $v_j^{(\ell,i)}$ (resp. $p_j^{(\ell,i)}$), and stick to the notation $v_j^{(i)}$ (resp. $p_j^{(i)}$). Note that the values of (ℓ, i) and the session index s are completely interchangeable (in particular, $\ell = s$ div n and $i = s$ mod n).

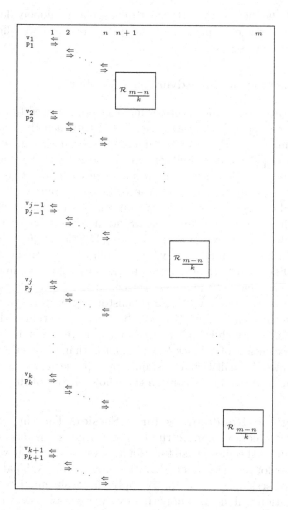

Fig. 7.4. The recursive schedule $\mathcal{R}_m$ for m sessions. Columns correspond to m individual sessions and rows correspond to the time progression.

Definition 7.2.1 (Identifiers of next message) *The schedule defines a mapping from partial execution transcripts ending with a prover message to the identifiers of the next verifier message; that is, the session and round number to which the next verifier message belongs. (Recall that such partial execution transcripts correspond to queries of a black-box simulator and so the mapping* defines the identifier of the answer.) *For such a query* $\overline{q} = (b_1, a_1, \ldots, b_t, a_t)$, *we denote by* $\pi_{\mathrm{sn}}(\overline{q}) = (\ell, i) \in \{1, \ldots, n\} \times \{1, \ldots, n\}$ *the session to which the next verifier message belongs, and by* $\pi_{\mathrm{msg}}(\overline{q}) = j \in \{1, \ldots, k+1\}$ *its index within the verifier's messages in this session.*

We stress that the identifiers of the next message are uniquely determined by the number of messages appearing in the query (and are not affected by the contents of these messages).

Towards Constructing an Adversarial Verifier

Once the identifiers of the next verifier message are deduced from the query's length, one has to specify a strategy according to which the contents of the next verifier message will be determined. Loosely speaking, our adversary verifier has two options. It will either send the answer that would have been sent by an honest verifier (given the messages in the query that are relevant to the current session), or it will choose to deviate from the honest verifier strategy and abort the interaction in the current session (this will be done by answering with a special ABORT message). Since in a non-trivial zero-knowledge proof system the honest verifier is always probabilistic (cf. [67]), and since the "abort behavior" of the adversary verifier should be "unpredictable" for the simulator, we have that both options require a source of randomness (either for computing the contents of the honest verifier answer or for deciding whether to abort the conversation). As is already customary in works of this sort [63, 83, 97], we let the source of randomness be a hash function with sufficiently high independence (which is "hard-wired" into the verifier's description), and consider the execution of a black-box simulator that is given access to such a random verifier. (Recall that the simulator's queries correspond to partial execution transcripts and thus contain the whole history of the interaction so far.)

Determining the Randomness for a Session. Focusing (first) on the randomness required to compute the honest verifier's answers, we ask what should the input of the above hash function be. A naive solution would be to let the randomness for a session depend on the session's index. That is, to obtain randomness for session $(\ell, i) = \pi_{\mathrm{sn}}(\overline{q})$ apply the hash function on the value (ℓ, i). This solution will indeed imply that every two sessions have independent randomness (as the hash function will have different inputs). However, the solution seems to fail to capture the difficulty arising in the simulation (of multiple concurrent sessions). What we would like to have is a situation in which whenever the simulator rewinds a session (that is, feeds the adversary verifier with a different query of the same length), it causes the randomness of some other session (say, one level down in the recursive schedule) to be completely modified. To achieve this, we must cause the randomness of a session to depend also on the history of the entire interaction. Changing even a single message in this history would immediately result in an unrelated instance of the current session, and would thus force the simulator to redo the simulation work on this session all over again.

So where in the schedule should the randomness of session (ℓ, i) be determined? On the one hand, we would like to determine the randomness of a session as late as possible (in order to maximize the effect of changes in the history of the interaction on the randomness of the session). On the other hand, we cannot afford to determine the randomness after the session's initiating message is scheduled (since the protocol's specification may require that the verifier's randomness is completely determined before the first verifier message is sent). For technical reasons, the point in which we choose to determine the randomness of session (ℓ, i) is the point in which recursive block number ℓ is invoked. That is, to obtain the randomness of session $(\ell, i) = \pi_{\mathrm{sn}}(\overline{q})$ we feed the hash function with the prefix of query $\overline{q}$ that ends just before the first message in block number ℓ (this prefix is called the block prefix of query $\overline{q}$ and is defined below). In order to achieve independence with other sessions in block number ℓ, we will also feed the hash function with the value of i. This (together with the above choice) guarantees us the following properties. (1) The input to the hash function (and thus the randomness for session (ℓ, i)) does not change once the interaction in the session begins (that is, once the first verifier message is sent). (2) For every pair of different sessions, the input to the hash function is different (and thus the randomness for each session is independent). (3) Even a single modification in the prefix of the interaction up to the first message in block number ℓ, induces fresh randomness for all sessions in block number ℓ.

Definition 7.2.2 (Block prefix) *The* block prefix *of a query $\overline{q}$ satisfying $\pi_{\mathrm{sn}}(\overline{q}) = (\ell, i)$, is the prefix of $\overline{q}$ that is answered with the first verifier message of session $(\ell, 1)$ (that is, the first main session in block number ℓ). More formally, $bp(\overline{q}) = (b_1, a_1, \ldots, b_\gamma, a_\gamma)$ is the block prefix of $\overline{q} = (b_1, a_1, \ldots, b_t, a_t)$ if $\pi_{\mathrm{sn}}(bp(\overline{q})) = (\ell, 1)$ and $\pi_{\mathrm{msg}}(bp(\overline{q})) = 1$. The block prefix will be said to correspond to recursive block number ℓ.[5] (Note that i may be any index in $\{1, \ldots, n\}$, and that a_t need not belong to session (ℓ, i).)*

Determining Whether and When to Abort Sessions. Whereas the randomness that is used to compute the honest verifier's answers in each session is determined before a session begins, the randomness that is used in order to decide whether to abort a session is chosen independently every time the execution of the schedule reaches the next verifier message in this session. As before, the required randomness is obtained by applying a hash function on the suitable prefix of the execution transcript. This time, however, the length of the prefix increases each time the execution of the session reaches the next verifier message (rather than being fixed for the whole execution of the session). This way, the decision of whether to abort a session also depends

---

[5]In the special case that $\ell = 1$ (that is, we are in the first block of the schedule), we define $bp(\overline{q}) = \perp$.

on the contents of messages that were exchanged after the initiation of the session has occurred. Specifically, in order to decide whether to abort session $(\ell, i) = \pi_{\mathrm{sn}}(\bar{q})$ at the jth message (where $j = \pi_{\mathrm{msg}}(\bar{q})$), we feed the hash function with the prefix (of query $\bar{q}$) that ends with the $(j-1)^{\mathrm{st}}$ prover message in the nth main session of block number ℓ. (As before, the hash function is also fed with the value of i in order to achieve independence from other sessions in the block.) This prefix is called the iteration prefix of query $\bar{q}$ and is defined next (see Fig. 7.5 for a graphical description of the block prefix and iteration prefix of a query).

Definition 7.2.3 (Iteration prefix) *The* iteration prefix *of a query $\bar{q}$ satisfying $\pi_{\mathrm{sn}}(\bar{q}) = (\ell, i)$ and $\pi_{\mathrm{msg}}(\bar{q}) = j > 1$, is the prefix of $\bar{q}$ that ends with the $(j-1)^{\mathrm{st}}$ prover message in session (ℓ, n) (that is, the nth main session in block number ℓ). More formally, $ip(\bar{q}) = (b_1, a_1, \ldots, b_\delta, a_\delta)$ is the iteration prefix of $\bar{q} = (b_1, a_1, \ldots, b_t, a_t)$ if a_δ is of the form $\mathrm{p}_{j-1}^{(n)}$ (where $\mathrm{p}_{j-1}^{(n)}$ denotes the $(j-1)^{\mathrm{st}}$ prover message in the nth main session of block number ℓ). This iteration prefix is said to correspond to the block prefix of $\bar{q}$. (Again, note that i may be any index in $\{1, \ldots, n\}$, and that a_t need not belong to session (ℓ, i). Also, note that the iteration prefix is defined only for $\pi_{\mathrm{msg}}(\bar{q}) > 1$.)*

We stress that two queries $\bar{q}_1, \bar{q}_2$ may have the same iteration prefix even if they do not correspond to the same session. This could happen whenever $bp(\bar{q}_1) = bp(\bar{q}_2)$ and $\pi_{\mathrm{msg}}(\bar{q}_1) = \pi_{\mathrm{msg}}(\bar{q}_2)$ (which is possible even if $\pi_{\mathrm{sn}}(\bar{q}_1) \neq \pi_{\mathrm{sn}}(\bar{q}_2)$).

Motivating Definitions 7.2.2 and 7.2.3. The choices made in Definitions 7.2.2 and 7.2.3 are designed to capture the difficulties encountered whenever many sessions are to be simulated concurrently. As was previously mentioned, we would like to create a situation in which every attempt of the simulator to rewind a specific session will result in loss of work done for other sessions (and so will cause the simulator to do the same amount of work all over again). In order to force the simulator to repeat each such rewinding attempt many times, we make each rewinding attempt fail with some predetermined probability (by letting the verifier send an ABORT message instead of a legal answer).[6]

To see that Definitions 7.2.2 and 7.2.3 indeed lead to the fulfillment of the above requirements, we consider the following example. Suppose that at some point during the simulation, the adversary verifier aborts session (ℓ, i) at the jth message (while answering query $\bar{q}$). Further suppose that (for some unspecified reason) the simulator wants to get a "second chance" in receiving a legal answer to the jth message in session (ℓ, i) (hoping that it will not receive the ABORT message again). Recall that the decision of whether to abort a session depends on the outcome of a hash function when applied to the

---

[6]Recall that all of the above is required in order to make the simulator's work accumulate to too much, and eventually cause its running time to be super-polynomial.

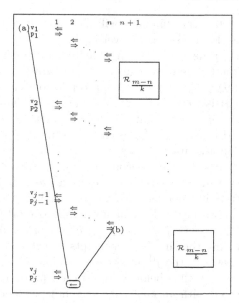

Fig. 7.5. Determining the prefixes of query $\bar{q}$ (in this example, query $\bar{q}$ ends with a $p_j^{(1)}$ message and is to be answered by $v_j^{(2)}$, represented by the marked arrow): (a) indicates the **block prefix** of $\bar{q}$ (i.e., messages up to this point are used by $V_{g,h}$ to determine the randomness to be used for computing message $v_j^{(2)}$). (b) indicates the **iteration prefix** of $\bar{q}$ (i.e., messages up to this point are used by $V_{g,h}$ to determine whether or not message $v_j^{(2)}$ will be set to ABORT).

iteration prefix $ip(\bar{q})$, of query $\bar{q}$. In particular, to obtain a "second chance", the black-box simulator has no choice but to change at least one prover message in the above iteration prefix (in other words, the simulator must rewind the interaction to some message occurring in iteration prefix $ip(\bar{q})$). At first glance it may seem that the effect of changes in the iteration prefix of query $\bar{q}$ is confined to the messages that belong to session $(\ell, i) = \pi_{\mathrm{sn}}(\bar{q})$ (or at most, to messages that belong to other sessions in block number ℓ). However, taking a closer look at the schedule, we observe that every iteration prefix (and in particular $ip(\bar{q})$) can also be viewed as the block prefix of a recursive block one level down in the recursive construction. Viewed this way, it is clear that the effect of changes in $ip(\bar{q})$ is not confined only to messages that correspond to recursive block number ℓ, but rather extends also to sessions at lower levels in the recursive schedule. By changing even a single message in iteration prefix $ip(\bar{q})$, the simulator is actually modifying the block prefix of all recursive blocks in a subschedule one level down in the recursive construction. This means that the randomness for all sessions in these blocks is completely modified (recall that the randomness of a session is determined by applying a hash function on the corresponding block prefix), and that all the simulation work done for these sessions is lost. In particular, by changing even a single message in iteration prefix $ip(\overline{q})$, the simulator will find himself doing the simulation work for these lower-level sessions all over again.

Having established the effect of changes in iteration prefix $ip(\overline{q})$ on sessions at lower levels in the recursive schedule, we now turn to examine the actual effect on session $(\ell, i) = \pi_{\mathrm{sn}}(\overline{q})$ itself. One possible consequence of changes in iteration prefix $ip(\overline{q})$ is that they may also affect the contents of the block prefix $bp(\overline{q})$ of query $\overline{q}$ (notice that, by definition, the block prefix $bp(\overline{q})$ of query $\overline{q}$ is contained in the iteration prefix $ip(\overline{q})$ of query $\overline{q}$). Whenever this happens, the randomness used for session (ℓ, i) is completely modified, and all simulation work done for this session will be lost. A more interesting consequence of a change in the contents of iteration prefix $ip(\overline{q})$, is that it will result in a completely independent decision of whether session (ℓ, i) is to be aborted at the jth message (the decision of whether to abort is taken whenever the simulator makes a query $\overline{q}$ satisfying $\pi_{\mathrm{sn}}(\overline{q}) = (\ell, i)$, and $\pi_{\mathrm{msg}}(\overline{q}) = j$). In other words, each time the simulator attempts to get a "second chance" in receiving a legal answer to the jth message in session (ℓ, i) (by rewinding the interaction to a message that belongs to iteration prefix $ip(\overline{q})$), it faces the risk of being answered with an ABORT message independently of all previous rewinding attempts.

7.2.2 The Actual Verifier Strategy $V_{g,h}$

We consider what happens when a simulator S (for the above schedule) is given oracle access to a verifier strategy $V_{g,h}$ defined as follows (depending on hash functions g, h and the input x). Recall that we may assume that S runs in strict polynomial time: we denote such time bound by $t_S(\cdot)$. Let G denote a small family of $t_S(n)$-wise independent hash functions mapping $\mathrm{poly}(n)$-bit long sequences into a single bit of output, so that for every α we have $\mathrm{Pr}_{g \leftarrow G}[g(\alpha) = 1] = n^{-1/2k}$. Let H denote a small family of $t_S(n)$-wise independent hash functions mapping $\mathrm{poly}(n)$-bit long sequences to $\rho_V(n)$-bit sequences, so that for every α we have $\mathrm{Pr}_{h \leftarrow H}[h(\alpha) = 1] = 2^{-\rho_V(n)}$ (where $\rho_V(n)$ is the number of random bits used by an honest verifier V on an input $x \in \{0,1\}^n$).[7] We describe a family $\{V_{g,h}\}_{g \in G, h \in H}$ of adversarial verifier strategies (where x is implicit in $V_{g,h}$). On query $\overline{q} = (b_1, a_1, \ldots, a_{t-1}, b_t, a_t)$, the verifier acts as follows:

1. First, $V_{g,h}$ checks if the execution transcript given by the query is legal (i.e., corresponds to a possible execution prefix), and halts with a special ERROR message if the query is not legal.[8]

---

[7]We stress that functions in such families can be described by strings of polynomial length in a way that enables polynomial time evaluation (cf. [79, 32, 33, 2]).

[8]In particular, $V_{g,h}$ checks whether the query is of the prescribed format (as described in Sect. 3.7, and as determined by the schedule), and that the contents of its messages is consistent with $V_{g,h}$'s prior answers. (That is, for every proper prefix $\overline{q}' = (b_1, a_1, \ldots, b_u, a_u)$ of query $\overline{q} = (b_1, a_1, \ldots, b_t, a_t)$, the verifier checks whether the value of b_{u+1} (as it appears in $\overline{q}$) is indeed equal to the value of $V_{g,h}(\overline{q}')$.)

2. Next, $V_{g,h}$ determines the block prefix, $bp(\bar{q}) = (b_1, a_1, \ldots, b_\gamma, a_\gamma)$, of query $\bar{q}$. It also determines the identifiers of the next-message $(\ell, i) = \pi_{\mathrm{sn}}(\bar{q})$ and $j = \pi_{\mathrm{msg}}(\bar{q})$, the iteration prefix $ip(\bar{q}) = (b_1, a_1, \ldots, b_\delta, \mathrm{p}_{j-1}^{(n)})$, and the $j-1$ prover messages of session i appearing in query $\bar{q}$ (which we denote by $\mathrm{p}_1^{(i)}, \ldots, \mathrm{p}_{j-1}^{(i)}$).

(**Motivating Discussion.** The next message is the jth verifier message in the ith session of block ℓ. The value of the block prefix, $bp(\bar{q})$, is used in order to determine the randomness of session (ℓ, i), whereas the value of the iteration prefix, $ip(\bar{q})$, is used in order to determine whether session (ℓ, i) is about to be aborted at this point (i.e., j^{th} message) in the schedule, by answering with a special ABORT message.)

3. If $j = 1$, then $V_{g,h}$ answers with the verifier's fixed initiation message for session i (i.e., $\mathrm{v}_1^{(i)}$).

4. If $j > 1$, then $V_{g,h}$ determines $b_{i,j} = g(i, ip(\bar{q}))$ (i.e., a bit deciding whether to abort session i):

   a) If $b_{i,j} = 0$, then $V_{g,h}$ sets $\mathrm{v}_j^{(i)} = \texttt{ABORT}$ (indicating that $V_{g,h}$ aborts session i).

   b) If $b_{i,j} = 1$, then $V_{g,h}$ determines $r_i = h(i, bp(\bar{q}))$ (as coins to be used by V), and computes the message $\mathrm{v}_j^{(i)} = V(x, r_i; \mathrm{p}_1^{(i)}, \ldots, \mathrm{p}_{j-1}^{(i)})$ that would have been sent by the honest verifier on common input x, random-pad r_i, and prover's messages $\mathrm{p}_1^{(i)}, \ldots, \mathrm{p}_{j-1}^{(i)}$.

   c) Finally, $V_{g,h}$ answers with $\mathrm{v}_j^{(i)}$.

Dealing with ABORT Messages. Note that, once $V_{g,h}$ has aborted a session, the interaction in this session essentially stops, and there is no need to continue exchanging messages in this session. However, for simplicity of exposition we assume that the verifier and prover stick to the fixed schedule of Sect. 7.2.1 and exchange ABORT messages whenever an aborted session is scheduled. Specifically, if the jth verifier message in session i is ABORT then all subsequent prover and verifier messages in that session will also equal ABORT.

On the Arguments to g and h. The hash function h, which determines the random input for V in a session, is applied both on i (the identifier of the relevant session within the current block) and on the entire block prefix of the query $\bar{q}$. This means that even though all sessions in a specific block have the same block prefix, for every pair of two different sessions, the corresponding random inputs of V will be independent of each other (as long as the number of applications of h does not exceed $t_S(n)$, which is indeed the case in our application). The hash function g, which determines whether and when the verifier aborts sessions, is applied both on i and on the entire iteration prefix of the query $\bar{q}$. As in the case of h, the decision whether to abort a session is independent from the same decision for other sessions (again, as long as g is not applied more than $t_S(n)$ times). However, there is a significant difference between the inputs of h and g: Whereas the input of h is *fixed* once i

and the block prefix are fixed (and is unaffected by messages that belong to that session), the input of g *varies* depending on previous messages sent in that session. In particular, whereas the randomness of a session is completely determined once the session begins, the decision of whether to abort a session is taken independently each time that the schedule reaches the next verifier message of this session.

On the Number of Different Prefixes that Occur in Interactions with $V_{g,h}$. Since the number of recursive blocks in the schedule is equal to n, and since there is a one-to-one correspondence between recursive blocks and block prefixes, we have that the number of different block prefixes that occur during an interaction between an *honest prover* P and the verifier $V_{g,h}$ is always equal to n. Since the number of iterations in the message exchange phase of a recursive invocation of the schedule equals $k+1$, and since there is a one-to-one correspondence between such iterations and iteration prefixes[9] we have that the number of different iteration prefixes that occur during an interaction between and honest prover P and the verifier $V_{g,h}$, is always equal to $k \cdot n$ (that is, k different iteration prefixes for each one of the n recursive invocations of the schedule). In contrast, the number of different block prefixes (resp., iteration prefixes), that occur during an execution of a black-box simulator S that is given oracle access to $V_{g,h}$, may be considerably larger than n (resp., $k \cdot n$). The reason for this is that there is nothing that prevents the simulator from feeding $V_{g,h}$ with different queries of the same length (this corresponds to the so called rewinding of an interaction). Still, the number of different prefixes in an execution of S is always upper bounded by the running time of S; that is, $t_S(n)$.

On the Probability That a Session Is Never Aborted. A typical interaction between an honest prover P and the verifier $V_{g,h}$ will contain sessions whose execution has been aborted prior to completion. Recall that at each point in the schedule, the decision of whether or not to abort the next scheduled session depends on the outcome of g. Since the function g returns 1 with probability $n^{-1/2k}$, a specific session is never aborted with probability $(n^{-1/2k})^k = n^{-1/2}$. Using the fact that whenever a session is not aborted, $V_{g,h}$ operates as the honest verifier, we infer that the probability that a specific session is eventually accepted by $V_{g,h}$ is at least $1/2$ times the probability that the very same session is never aborted (where $1/2$ is an arbitrary lower bound on the completeness probability of the protocol). In other words, the probability that a session is accepted by $V_{g,h}$ is at least $\frac{n^{-1/2}}{2}$. In particular, for every set of n sessions, the expected number of sessions that are eventually accepted by $V_{g,h}$ (when interacting with the honest prover P) is at least

---

[9]The only exception is the first iteration in the message exchange phase. Since only queries $\bar{q}$ that satisfy $\pi_{\mathrm{msg}}(\bar{q}) > 1$ have an iteration prefix, the first iteration will never have a corresponding iteration prefix.

$n \cdot \frac{n^{-1/2}}{2} = \frac{n^{1/2}}{2}$, and with overwhelming high probability at least $\frac{n^{1/2}}{4}$ sessions are accepted by $V_{g,h}$.

A Slight Modification of the Verifier Strategy. To facilitate the analysis, we slightly modify the verifier strategy $V_{g,h}$ so that it does not allow the number of accepted sessions in the history of the interaction to deviate much from its "expected behavior". Loosely speaking, given a prefix of the execution transcript (ending with a prover message), the verifier will check whether the recursive block that has just been completed contains at least $\frac{n^{1/2}}{4}$ accepted sessions. (To this end, it will be sufficient to inspect the history of the interaction only when the execution of the schedule reaches the end of a recursive block. That is, whenever the schedule reaches the last prover message in the last session of a recursive block, i.e., some $p_{k+1}^{(n)}$ message.) The modified verifier strategy (which we continue to denote by $V_{g,h}$), is obtained by adding to the original strategy an additional Step 1' (to be executed after Step 1 of $V_{g,h}$):

1'. If a_t is of the form $p_{k+1}^{(n)}$ (i.e., in case query $\bar{q} = (b_1, a_1, \ldots, b_t, a_t)$ ends with the last prover message of the nth main session of a recursive block), $V_{g,h}$ checks whether the transcript $\bar{q} = (b_1, a_1, \ldots, b_t, p_{k+1}^{(n)})$ contains the accepting conversations of at least $\frac{n^{1/2}}{4}$ main sessions in the block that has just been completed. In case it does not, $V_{g,h}$ halts with a special DEVIATION message (indicating that the number of accepted sessions in the block that has just been completed deviates from its expected value).

Motivating Discussion. Since the expected number of accepted sessions in a specific block is at least $\frac{n^{1/2}}{2}$, the probability that the block contains less than $\frac{n^{1/2}}{4}$ accepted sessions is negligible (see the proof of Lemma 7.2.4). Still, the above modification is not superfluous (even though it refers to events that occur only with negligible probability): it allows us to assume that every recursive block that is completed *during the simulation* (including those that *do not* appear in the simulator's output) contains at least $\frac{n^{1/2}}{4}$ accepted sessions. In particular, whenever the simulator feeds $V_{g,h}$ with a partial execution transcript (i.e., a query), we are guaranteed that for every completed block in this transcript, the simulator has indeed "invested work" to simulate the at least $\frac{n^{1/2}}{4}$ accepted sessions in the block.

A Slight Modification of the Simulator. Before presenting the decision procedure, we slightly modify the simulator so that it never makes a query that is answered with either the ERROR or DEVIATION messages by the verifier $V_{g,h}$. Note that the corresponding condition can be easily checked by the simulator (which can easily produce this special message by itself),[10] and that the modification does not affect the simulator's output. From this point

---

[10] We stress that, as opposed to the ERROR and DEVIATION messages, the simulator cannot predict whether its query is about to be answered with the ABORT message.

on, when we talk of the simulator (which we continue to denote by S) we mean the modified one.

7.2.3 The Decision Procedure for L

We are now ready to describe a probabilistic polynomial-time decision procedure for L, based on the black-box simulator S and the verifier strategies $V_{g,h}$. On input $x \in \{0,1\}^n$, the procedure operates as follows:

1. Uniformly select hash functions $g \overset{\text{R}}{\leftarrow} G$ and $h \overset{\text{R}}{\leftarrow} H$.
2. Invoke S on input x providing it black-box access to $V_{g,h}$ (as defined above). That is, the procedure emulates the execution of the oracle machine S on input x along with emulating the answers of $V_{g,h}$, where g and h are as determined in Step 1.
3. Accept if and only if S outputs a legal transcript (as determined by Steps 1 and $1\prime$ of $V_{g,h}$).[11]

By our hypothesis, the above procedure runs in probabilistic polynomial-time. We next analyze its performance.

Lemma 7.2.4 (Performance on YES-instances) *For all but finitely many $x \in L$, the above procedure accepts x with probability at least $2/3$.*

Proof Sketch Let $x \in L$, $g \overset{\text{R}}{\leftarrow} G$, $h \overset{\text{R}}{\leftarrow} H$, and consider the honest prover P. We show below that, except for negligible probability (where the probability is taken over the random choices of g, h, and P's coin tosses), when $V_{g,h}$ interacts with P, all recursive blocks in the resulting transcript contain the accepting conversations of at least $\frac{n^{1/2}}{4}$ main sessions. Since for *every* g and h the simulator $S^{V_{g,h}}(x)$ must generate a transcript whose deviation gap from $\langle P, V_{g,h} \rangle(x)$ is at most $1/4$, it follows that $S^{V_{g,h}}(x)$ has deviation gap at most $1/4$ from $\langle P, V_{g,h} \rangle(x)$ also when $g \overset{\text{R}}{\leftarrow} G$ and $h \overset{\text{R}}{\leftarrow} H$. Consequently, when S is run by the decision procedure for L, the transcript $S^{V_{g,h}}(x)$ will not be legal with probability at most $1/3$. Details follow.

Let τ denote the random variable describing the transcript of the interaction between the honest prover P and $V_{g,h}$, where the probability is taken over the choices of g, h, and P. Let $s \in \{1, \ldots, n^2\}$. We first calculate the probability that the sth session in τ is completed and accepted (i.e., $V_{g,h}$ sends the

---

[11] Recall that we are assuming that the simulator never makes a query that is ruled out by Steps 1 and $1\prime$ of $V_{g,h}$. Since before producing output $(b_1, a_1, \ldots, b_T, a_T)$ the simulator makes the query $(b_1, a_1, \ldots, b_T, a_T)$, checking the legality of the transcript in Step 3 is not really necessary (as, in case that the modified simulator indeed reaches the output stage "safely", we are guaranteed that it will produce a legal output). In particular, we are always guaranteed that the simulator either produces execution transcripts in which every recursive block contains at least $n^{1/2}/4$ sessions that were accepted by $V_{g,h}$, or it does not produce any output at all.

message $\mathrm{v}_{k+1}^{(s)} = \mathtt{ACCEPT}$), conditioned on the event that $V_{g,h}$ did not abandon the interaction beforehand (i.e., $V_{g,h}$ did not send the DEVIATION message before).[12] For uniformly selected $g \overset{\mathrm{R}}{\leftarrow} G$, the probability that $V_{g,h}$ does not abort the session in each of the k rounds, given that it has not already aborted, is $n^{-1/2k}$. Thus, conditioned on the event that $V_{g,h}$ did not output DEVIATION beforehand, the session is completed (without being aborted) with probability $(n^{-1/2k})^k = n^{-1/2}$.

The key observation is that if h is uniformly chosen from H then, conditioned on the event that $V_{g,h}$ did not output DEVIATION beforehand and the current session is not aborted, the conversation between $V_{g,h}$ and P is distributed identically to the conversation between the honest verifier V and P on input x. By the completeness requirement for zero-knowledge protocols, we have that V accepts in such an interaction with probability at least $1/2$ (this probability is actually higher, but $1/2$ is more than enough for our purposes). Consequently, for uniformly selected g and h, conditioned on the event that $V_{g,h}$ did not output DEVIATION beforehand, the probability that a session is accepted by $V_{g,h}$ is at least $\frac{n^{-1/2}}{2}$.

We calculate the probability that τ contains a block such that less than $\frac{n^{1/2}}{4}$ of its sessions are accepted. Say that a block B in a transcript has been completed if all the messages of sessions in B have been sent during the interaction. Say that B is admissible if the number of accepted sessions that belong to block B in the transcript is at least $\frac{n^{1/2}}{4}$. Enumerating blocks in the order in which they are completed (that is, when we refer to the ℓth block in τ, we mean the ℓth block that is completed in τ), we denote by γ_ℓ the event that all the blocks up to and including the ℓth block are admissible in τ.

For $i \in \{1, \ldots, n\}$ define a Boolean indicator α_i^ℓ to be 1 if and only if the ith session in the ℓth block is accepted by $V_{g,h}$. We have seen that, conditioned on the event $\gamma_{\ell-1}$, each α_i^ℓ is 1 w.p. at least $\frac{n^{-1/2}}{2}$. As a consequence, for every ℓ, the expectation of $\sum_{i=1}^n \alpha_i^\ell$ (i.e., the number of accepted main sessions in block number ℓ) is at least $\frac{n^{1/2}}{2}$. Since, conditioned on $\gamma_{\ell-1}$, the α_i^ℓ's are independent of each other, we can apply the Chernoff bound, and infer that

$$\Pr\left[\gamma_\ell | \gamma_{\ell-1}\right] > 1 - e^{-\Omega(n^{1/2})}.$$

Furthermore, since no session belongs to more than one block, we have:

$$\Pr\left[\gamma_\ell\right] \geq \Pr\left[\gamma_l | \gamma_{\ell-1}\right] \cdot \Pr\left[\gamma_{l-1}\right].$$

It follows (by induction on the number of completed blocks in a transcript), that all blocks in τ are admissible with probability at least $(1 - e^{-\Omega(n^{1/2})})^n > 1 - n \cdot e^{-\Omega(n^{1/2})}$. The lemma follows. ∎

---

[12]Note that, since we are dealing with the honest prover P, there is no need to consider the ERROR message at all (since in an interaction with the honest prover P, the adversary verifier $V_{g,h}$ will never output ERROR anyway).

Lemma 7.2.5 (Performance on NO-instances) *For all but finitely many $x \notin L$, the above procedure rejects x with probability at least 2/3.*

We can actually prove that for every positive polynomial $p(\cdot)$ and for all but finitely many $x \notin L$, the above procedure accepts x with probability at most $1/p(|x|)$. Assuming towards contradiction that this is not the case, we will construct a (probabilistic polynomial-time) strategy for a cheating prover that fools the honest verifier V with success probability at least $1/\mathrm{poly}(n)$ in contradiction to the soundness (and even computational-soundness) of the proof system.

7.3 Performance on NO-instances

We now turn to prove Lemma 7.2.5. Let us fix an $x \in \{0,1\}^n \setminus L$ as above.[13] Denote by $\mathtt{AC} = \mathtt{AC}_x$ the set of triplets (σ, g, h) so that on input x, internal coins σ and oracle access to $V_{g,h}$, the simulator outputs a legal transcript (which we denote by $S_\sigma^{V_{g,h}}(x)$). Recall that our contradiction assumption is that $\mathrm{Pr}_{\sigma,g,h}[(\sigma,g,h) \in \mathtt{AC}] > 1/p(n)$, for some fixed positive polynomial $p(\cdot)$. Before proceeding with the proof of Lemma 7.2.5, we formalize what we mean by referring to the "execution of the simulator".

Definition 7.3.1 (Execution of simulator) *Let $x, \sigma \in \{0,1\}^*$, $g \in G$ and $h \in H$. The* execution *of simulator S, denoted $\mathrm{EXEC}_x(\sigma, g, h)$, is the sequence of queries made by S, given input x, random coins σ, and oracle access to $V_{g,h}(x)$.*

Since the simulator has the ability to "rewind" the verifier $V_{g,h}$ and explore $V_{g,h}$'s output on various execution prefixes (i.e., queries) of the same length, the number of distinct block prefixes that appear in $\mathrm{EXEC}_x(\sigma, g, h)$ may be strictly larger than n (recall that the schedule consists of n invocations to recursive blocks, and that in an interaction between the honest prover P and $V_{g,h}$ there is a one-to-one correspondence between recursive blocks and block prefixes). As a consequence, the ℓth distinct block prefix appearing in $\mathrm{EXEC}_x(\sigma, g, h)$ does not necessarily correspond to the ℓth recursive block in the schedule. Nevertheless, given $\mathrm{EXEC}_x(\sigma, g, h)$ and ℓ, one can easily determine for the ℓth distinct block prefix in the execution of the simulator the index of its corresponding block in the schedule (say, by extracting the ℓth distinct block prefix in $\mathrm{EXEC}_x(\sigma, g, h)$, and then analyzing its length).

In the sequel, given a specific block prefix $\overline{bp}$, we let $\ell^{(\overline{bp})} \in \{1, \ldots, n\}$ denote the index of its corresponding block in the schedule (as determined by $\overline{bp}$'s length). Note that two different block prefixes $\overline{bp}_1$ and $\overline{bp}_2$ in $\mathrm{EXEC}_x(\sigma, g, h)$ may satisfy $\ell^{(\overline{bp}_1)} = \ell^{(\overline{bp}_2)}$ (as they may correspond to two different instances of the same recursive block). In particular, session $(\ell^{(\overline{bp}_1)}, i)$ may have more

---

[13] Actually, we need to consider infinitely many such x's.

than a single occurrence during the execution of the simulator (whereas in an interaction of the honest prover P with $V_{g,h}$ each session index will occur exactly once). This means that whenever we refer to an instance of session (ℓ, i) in the simulation, we will also have to explicitly specify to which block prefix this instance corresponds.

In order to avoid cumbersome statements, we will abuse the notation $\ell^{(\overline{bp})}$ and also use it in order to specify to which instance the recursive block $\ell^{(\overline{bp})}$ corresponds. That is, whenever we refer to recursive block number $\ell^{(\overline{bp})}$ we will actually mean: "the specific instance of recursive block number ℓ $(= \ell^{(\overline{bp})})$ that corresponds to block prefix $\overline{bp}$ in $\text{EXEC}_x(\sigma, g, h)$". Viewed this way, for $\ell^{(\overline{bp_1})} = \ell^{(\overline{bp_2})}$, sessions $(\ell^{(\overline{bp_1})}, i)$ and $(\ell^{(\overline{bp_2})}, i)$ actually correspond to two different instances of the same session in the schedule.

7.3.1 The Cheating Prover

The cheating prover (denoted P^*) starts by uniformly selecting a triplet (σ, g, h) while hoping that $(\sigma, g, h) \in \text{AC}$. It next selects uniformly a pair $(\xi, \eta) \in \{1, \ldots, t_S(n)\} \times \{1, \ldots, n\}$, where the simulator's running time, $t_S(n)$, acts as a bound on the number of (different block prefixes induced by the) queries made by S on input $x \in \{0,1\}^n$. The prover next emulates an execution of $S_\sigma^{V_{g,h^{(r)}}}(x)$ (where $h^{(r)}$, which is essentially equivalent to h, will be defined below), while interacting with $V(x, r)$ (that is, the honest verifier, running on input x and using coins r). The prover handles the simulator's queries as well as the communication with the verifier as follows: Suppose that the simulator makes query $\overline{q} = (b_1, a_1, \ldots, b_t, a_t)$, where the a's are prover messages.

1. Operating as $V_{g,h}$, the cheating prover determines the block prefix $bp(\overline{q}) = (b_1, a_1, \ldots, b_\gamma, a_\gamma)$. It also determines $(\ell, i) = \pi_{\text{sn}}(\overline{q})$, $j = \pi_{\text{msg}}(\overline{q})$, the iteration prefix $ip(\overline{q}) = (b_1, a_1, \ldots, b_\delta, \text{p}_{j-1}^{(n)})$, and the $j-1$ prover messages $\text{p}_1^{(i)}, \ldots, \text{p}_{j-1}^{(i)}$ appearing in the query $\overline{q}$ (as done by $V_{g,h}$ in Step 2). (Note that by the modification of S there is no need to perform Steps 1 and 1' of $V_{g,h}$.)
2. If $j = 1$, the cheating prover answers the simulator with the verifier's fixed initiation message for session i (as done by $V_{g,h}$ in Step 3).
3. If $j > 1$, the cheating prover determines $b_{i,j} = g(i, ip(\overline{q}))$ (as done by $V_{g,h}$ in Step 4).
4. If $bp(\overline{q})$ is the ξth distinct block prefix resulting from the simulator's queries so far and if, in addition, i equals η, then the cheating prover operates as follows:
   a) If $b_{i,j} = 0$, then the cheating prover answers the simulator with ABORT.
   Motivating Discussion for Substeps b and c: The cheating prover has now reached a point in the schedule in which it is supposed to feed the simulator with $\text{v}_j^{(i)}$. To do so, it first forwards $\text{p}_{j-1}^{(i)}$ to the honest verifier

$V(x, r)$, and only then feeds the simulator with the verifier's answer $v_j^{(i)}$ (as if it were the answer given by $V_{g, h(r)}$). We stress the following two points: (1) The cheating prover cannot forward more than one $p_{j-1}^{(i)}$ message to V (since P^* and V engage in an actual execution of the protocol $\langle P, V \rangle$). (2) The cheating prover will wait and forward $p_{j-1}^{(i)}$ to the verifier only when $v_j^{(i)}$ is the next scheduled message.

b) If $b_{i,j} = 1$ and the cheating prover has only sent $j-2$ messages to the actual verifier, the cheating-prover forwards $p_{j-1}^{(i)}$ to the verifier, and feeds the simulator with the verifier's response (i.e., which is of the form $v_j^{(i)}$).[14]

(We comment that by our conventions regarding the simulator, it cannot be the case that the cheating prover has sent less than $j-2$ prover messages to the actual verifier. The prefixes of the current query dictate $j-2$ sequences of prover messages with distinct lengths, so that none of these sequences was answered with ABORT. In particular, the last message of each one of these sequences was already forwarded to the verifier.)

c) If $b_{i,j} = 1$ and the cheating prover has already sent $j-1$ messages (or more) to the actual verifier then it retrieves the $(j-1)^{\text{st}}$ answer it has received and feeds it to the simulator.

(We comment that this makes sense provided that the simulator never makes two queries with the same block prefix and the same number of prover messages, but with a different sequence of such messages. However, for $j \geq 2$ it may be the case that a previous query regarding the same block prefix had a different $p_{j-1}^{(i)}$ message. This is the case in which the cheating prover may fail to conduct Step 4c; see further discussion below.)

5. If either $bp(\bar{q})$ is NOT the ξth distinct block prefix resulting from the queries so far, or if i is NOT equal to η, the prover emulates $V_{g,h}$ in the obvious manner (i.e., as in Step 4 of $V_{g,h}$):

a) If $b_{i,j} = 0$, then the cheating prover answers the simulator with ABORT.

b) If $b_{i,j} = 1$, then the cheating prover determines $r_i = h(i, bp(\bar{q}))$, and then answers the simulator with $V(x, r_i; p_1^{(i)}, \ldots, p_{j-1}^{(i)})$, where all notations are as above.

On the Efficiency of the Cheating Prover. Notice that the strategy of the cheating prover can be implemented in polynomial-time (that is, given that the simulator's running time, $t_S(\cdot)$, is polynomial as well). Thus, Lemma 7.2.5 (and so Theorem 7.1) will also hold if $\langle P, V \rangle$ is an *argument* system (since,

---

[14] Note that in the special case that $j = 1$ (i.e., when the verifier's response is the fixed initiation message $v_1^{(i)}$), the cheating prover cannot really forward $p_{j-1}^{(i)}$ to the honest verifier (since no such message exists). Still, since $v_1^{(i)}$ is a fixed initiation message, the cheating prover can produce $v_1^{(i)}$ without actually having to interact with the honest verifier (as it indeed does in Step 2 of the cheating prover strategy).

in the case of argument systems, the existence of an *efficient* P^* leads to contradiction of the (strong) computational soundness of $\langle P, V \rangle$).

The Cheating Prover May "Do Nonsense" in Step 4c. The cheating prover is hoping to convince an honest verifier by focusing on the ηth session in recursive block number $\ell^{(\overline{bp}_\xi)}$, where $\overline{bp}_\xi$ denotes the ξth distinct block prefix in the simulator's execution. Prover messages in session $(\ell^{(\overline{bp}_\xi)}, \eta)$ are received from the (multi-session) simulator and are forwarded to the (single-session) verifier. The honest verifier's answers are then fed back to the simulator as if they were answers given by $V_{g,h^{(r)}}$ (defined below). For the cheating prover to succeed in convincing the honest verifier the following two conditions must be satisfied: (1) session $(\ell^{(\overline{bp}_\xi)}, \eta)$ is eventually accepted by $V_{g,h^{(r)}}$; (2) the cheating prover never "does nonsense" in Step 4c during its execution. Let us clarify the meaning of this "nonsense".

One main problem that the cheating prover is facing while conducting Step 4c emerges from the following fact. Whereas the black-box simulator is allowed to "rewind" $V_{g,h^{(r)}}$ (impersonated by the cheating prover) and attempt different execution prefixes before proceeding with the interaction of a session, the prover cannot do so while interacting with the actual verifier. In particular, the cheating prover may reach Step 4c with a $\mathsf{p}_{j-1}^{(\eta)}$ message that is different from the $\mathsf{p}_{j-1}^{(\eta)}$ message that was previously forwarded to the honest verifier (in Step 4b). Given that the verifier's answer to the current $\mathsf{p}_{j-1}^{(\eta)}$ message is most likely to be different than the answer which was given to the "previous" $\mathsf{p}_{j-1}^{(\eta)}$ message, by answering (in Step 4c) in the same way as before, the prover action "makes no sense".[15]

We stress that, at this point in its execution, the cheating prover might as well have stopped with some predetermined "failure" message (rather than "doing nonsense"). However, for simplicity of presentation, it is more convenient for us to let the cheating prover "do nonsense".

The punchline of the analysis is that with noticeable probability (over choices of (σ, g, h)), there exists a choice of (ξ, η) so that the above "bad" event will not occur for session $(\ell^{(\overline{bp}_\xi)}, \eta)$. That is, using the fact that the success of a "rewinding" also depends on the output of g (which determines whether and when sessions are aborted) we show that, with non-negligible probability, Step 4c is never reached with two different $\mathsf{p}_{j-1}^{(\eta)}$ messages. Specifically, for every $j \in \{2, \ldots, k+1\}$, once a $\mathsf{p}_{j-1}^{(\eta)}$ message is forwarded to the verifier

---

[15]We stress that the cheating prover does not know the random coins of the honest verifier, and so it cannot compute the verifier's answers by himself. In addition, since P^* and V are engaging in an actual execution of the specified protocol $\langle P, V \rangle$ (in which every message is sent exactly once), the cheating prover cannot forward the "recent" $\mathsf{p}_{j-1}^{(\eta)}$ message to the honest verifier in order to obtain the corresponding answer (because it has already forwarded the previous $\mathsf{p}_{j-1}^{(\eta)}$ message to the honest verifier).

(in Step 4b), all subsequent $\mathrm{p}_{j-1}^{(\eta)}$ messages are either equal to the forwarded message or are answered with ABORT (here we assume that session $(\ell^{(\overline{bp}_\xi)}, \eta)$ is eventually accepted by $V_{g,h^{(r)}}$, and every $\mathrm{p}_{j-1}^{(\eta)}$ message is forwarded to the verifier at least once).

Defining $h^{(r)}$ (Mentioned Above). Let (σ, g, h) and (ξ, η) be the initial choices made by the cheating prover, let $\overline{bp}_\xi$ be the ξth block prefix appearing in $\text{EXEC}_x(\sigma, g, h)$, and suppose that the honest verifier uses coins r. Then, the function $h^{(r)} = h^{(r,\sigma,g,h,\xi,\eta)}$ is defined to be uniformly distributed among the functions h' which satisfy the following conditions: The value of h' when applied on $(\eta, \overline{bp}_\xi)$ equals r, whereas for $(\eta', \xi') \neq (\eta, \xi)$ the value of h' when applied on $(\eta', \overline{bp}_{\xi'})$ equals the value of h on this prefix. (The set of such functions h' is not empty due to the hypothesis that the functions are selected in a family of $t_S(n)$-wise independent hash functions.) We note that replacing h by $h^{(r)}$ does not affect Step 5 of the cheating prover, and that the cheating prover does not know $h^{(r)}$. In particular, whenever the honest verifier V uses coins r, one may think of the cheating prover as if it is answering the simulator's queries with the answers that would have been given by $V_{g,h^{(r)}}$.

Claim 7.3.2 *For every value of σ, g, ξ and η, if h and r are uniformly distributed then so is $h^{(r)}$.*

Proof Sketch Fix some simulator coins $\sigma \in \{0,1\}^*$, $g \in G$, block prefix index $\xi \in \{1, \ldots, t_S(n)\}$, and session index $\eta \in \{1, \ldots, n\}$. The key for proving Claim 7.3.2 is to view the process of picking a function $h \in H$ as consisting of two stages. The first stage is an iterative process in which up to $t_S(n)$ different arguments are adversarially chosen, and for each such argument the value of h on this argument is uniformly selected in its range. In the second stage, a function h is chosen uniformly from all h's in H under the constraints that are introduced in the first stage. The iterative process in which the arguments are chosen (that is, the first stage above) corresponds the simulator's choice of the various block prefixes $\overline{bp}$ (along with the indices i), on which h is applied.

At first glance, it seems obvious that the function $h^{(r)}$, which is uniformly distributed amongst all functions that are defined to be equal to h on all inputs (except for the input $(\eta, \overline{bp}_\xi)$ on which it equals r) is uniformly distributed in H. Taking a closer look, however, one realizes that a rigorous proof for the above claim is more complex than one may initially think, since it is not even clear that a h that is defined by the above process actually belongs to the family H.

The main difficulty in proving the above lies in the fact that the simulator's queries may "adaptively" depend on previous answers it has received (which, in turn, may depend on previous outcomes of h). The key observation used in order to overcome this difficulty is that for *every* family of $t_S(n)$-wise independent functions and for *every* sequence of at most $t_S(n)$ arguments (and in particular, for an adaptively chosen sequence), the values of a uniformly chosen function when applied to the arguments in the sequence are uniformly and independently distributed. Thus, as long as the values assigned to the function in the first stage of the above process are uniformly and independently distributed (which is indeed the case, even if we constraint one output to be equal to r), the process will yield a uniformly distributed function from H. ∎

7.3.2 The Success Probability of the Cheating Prover

We start by introducing two important notions that will play a central role in the analysis of the success probability of the cheating prover.

Grouping Queries According to Their Iteration Prefixes

In the sequel, it will be convenient to group the queries of the simulator into different classes based on different iteration prefixes. (Recall that the iteration prefix of a query $\bar{q}$ (satisfying $\pi_{\mathrm{sn}}(\bar{q}) = (\ell, i)$ and $\pi_{\mathrm{msg}}(\bar{q}) = j > 1$) is the prefix of $\bar{q}$ that ends with the $(j-1)^{\mathrm{st}}$ prover message in session (ℓ, n).). Grouping by iteration prefixes particularly makes sense in the case that two queries are of the same length (see discussion below). Nevertheless, by Definition 7.2.3, two queries may have the same iteration prefix even if they are of *different* lengths (see below).

Definition 7.3.3 (ip-different queries) *Two queries, $\bar{q}_1$ and $\bar{q}_2$ (of possibly different lengths), are said to be ip-different, if and only if they have different iteration prefixes (that is, $ip(\bar{q}_1) \neq ip(\bar{q}_2)$).*

By Definition 7.2.3, if two queries, $\bar{q}_1$ and $\bar{q}_2$, satisfy $ip(\bar{q}_1) = ip(\bar{q}_2)$, then the following two conditions must hold: (1) $\pi_{\mathrm{sn}}(\bar{q}_1) = (\ell, i_1)$, $\pi_{\mathrm{sn}}(\bar{q}_2) = (\ell, i_2)$ and; (2) $\pi_{\mathrm{msg}}(\bar{q}_1) = \pi_{\mathrm{msg}}(\bar{q}_2)$. However, it is not necessarily true that $i_1 = i_2$. In particular, it may very well be the case that q_1, q_2 have different lengths (i.e., $i_1 \neq i_2$) but are *not* ip-different (note that if $i_1 = i_2$ then q_1 and q_2 are of equal length). Still, even if two queries are of the same length and have the same iteration prefix, it is not necessarily true that they are equal, as they may be different at some message which occurs after their iteration prefixes.

Motivating Definition 7.3.3. Recall that a necessary condition for the success of the cheating prover is that for every j, once a $p_{j-1}^{(n)}$ message has been forwarded to the verifier (in Step 4b), all subsequent $p_{j-1}^{(n)}$ messages (that are not answered with ABORT) are equal to the forwarded message. In order to satisfy the above condition it is sufficient to require that the cheating prover never reaches Steps 4b and 4c with two ip-different queries of equal length. The reason for this is that if two queries of the same length have the same iteration prefix, then they contain the *same* sequence of prover messages for the corresponding session (since all such messages are contained in the iteration prefix), and so they agree on their $p_{j-1}^{(n)}$ message. In particular, once a

$\mathsf{p}_{j-1}^{(\eta)}$ message has been forwarded to the verifier (in Step 4b), all subsequent queries that reach Step 4c and are of the same lenght will have the same $\mathsf{p}_{j-1}^{(\eta)}$ messages as the first such query (since they have the same iteration prefix).

In light of the above discussion, it is only natural to require that the number of ip-different queries that reach Step 4c of the cheating prover is exactly one (as, in such a case, the above necessary condition is indeed satified).[16] Jumping ahead, we comment that the smaller is the number of ip-different queries that correspond to block prefix $\overline{bp}_\xi$, the smaller is the probability that more than one ip-different query reaches Step 4c. The reason for this lies in the fact that the number of ip-different queries that correspond to block prefix $\overline{bp}_\xi$ is equal to the number of different iteration prefixes that correspond to $\overline{bp}_\xi$. In particular, the smaller the number of such iteration prefixes, the smaller the probability that g will evaluate to 1 on more than a single iteration prefix (thus reaching Step 4c with more than one ip-different query).

Useful Block Prefixes

The probability that the cheating prover makes the honest verifier accept will be lower bounded by the probability that the ξth distinct block prefix in $\mathrm{EXEC}_x(\sigma, g, h)$ is η-useful (in the sense hinted above and defined next):

Definition 7.3.4 (Useful block prefix) *A block prefix $\overline{bp} = (b_1, a_1, \ldots, b_\gamma, a_\gamma)$, that appears in $\mathrm{EXEC}_x(\sigma, g, h)$, is called i-useful if it satisfies the following two conditions:*

1. *For every $j \in \{2, \ldots, k+1\}$, the number of ip-different queries $\overline{q}$ in $\mathrm{EXEC}_x(\sigma, g, h)$ that correspond to block prefix $\overline{bp}$ and satisfy $\pi_{\mathrm{sn}}(\overline{q}) = (\ell^{(\overline{bp})}, i)$, $\pi_{\mathrm{msg}}(\overline{q}) = j$, and $g(i, ip(\overline{q})) = 1$, is exactly one.*
2. *The (only) query $\overline{q}$ in $\mathrm{EXEC}_x(\sigma, g, h)$ that corresponds to block prefix $\overline{bp}$ and that satisfies $\pi_{\mathrm{sn}}(\overline{q}) = (\ell^{(\overline{bp})}, i)$, $\pi_{\mathrm{msg}}(\overline{q}) = k+1$, and $g(i, ip(\overline{q})) = 1$, is answered with ACCEPT by $V_{g,h}$.*

If there exists an $i \in \{1, \ldots, n\}$, so that a block prefix is i-useful, then this block prefix is called useful.

Condition 1 in Definition 7.3.4 states that for every fixed value of j there exists exactly one iteration prefix, $\overline{ip}$, that corresponds to queries of the block prefix $\overline{bp}$ and the jth message so that $g(i, \overline{ip})$ evaluates to 1. Condition 2 asserts that the last verifier message in the ith main session of recursive block number $\ell = \ell^{(\overline{bp})}$ is equal to ACCEPT. It follows that if the cheating prover happens to select $(\sigma, g, h, \xi, \eta)$ so that block prefix $\overline{bp}_\xi$ (i.e., the ξth distinct block prefix in $\mathrm{EXEC}_x(\sigma, g, h^{(r)})$) is η-useful, then it convinces $V(x, r)$; the reason being that (by Condition 2) the last message in session $(\ell^{(\overline{bp}_\xi)}, \eta)$ is answered with

---

[16] In order to ensure the cheating prover's success, the above requirement should be augmented by the condition that session $(\ell^{(\overline{bp}_\xi)}, \eta)$ is accepted by $V_{g, h^{(r)}}$.

ACCEPT,[17] and that (by Condition 1) the emulation does not get into trouble in Step 4c of the cheating prover (to see this, notice that each prover message in session $(\ell^{(\overline{bp}_\xi)}, \eta)$ will end up reaching Step 4c only once).

Let $\langle P^*, V \rangle(x) = \langle P^*(\sigma, g, h, \xi, \eta), V(r) \rangle(x)$ denote the random variable representing the (local) output of the honest verifier V when interacting with the cheating prover P^* on common input x, where σ, g, h, ξ, η are the initial random choices made by the cheating prover P^*, and r is the randomness used by the honest verifier V. Adopting this notation, we will say that the cheating prover $P^* = P^*(x, \sigma, g, h, \xi, \eta)$ has convinced the honest verifier $V = V(x, r)$ if $\langle P^*, V \rangle(x) = \text{ACCEPT}$. With these notations, we are ready to formalize the above discussion.

Claim 7.3.5 *If the cheating prover happens to select $(\sigma, g, h, \xi, \eta)$ so that the ξth distinct block prefix in $\text{EXEC}_x(\sigma, g, h^{(r)})$ is η-useful, then the cheating prover convinces $V(x, r)$ (i.e., $\langle P^*, V \rangle(x) = \text{ACCEPT}$).*

Proof Let us fix $x \in \{0,1\}^n$, $\sigma \in \{0,1\}^*$, $g \in G$, $h \in H$, $r \in \{1, \ldots, \rho_V(n)\}$, $\eta \in \{1, \ldots, n\}$, and $\xi \in \{1, \ldots, t_S(n)\}$. We show that if the ξth distinct block prefix in $\text{EXEC}_x(\sigma, g, h^{(r)})$ is η-useful, then the cheating prover $P^*(x, \sigma, g, h, \xi, \eta)$ convinces the honest verifier $V(x, r)$.

By definition of the cheating-prover, the prover messages that are actually forwarded to the honest verifier (in Step 4b) correspond to session $(\ell^{(\overline{bp}_\xi)}, \eta)$. Specifically, messages that are forwarded by the cheating prover are of the form $\mathbf{p}_{j-1}^{(\eta)}$, and correspond to queries $\overline{q}$, that satisfy $\pi_{\text{sn}}(\overline{q}) = (\ell^{(\overline{bp}_\xi)}, \eta)$, $\pi_{\text{msg}}(\overline{q}) = j$ and $g(\eta, ip(\overline{q})) = 1$. Since the ξth distinct block prefix in $\text{EXEC}_x(\sigma, g, h^{(r)})$ is η-useful, we have that for every $j \in \{2, \ldots, k+1\}$, there is exactly one query $\overline{q}$ that satisfies the above conditions. Thus, for every $j \in \{2, \ldots, k+1\}$, the cheating prover never reaches Step 4c with two different $\mathbf{p}_{j-1}^{(\eta)}$ messages. Here we use the fact that if two queries of the same length are not ip-different (i.e., have the same iteration prefix) then the answers given by $V_{g,h^{(r)}}$ to these queries are identical (see discussion above). This in particular means that P^* is answering the simulator's queries with the answers that would have been given by $V^{g,h^{(r)}}$ itself. (Put in other words, whenever the ξth distinct block prefix in $\text{EXEC}_x(\sigma, g, h^{(r)})$ is η-useful, the emulation does not "get into trouble" in Step 4c of the cheating prover.)

At this point, we have that the cheating prover never fails to perform Step 4c, and so the interaction that it is conducting with $V(x, r)$ reaches "safely" the $(k+1)^{\text{st}}$ verifier message in the protocol. To complete the proof we have to show that at the end of the interaction with the cheating-prover, $V(x, r)$ outputs ACCEPT. This is true since, by Condition 2 of Definition 7.3.4, the query $\overline{q}$, that corresponds to block prefix $\overline{bp}_\xi$, satisfies $\pi_{\text{sn}}(\overline{q}) = (\ell^{(\overline{bp}_\xi)}, \eta)$, $\pi_{\text{msg}}(\overline{q}) = j$ and $g(\eta, ip(\overline{q})) = 1$, is answered with ACCEPT. Here we use the

---

[17]Notice that $V(x, r)$ behaves exactly as $V_{g,h^{(r)}}$ behaves on queries that correspond to the ξth distinct iteration prefix in $\text{EXEC}_x(\sigma, g, h^{(r)})$.

fact that $V(x, r)$ behaves exactly as $V_{g,h^{(r)}}$ behaves on queries that correspond to the ξth distinct block prefix in $\text{EXEC}_x(\sigma, g, h^{(r)})$. ∎

Reduction to Rareness of Legal Transcripts Without Useful Block Prefixes

The following lemma (Lemma 7.3.6) establishes the connection between the success probability of the simulator and the success probability of the cheating-prover. Loosely speaking, the lemma asserts that if S outputs a legal transcript with non-negligible probability, then the cheating prover will succeed in convincing the honest verifier with non-negligible probability. Since this is in contradiction to the computational soundness of the proof system, we have that Lemma 7.3.6 actually implies the correctness of Lemma 7.2.5 (recall that the contradiction hypothesis of Lemma 7.2.5 is that the probability that the simulator outputs a legal transcript is non-negligible).

Lemma 7.3.6 *Suppose that* $\text{Pr}_{\sigma,g,h}[(\sigma, g, h) \in \text{AC}] > 1/p(n)$ *for some fixed polynomial* $p(\cdot)$. *Then the probability (taken over* $\sigma, g, h, \xi, \eta, r$), *that* $\langle P^*, V \rangle(x)$ *equals* ACCEPT *is at least* $\frac{1}{2 \cdot p(n) \cdot t_S(n) \cdot n}$.

Proof Define a Boolean indicator $\text{useful}_{\xi,\eta}(\sigma, g, h)$ to be true if and only if the ξth distinct block prefix in $\text{EXEC}_x(\sigma, g, h)$ is η-useful. Using Claim 7.3.5, we have:

$$\text{Pr}_{\sigma,g,h,\xi,\eta,r}\left[\langle P^*, V \rangle(x) = \text{ACCEPT}\right] \geq \text{Pr}_{\sigma,g,h,\xi,\eta,r}\left[\text{useful}_{\xi,\eta}(\sigma, g, h^{(r)})\right] \quad (7.2)$$

where the second probability refers to an interaction between S and $V_{g,h^{(r)}}$. Since for every value of σ, g, η and ξ, when h and r are uniformly selected the function $h^{(r)}$ is uniformly distributed (see Claim 7.3.2), we infer that:

$$\text{Pr}_{\sigma,g,h,\xi,\eta,r}\left[\text{useful}_{\xi,\eta}(\sigma, g, h^{(r)})\right] = \text{Pr}_{\sigma,g,h',\xi,\eta}\left[\text{useful}_{\xi,\eta}(\sigma, g, h')\right]. \quad (7.3)$$

On the other hand, since ξ and η are distributed independently of (σ, g, h), we have that $\text{Pr}_{\sigma,g,h,\xi,\eta}\left[\text{useful}_{\xi,\eta}(\sigma, g, h)\right]$ equals

$$\sum_{\ell=1}^{t_S(n)} \sum_{i=1}^{n} \text{Pr}_{\sigma,g,h,\xi,\eta}\left[\text{useful}_{\ell,i}(\sigma, g, h) \,\&\, (\xi = \ell \,\&\, \eta = i)\right] \quad (7.4)$$

$$= \sum_{\ell=1}^{t_S(n)} \sum_{i=1}^{n} \text{Pr}_{\sigma,g,h}\left[\text{useful}_{\ell,i}(\sigma, g, h)\right] \cdot \text{Pr}_{\xi,\eta}\left[\xi = \ell \,\&\, \eta = i\right]$$

$$= \sum_{\ell=1}^{t_S(n)} \sum_{i=1}^{n} \text{Pr}_{\sigma,g,h}\left[\text{useful}_{\ell,i}(\sigma, g, h)\right] \cdot \frac{1}{t_S(n) \cdot n}$$

$$\geq \text{Pr}_{\sigma,g,h}\left[\exists \ell, i \text{ s.t. useful}_{\ell,i}(\sigma, g, h)\right] \cdot \frac{1}{t_S(n) \cdot n} \quad (7.5)$$

where $t_S(n)$ is the bound used by the cheating prover (for the number of distinct block prefixes in $\text{EXEC}_x(\sigma, g, h)$). Combining (7.2), (7.3), and (7.4) we get:

$$\text{Pr}_{\sigma,g,h,\xi,\eta,r}\left[\langle P^*, V\rangle(x) = \text{ACCEPT}\right]$$

$$\geq \text{Pr}_{\sigma,g,h}\left[\exists \ell, i \text{ s.t. useful}_{\ell,i}(\sigma, g, h)\right] \cdot \frac{1}{t_S(n) \cdot n}. \tag{7.6}$$

Recall that by our hypothesis, $\text{Pr}[(\sigma, g, h) \in \text{AC}] > 1/p(n)$ for some fixed polynomial $p(\cdot)$. We can thus lower bound $\text{Pr}_{\sigma,g,h}\left[\exists \ell, i \text{ s.t. useful}_{\ell,i}(\sigma, g, h)\right]$ in the following way:

$$\text{Pr}\left[\exists \ell, i \text{ s.t. useful}_{\ell,i}(\sigma, g, h)\right]$$

$$= 1 - \text{Pr}\left[\forall \ell, i \ \neg\text{useful}_{\ell,i}(\sigma, g, h)\right]$$

$$= 1 - \text{Pr}\left[(\forall \ell, i \ \neg\text{useful}_{\ell,i}(\sigma, g, h)) \ \& \ ((\sigma, g, h) \notin \text{AC})\right]$$

$$\quad - \text{Pr}\left[(\forall \ell, i \ \neg\text{useful}_{\ell,i}(\sigma, g, h)) \ \& \ ((\sigma, g, h) \in \text{AC})\right]$$

$$\geq 1 - \text{Pr}\left[(\sigma, g, h) \notin \text{AC}\right] - \text{Pr}\left[(\forall \ell, i \ \neg\text{useful}_{\ell,i}(\sigma, g, h)) \ \& \ (\sigma, g, h) \in \text{AC}\right]$$

$$> 1/p(n) - \text{Pr}\left[(\forall \ell, i \ \neg\text{useful}_{\ell,i}(\sigma, g, h)) \ \& \ (\sigma, g, h) \in \text{AC}\right]$$

where all the above probabilities are taken over (σ, g, h). It follows that in order to show that $\text{Pr}_{\sigma,g,h,\xi,\eta,r}\left[\langle P^*, V\rangle(x) = \text{ACCEPT}\right] > \frac{1}{2 \cdot p(n) \cdot t_S(n) \cdot n}$, it will be sufficient to prove that for every fixed polynomial $p'(\cdot)$ it holds that:

$$\text{Pr}_{\sigma,g,h}\left[(\forall \ell, i \ \neg\text{useful}_{\ell,i}(\sigma, g, h)) \ \& \ (\sigma, g, h) \in \text{AC}\right] < 1/p'(n) \tag{7.7}$$

Thus, Lemma 7.3.6 is true provided that

$$\text{Pr}_{\sigma,g,h}\left[\forall \ell, i \ \neg\text{useful}_{\ell,i}(\sigma, g, h) \ \& \ (\sigma, g, h) \in \text{AC}\right]$$

is negligible.

Lemma 7.3.7 *For every $\sigma \in \{0,1\}^*$ and every $h \in H$, the probability (taken over g), that for all pairs (ℓ, i) useful$_{\ell,i}(\sigma, g, h)$ does not hold **and** that $(\sigma, g, h) \in \text{AC}$, is negligible. That is, the probability that $\text{EXEC}_x(\sigma, g, h)$ does not contain a useful block prefix and S outputs a legal transcript is negligible.*

Notice that Lemma 7.3.7 is actually stronger than what we need, since it asserts that (7.7) is negligible for *every* choice of σ, h. This completes the proof of Lemma 7.3.6. In the rest of this section we prove Lemma 7.3.7. ∎

7.3.3 Legal Transcripts Yield Useful Block Prefixes

We now prove Lemma 7.3.7. The proof will proceed as follows. We first define a special kind of block prefix, called **potentially useful** block prefixes. Loosely speaking, these are block prefixes in which the simulator does not make too many "rewinding" attempts (each "rewinding" corresponds to a different iteration prefix). Intuitively, the larger the number of "rewinds" is, the smaller is the probability that a specific block prefix is useful. A block prefix with a small number of "rewinds" is thus more likely to cause its block prefix to be useful. Thus our basic approach will be to show that:

1. In *every* "successful" execution (i.e., producing a legal transcript), the simulator generates a potentially useful block prefix. This is proved by demonstrating, based on the structure of the schedule, that if no potentially useful block prefix exists, then the simulation must take super-polynomial time.

2. Any potentially useful block prefix is in fact useful with considerable probability. The argument that demonstrates this claim proceeds basically as follows. Consider a specific block prefix $\overline{bp}$, let $\ell = \ell^{(\overline{bp})}$, and focus on a specific instance of session (ℓ, i) (that is, the specific instance of session (ℓ, i) that corresponds to block prefix $\overline{bp}$). Suppose that block prefix $\overline{bp}$ is potentially useful and that the above instance of session (ℓ, i) happens to be accepted by $V_{g,h}$. This means that there exist k queries with block prefix $\overline{bp}$ that consist of the "main thread" that leads to acceptance (i.e., all queries that were not answered with ABORT). Recall that the decision to abort a session (ℓ, i) is made by applying the function g to i and the iteration prefix of the corresponding query. Thus, if there are only few different iteration prefixes that correspond to block prefix $\overline{bp}$ (which, as we said, is potentially useful), then there is considerable probability that *all* the queries having block prefix $\overline{bp}$, but which do not belong to that "main thread", will be answered with ABORT (that is, g will evaluate to 0 on the corresponding input). If this lucky event occurs, then block prefix $\overline{bp}$ will indeed be useful (recall that for a block prefix to be useful we require that there exists a corresponding session that is accepted by $V_{g,h}$ and satisfies that for every $j \in \{2, \ldots, k+1\}$ there is a single iteration prefix that makes g evaluate to 1 at the jth message of this session).

Returning to the actual proof, we start by introducing the necessary definition (of a potentially useful block prefix). Recall that, for any $g \in G$ and $h \in H$, the running time of the simulator S with oracle access to $V_{g,h}$ is bounded by $t_S(n)$. Let c be a constant such that $t_S(n) \le n^c$ for all sufficiently large n.

Definition 7.3.8 (Potentially useful block prefix) *A block prefix $\overline{bp} = (b_1, a_1, \ldots, b_\gamma, a_\gamma)$, that appears in $\mathrm{EXEC}_x(\sigma, g, h)$, is called* **potentially useful** *if it satisfies the following two conditions:*

1. *The number of* ip*-different queries that correspond to block prefix $\overline{bp}$ is at most k^{c+1}.*

2. *The execution of the simulator reaches the end of the block that corresponds to block prefix $\overline{bp}$. That is,* $\text{EXEC}_x(\sigma, g, h)$ *contains a query $\overline{q}$, that ends with the $(k{+}1)^{\text{st}}$ prover message in the nth main session of recursive block number $\ell^{(\overline{bp})}$ (i.e., some* $\mathbf{p}_{k+1}^{(\ell^{(\overline{bp})}, n)}$ *message).*

We stress that the bound k^{c+1} in Condition 1 above refers to the same constant $c > 0$ that is used in the time bound $t_S(n) \leq n^c$. Using Definition 7.3.3 (of ip-different queries), we have that a bound of k^{c+1} on the number of ip-different queries that correspond to block prefix $\overline{bp}$ induces an upper bound on the total number of iteration prefixes that correspond to block prefix $\overline{bp}$. Note that this is in contrast to the definition of a useful block prefix (Definition 7.3.4), in which we only have a bound on the number of ip-different queries of a specific length (i.e., the number of ip-different queries that correspond to specific message in a specific session).

Turning to Condition 2 of Definition 7.3.8 we recall that the query $\overline{q}$ ends with a $\mathbf{p}_{k+1}^{(\ell^{(\overline{bp})}, n)}$ message (i.e., the last prover message of recursive block number $\ell^{(\overline{bp})}$). Technically speaking, this means that $\overline{q}$ does not actually correspond to block prefix $\overline{bp}$ (since, by definition of the recursive schedule, the answer to query $\overline{q}$ is a message that does not belong to recursive block number $\ell^{(\overline{bp})}$). Nevertheless, since before making query $\overline{q}$, the simulator has made queries to all prefixes of $\overline{q}$, we are guaranteed that for every $i \in \{1, \ldots, n\}$ and $j \in \{1, \ldots, k{+}1\}$, the simulator has made a query $\overline{q}_{i,j}$ that is a prefix of $\overline{q}$, corresponds to block prefix $\overline{bp}$, and satisfies $\pi_{\text{sn}}(\overline{q}) = (\ell^{(\overline{bp})}, i)$ and $\pi_{\text{msg}}(\overline{q}) = j$. (In other words, all messages of all sessions in recursive block number $\ell^{(\overline{bp})}$ have occurred during the execution of the simulator.) Furthermore, since the (modified) simulator does not make a query that is answered with a DEVIATION message (in Step 1' of $V_{g,h}$) and it does make the query $\overline{q}$, we are guaranteed that the partial execution transcript induced by the query $\overline{q}$ contains the accepting conversations of at least $\frac{n^{1/2}}{4}$ sessions in recursive block number $\ell^{(\overline{bp})}$. (The latter observation will be used only at a later stage, while proving Lemma 7.3.7.)

It is worth noting that whereas the definition of a useful block prefix refers to the contents of iteration prefixes (induced by the queries) that are sent by the simulator, the definition of a potentially useful block prefix refers only to their quantity (neither to their contents nor to the effect of the application of g on them).[18] It is thus natural that statements referring to potentially useful block prefixes tend to have a combinatorial flavor. The following lemma is no exception. It asserts that *every* "successful" execution of the simulator must

---

[18]In particular, whereas the definition of a useful block prefix refers to the outcome of g on iteration prefixes that correspond to the relevant block prefix, the definition of a potentially useful block prefix refers only to the number of ip-different queries that correspond to the block prefix (ignoring the outcomes of g on the relevant iteration prefixes).

contain a potentially useful block prefix (or, otherwise, the simulator will run in super-polynomial time).

Lemma 7.3.9 *For any* $(\sigma, g, h) \in \mathsf{AC}_x$, $\mathrm{EXEC}_x(\sigma, g, h)$ *contains a potentially useful block prefix.*

7.3.4 Existence of Potentially Useful Block Prefixes

We now prove Lemma 7.3.9. The proof is by contradiction. We assume the existence of a triplet $(\sigma, g, h) \in \mathsf{AC}$ so that every block prefix in $\mathrm{EXEC}_x(\sigma, g, h)$ is not potentially useful, and show that this implies that $S_\sigma^{V_h}(x)$ made strictly more than n^c queries (which contradicts the explicit hypothesis that the running time of S is bounded by n^c).

The Query-And-Answer Tree. Throughout the proof of Lemma 7.3.9, we will fix an arbitrary $(\sigma, g, h) \in \mathsf{AC}$ as above, and study the corresponding $\mathrm{EXEC}_x(\sigma, g, h)$. A key vehicle in this study is the notion of a query-and-answer tree introduced in [83] (and also used in [97]).[19] This is a rooted tree (corresponding to $\mathrm{EXEC}_x(\sigma, g, h)$) in which vertices are labeled with verifier messages and edges are labeled with prover's messages. The root is labeled with the fixed verifier message initializing the first session, and has outgoing edges corresponding to the prover's messages initializing this session. In general, paths down the tree (i.e., from the root to some vertices) correspond to queries. The query associated with such a path is obtained by concatenating the labeling of the vertices and edges along the path in the order traversed. We stress that each vertex in the query-and-answer tree corresponds to a query actually made by the simulator.

The index of the verifier (resp., prover) message labelling a specific vertex (resp., edge) in the tree is completely determined by the level in which the vertex (resp., edge) lies. That is, all vertices (resp., edges) in the ωth level of the tree are labeled with the ωth verifier (resp., prover) message in the schedule (out of a total of $n^2 \cdot (k+1)$ scheduled messages). For example, if $\omega = n^2 \cdot (k+1)$ all vertices (resp., edges) at the ωth level (which is the lowest possible level in the tree) are labeled with $v_{k+1}^{(1,n)}$ (resp., $p_{k+1}^{(1,n)}$). The difference between "sibling" vertices in the same level of the tree lies in the difference in the labels of their incoming edges (as induced by the simulator's "rewinds"). Specifically, whenever the simulator "rewinds" the interaction to the ωth verifier message in the schedule (i.e., makes a new query that is answered with the ωth verifier message), the corresponding vertex in the tree (which lies at the ωth level) will have multiple descendants one level down in the tree (i.e., at the $(\omega+1)^{\text{st}}$ level). The edges to each one of these descendants will be labeled with a different

---

[19] The query-and-answer tree should not be confused with the tree that is induced by the recursive schedule.

prover message.[20] We stress that the difference between these prover messages lies in the contents of the corresponding message (and not in its index).

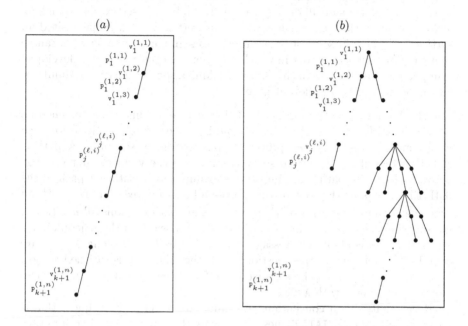

Fig. 7.6. The query-and-answer-tree. (a) Interaction with P. (b) Simulation.

By the above discussion, the outdegree of every vertex in the query-and-answer tree corresponds to the number of "rewinds" that the simulator has made to the relevant point in the schedule (the order in which the outgoing edges appear in the tree does not necessarily correspond to the order in which the "rewinds" were actually performed by the simulator). Vertices in which the simulator does not perform a "rewinding" will thus have a single outgoing edge. In particular, in case that the simulator follows the prescribed prover strategy P (sending each scheduled message exactly once), all vertices in the tree will have outdegree one, and the tree will actually consist of a single path of total length $n^2 \cdot (k+1)$ (ending with an edge that is labeled with a $p_{k+1}^{(n,n)}$ message).

Recall that, by our conventions regarding the simulator, before making a query $\bar{q}$ the simulator has made queries to all prefixes of $\bar{q}$. Since every query corresponds to a path down the tree, we have that every particular path down the query-and-answer tree is developed from the root downwards

---

[20]In particular, the shape of the query-and-answer tree is completely determined by the contents of prover messages in $\text{EXEC}_x(\sigma, g, h)$ (whereas the contents of verifier answers given by $V_{g,h}$ have no effect on the shape of the tree).

(that is, within a specific path, a level $\omega < \omega'$ vertex is always visited before a level ω' vertex). However, we cannot say anything about the order in which *different* paths in the tree are developed (for example, we cannot assume that the simulator has made all queries that end at a level ω vertex before making any other query that ends at a level $\omega' > \omega$ vertex, or that it has visited all vertices of level ω in some specific order). To summarize, the only guarantee that we have about the order in which the query-and-answer tree is developed is implied by the convention that before making a specific query, the simulator has made queries to all relevant prefixes.

Satisfied Path. A path from one node in the tree to some of its descendants is said to **satisfy session i** if the path contains edges (resp., vertices) for each of the messages sent by the prover (resp., verifier) in session i. A path is called **satisfied** if it satisfies all sessions for which the verifier's first message appears along the path. One important example for a satisfied path is the path that starts at the root of the query-and-answer tree and ends with an edge that is labeled with a $\mathbf{p}_{k+1}^{(n,n)}$ message. This path contains all $n^2 \cdot (k+1)$ messages in the schedule (and so satisfies all n^2 sessions in the schedule). We stress that the contents of messages (occurring as labels) along a path are completely irrelevant to the question of whether the path is satisfied or not. In particular, a path may be satisfied even if some (or even all) of the vertices along it are labeled with ABORT.

Recall that, by our conventions, the simulator never makes a query that is answered with the DEVIATION message. We are thus guaranteed that, for every completed block along a path in the tree, at least $\frac{n^{1/2}}{4}$ sessions are accepted by $V_{g,h}$. In particular, the vertices corresponding to messages of these accepted sessions cannot be labeled with ABORT.

Good Subtree. Consider an arbitrary subtree (of the query-and-answer tree) that satisfies the following two conditions:

1. The subtree is rooted at a vertex corresponding to the first message of some session so that this session is the first main session of some recursive invocation of the schedule.
2. Each path in the subtree is truncated at the last message of the relevant recursive invocation.

The full tree (i.e., the tree rooted at the vertex labeled with the first message in the schedule) is indeed such a tree, but we will need to consider subtrees which correspond to m sessions in the recursive schedule construction (i.e., correspond to $\mathcal{R}_m$). We call such a subtree m-**good** if it contains a satisfied path starting at the root of the subtree. Since $(\sigma, g, h) \in$ AC, we have that the simulator has indeed produced a "legal" transcript as output. It follows that the full tree contains a path from the root to a leaf that contains vertices (resp., edges) for each of the messages sent by the verifier (resp., prover) in all n^2 sessions of the schedule (as otherwise the transcript $S_\sigma^{V_{g,h}}(x)$ would have not been legal). In other words, the full tree contains a satisfied path and is thus n^2-good.

Note that, by the definition of the recursive schedule, two m-good subtrees are always disjoint. On the other hand, if $m' < m$, it may be the case that an m'-good subtree is contained in another m-good subtree. As a matter of fact, since an m-good subtree contains all messages of all sessions in a recursive block corresponding to $\mathcal{R}_m$, then it must contain at least k disjoint $\frac{m-n}{k}$-good subtrees (i.e., that correspond to k the recursive invocations of $\mathcal{R}_{\frac{m-n}{k}}$ made by $\mathcal{R}_m$).

The next lemma (which can be viewed as the crux of the proof) states that, if the contradiction hypothesis of Lemma 7.3.9 is satisfied, then the number of disjoint $\frac{m-n}{k}$-good subtrees that are contained in an m-good subtree is actually considerably larger than k.

Lemma 7.3.10 *Suppose that every block prefix that appears in* EXEC$_x(\sigma, g, h)$ *is not potentially useful. Then for every $m \geq n$, every m-good subtree contains at least k^{c+1} disjoint $\frac{m-n}{k}$-good subtrees.*

Denote by $W(m)$ the size of an m-good subtree. (That is, $W(m)$ actually represents the work performed by the simulator on m concurrent sessions in our fixed scheduling.) It follows (from Lemma 7.3.10) that any m-good subtree must satisfy:

$$W(m) \geq \begin{cases} 1 & \text{if } m \leq n \\ k^{c+1} \cdot W\left(\frac{m-n}{k}\right) & \text{if } m > n. \end{cases} \tag{7.8}$$

Claim 7.3.11 *For all sufficiently large n, $W(n^2) > n^c$.*

Proof By applying (7.8) iteratively $\log_k(n-1)$ times, we get:

$$\begin{aligned} W(n^2) &\geq \left(k^{c+1}\right)^{\log_k(n-1)} \cdot W(n) \\ &\geq \left(k^{c+1}\right)^{\log_k(n-1)} \cdot 1 \\ &= (n-1)^{c+1} \\ &> n^c \end{aligned} \tag{7.9}$$

where 7.9 holds for all sufficiently large n. ∎

Since every vertex in the query-and-answer tree corresponds to a query actually made by the simulator, it follows that the hypothesis that the simulator runs in time that is bounded by n^c (and hence the full n^2-good tree must have been of size at most n^c) is contradicted. Thus, Lemma 7.3.9 will actually follow from Lemma 7.3.10.

Proof (of Lemma 7.3.10) Let T be an arbitrary m-good subtree of the query-and-answer tree. Considering the m sessions corresponding to an m-good subtree, we focus on the n main sessions of this level of the recursive construction. Let B_T denote the recursive block to which the indices of these n

sessions belong. A T-query is a query $\bar{q}$ whose corresponding path down the query-and-answer tree ends with a node that belongs to T (recall that every query $\bar{q}$ appearing in $\text{EXEC}_x(\sigma, g, h)$ corresponds to a path down the full tree), and that satisfies $\pi_{\text{sn}}(\bar{q}) \in B_T$.[21] We first claim that all T-queries $\bar{q}$ in $\text{EXEC}_x(\sigma, g, h)$ have the same block prefix. This block prefix corresponds to the path from the root of the full tree to the root of T, and is denoted by $\overline{bp}_T$.

Fact 7.3.12 *All T-queries in $\text{EXEC}_x(\sigma, g, h)$ have the same block prefix (denoted $\overline{bp}_T$).*

Proof Assume, towards contradiction, that there exist two different T-queries $\bar{q}_1, \bar{q}_2$ so that $bp(\bar{q}_1) \neq bp(\bar{q}_2)$. In particular, $bp(\bar{q}_1)$ and $bp(\bar{q}_2)$ must differ in a message that precedes the first message of the first main session in B_T. (Note that if two block prefixes are equal in all messages preceding the first message of the first session of the relevant block then, by definition, they are equal.[22]) This means that the paths that correspond to $\bar{q}_1$ and $\bar{q}_2$ split from each other before they reach the root of T (remember that T is rooted at a node corresponding to the first main session of recursive block B_T). But this contradicts the fact that both paths that correspond to these queries end with a node in T, and the fact follows. ∎

Using the hypothesis that no block prefix in $\text{EXEC}_x(\sigma, g, h)$ is potentially useful, we prove:

Claim 7.3.13 *Let T be an m-good subtree. Then the number of ip-different queries that correspond to block prefix $\overline{bp}_T$ is at least k^{c+1}.*

Proof Since all block prefixes that appear in $\text{EXEC}_x(\sigma, g, h)$ are not potentially useful (by the hypothesis of Lemma 7.3.10), this holds as a special case for block prefix $\overline{bp}_T$. Let $\ell = \ell^{(\overline{bp}_T)}$ be the index of the recursive block that corresponds to block prefix $\overline{bp}_T$ in $\text{EXEC}_x(\sigma, g, h)$. Since block prefix $\overline{bp}_T$ is not potentially useful, at least one of the two conditions of Definition 7.3.8 is violated. In other words, one of the following two conditions is satisfied:

1. The number of ip-different queries that correspond to block prefix $\overline{bp}_T$ is at least k^{c+1}.
2. The execution of the simulator does not reach the end of the block that corresponds to block prefix $\overline{bp}_T$ (i.e., there is no query in $\text{EXEC}_x(\sigma, g, h)$ that ends with a $\text{p}_{k+1}^{(\ell,n)}$ message that corresponds to block prefix $\overline{bp}_T$).

---

[21] Note that queries $\bar{q}$ that satisfy $\pi_{\text{sn}}(\bar{q}) \in B_T$ do not necessarily correspond to a path that ends with a node in T (as $\text{EXEC}_x(\sigma, g, h)$ may contain a different subtree T' that satisfies $B_T = B_{T'}$). Also note that there exist queries $\bar{q}$, whose corresponding path ends with a node that belongs to T, but satisfy $\pi_{\text{sn}}(\bar{q}) \notin B_T$. This is so, since T may also contain vertices that correspond to messages in sessions which are not main sessions of B_T (in particular, all sessions that belong to the lower level recursive blocks that are invoked by block B_T).

[22] Recall that the index of the relevant block is determined by the length of the corresponding block prefix.

Now, since T is an m-good subtree, then it must contain a satisfied path. Such a path starts at the root of T and satisfies all sessions whose first verifier message appears along the path. The key observation is that every satisfied path that starts at the root of subtree T must satisfy all the main sessions in B_T (to see this, notice that the first message of all main sessions in B_T will always appear along such a path), and so it contains all messages of all main session in recursive block B_T. In particular, the subtree T contains a path that starts at the root of T and ends with an edge that is labeled with the last prover message in session number (ℓ, n) (i.e., a $\mathrm{p}_{k+1}^{(\ell,n)}$ message). In other words, the execution of the simulator *does* reach the end of the block that corresponds to block prefix $\overline{bp}_T$ (since, for the above path to exist, the simulator must have made a query that ends with a $\mathrm{p}_{k+1}^{(\ell,n)}$ message that corresponds to block prefix $\overline{bp}_T$), and so Condition 2 above does not apply. Thus, the only reason that may cause block prefix $\overline{bp}_T$ not to be potentially useful is Condition 1. We conclude that the number of ip-different queries that correspond to block prefix $\overline{bp}_T$ is at least k^{c+1}, as required. ■

The following claim establishes the connection between the number of ip-different queries that correspond to block prefix $\overline{bp}_T$ and the number of $\frac{m-n}{k}$-good subtrees contained in T. Loosely speaking, this is achieved based on the following three observations: (1) Two queries are said to be ip-different if and only if they have different iteration prefixes. (2) Every iteration prefix is a block prefix of some sub-schedule one level down in the recursive construction (consisting of $\frac{m-n}{k}$ sessions). (3) Every such distinct block prefix yields a distinct $\frac{m-n}{k}$-good subtree.

Claim 7.3.14 *Let T be an m-good subtree. Then for every pair of* ip-*different queries that correspond to block prefix $\overline{bp}_T$, the subtree T contains two disjoint $\frac{m-n}{k}$-good subtrees.*

Once Claim 7.3.14 is proved, we can use it in conjunction with Claim 7.3.13 to infer that T contains at least k^{c+1} disjoint $\frac{m-n}{k}$-good subtrees.

Proof Before we proceed with the proof of Claim 7.3.14, we introduce the notion of an iteration suffix of a query $\overline{q}$. This is the suffix of $\overline{q}$ that starts at the ending point of the query's iteration prefix. A key feature satisfied by an iteration suffix of a query is that it contains all the messages of all sessions belonging to some invocation of the schedule one level down in the recursive construction (this follows directly from the structure of our fixed schedule).

Definition 7.3.15 (Iteration suffix) *The* iteration suffix *of a query $\overline{q}$ (satisfying $j = \pi_{\mathrm{msg}}(\overline{q}) > 1$), denoted $is(\overline{q})$, is the suffix of $\overline{q}$ that begins at the ending point of the iteration prefix of query $\overline{q}$. That is, for $\overline{q} = (b_1, a_1, \ldots, a_t, b_t)$ if $ip(\overline{q}) = (b_1, a_1, \ldots, b_{\delta-1}, a_\delta)$ then $is(\overline{q}) = (a_\delta, b_{\delta+1}, \ldots, a_t, b_t)$.*[23]

---

[23]This means that a_δ is of the form $\mathrm{p}_{j-1}^{(\ell,n)}$, where $(\ell, i) = \pi_{\mathrm{sn}}(\overline{q})$ and $j = \pi_{\mathrm{msg}}(\overline{q})$.

Let $\bar{q}$ be a query, and let $(\ell, i) = \pi_{\mathrm{sn}}(\bar{q})$, $j = \pi_{\mathrm{msg}}(\bar{q})$. Let $\mathcal{P}(\bar{q})$ denote the path corresponding to query $\bar{q}$ in the query-and-answer tree. Let $\mathcal{P}_{ip}(\bar{q})$ denote the subpath of $\mathcal{P}(\bar{q})$ that corresponds to the iteration prefix $ip(\bar{q})$ of $\bar{q}$, and let $\mathcal{P}_{is}(\bar{q})$ denote the subpath of $\mathcal{P}(\bar{q})$ that corresponds to the iteration suffix $is(\bar{q})$ of $\bar{q}$. That is, the subpath $\mathcal{P}_{ip}(\bar{q})$ starts at the root of the full tree, and ends at a $p_{j-1}^{(\ell,n)}$ message, whereas the subpath $\mathcal{P}_{is}(\bar{q})$ starts at a $p_{j-1}^{(\ell,n)}$ message and ends at a $v_j^{(\ell,i)}$ message (in particular, path $\mathcal{P}(\bar{q})$ can be obtained by concatenating $\mathcal{P}_{ip}(\bar{q})$ with $\mathcal{P}_{is}(\bar{q})$[24]).

Fact 7.3.16 *For every query $\bar{q} \in \mathrm{EXEC}_x(\sigma, g, h)$, the subpath $\mathcal{P}_{is}(\bar{q})$ is satisfied. Moreover:*

1. *The subpath $\mathcal{P}_{is}(\bar{q})$ satisfies all $\frac{m-n}{k}$ sessions of a recursive invocation one level down in the recursive construction (i.e., corresponding to $\mathcal{R}_{\frac{m-n}{k}}$).*

2. *If $\bar{q}$ corresponds to block prefix $\overline{bp}_T$, then the subpath $\mathcal{P}_{is}(\bar{q})$ is contained in T.*

Proof Let $(\ell, i) = \pi_{\mathrm{sn}}(\bar{q})$ and $j = \pi_{\mathrm{msg}}(\bar{q})$. By nature of our fixed scheduling, the vertex in which subpath $\mathcal{P}_{is}(\bar{q})$ begins precedes the first message of all (nested) sessions in the $(j-1)^{\mathrm{st}}$ recursive invocation made by recursive block number ℓ (i.e., an instance of $\mathcal{R}_{\frac{m-n}{k}}$ which is invoked by $\mathcal{R}_m$). Since query $\bar{q}$ is answered with a $v_j^{(\ell,i)}$ message, we have that the subpath $\mathcal{P}_{is}(\bar{q})$ eventually reaches a vertex labeled with $v_j^{(\ell,i)}$. In particular, the subpath $\mathcal{P}_{is}(\bar{q})$ (starting at a $p_{j-1}^{(\ell,n)}$ edge and ending at a $v_j^{(\ell,i)}$ vertex) contains the first and last messages of each of the above (nested) sessions, and so contains edges (resp., vertices) for each prover (resp., verifier) message in these sessions. But this means (by definition) that all these (nested) sessions are satisfied by $\mathcal{P}_{is}(\bar{q})$. Since the above (nested) sessions are the only sessions whose first message appears along the subpath $\mathcal{P}_{is}(\bar{q})$, we have that $\mathcal{P}_{is}(\bar{q})$ is satisfied. To see that whenever $\bar{q}$ corresponds to block prefix $\overline{bp}_T$ the subpath $\mathcal{P}_{is}(\bar{q})$ is contained in the subtree T, we observe that both its starting point (i.e., a $p_{j-1}^{(\ell,n)}$ edge) and its ending point (i.e., a $v_j^{(\ell,i)}$ vertex) are contained in T. ∎

Fact 7.3.17 *Let $\bar{q}_1, \bar{q}_2$ be two ip-different queries. Then $\mathcal{P}_{is}(\bar{q}_1)$ and $\mathcal{P}_{is}(\bar{q}_2)$ are disjoint.*

Proof Let $\bar{q}_1$ and $\bar{q}_2$ be two ip-different queries, let $(\ell_1, i_1) = \pi_{\mathrm{sn}}(\bar{q}_1)$, $(\ell_2, i_2) = \pi_{\mathrm{sn}}(\bar{q}_2)$, and let $j_1 = \pi_{\mathrm{msg}}(\bar{q}_1)$, $j_2 = \pi_{\mathrm{msg}}(\bar{q}_2)$. Recall that queries $\bar{q}_1$ and $\bar{q}_2$ are said to be ip-different if and only if they have different iteration prefixes. Since $\bar{q}_1$ and $\bar{q}_2$ are assumed to be ip-different, then so are iteration prefixes $ip(\bar{q}_1)$ and $ip(\bar{q}_2)$. In particular, the paths $\mathcal{P}_{ip}(\bar{q}_1)$ and $\mathcal{P}_{ip}(\bar{q}_2)$ are different. We distinguish between the following two cases:

---

[24]To be precise, one should delete from the resulting concatenation one of the two consecutive edges which are labeled with $a_\delta = p_{j-1}^{(\ell,n)}$ (one edge is the last in $\mathcal{P}_{ip}(\bar{q})$ and the other edge is the first in $\mathcal{P}_{is}(\bar{q})$).

1. **Path $\mathcal{P}_{ip}(\overline{q}_1)$ splits from $\mathcal{P}_{ip}(\overline{q}_2)$:** In such a case, the ending points of paths $\mathcal{P}_{ip}(\overline{q}_1)$ and $\mathcal{P}_{ip}(\overline{q}_2)$ must belong to different subtrees of the query-and-answer tree. Since the starting point of an iteration suffix is the ending point of the corresponding iteration prefix, we must have that paths $\mathcal{P}_{is}(\overline{q}_1)$ and $\mathcal{P}_{is}(\overline{q}_2)$ are disjoint.

2. **Path $\mathcal{P}_{ip}(\overline{q}_1)$ is a prefix of path $\mathcal{P}_{ip}(\overline{q}_2)$:** That is, both $\mathcal{P}_{ip}(\overline{q}_1)$ and $\mathcal{P}_{ip}(\overline{q}_2)$ reach a $v_{j_1-1}^{(\ell_1,n)}$ vertex, while path $\mathcal{P}_{ip}(\overline{q}_2)$ continues down the tree and reaches a $v_{j_2-1}^{(\ell_2,n)}$ vertex. The key observation in this case is that either ℓ_1 is strictly smaller than ℓ_2, or j_1 is strictly smaller than j_2. The reason for this is that in case both $\ell_1 = \ell_2$ and $j_1 = j_2$ hold, iteration prefix $ip(\overline{q}_1)$ must be equal to iteration prefix $ip(\overline{q}_2)$,[25] in contradiction to our hypothesis. Since path $\mathcal{P}_{is}(\overline{q}_1)$ starts at a $p_{j_1-1}^{(\ell_1,n)}$ vertex and ends with a $v_{j_1}^{(\ell_1,i_1)}$ vertex, and since path $\mathcal{P}_{is}(\overline{q}_2)$ starts with a $p_{j_2-1}^{(\ell_2,n)}$ vertex, we have that the ending point of path $\mathcal{P}_{is}(\overline{q}_1)$ precedes the starting point of path $\mathcal{P}_{is}(\overline{q}_2)$ (this is so since if $j_1 < j_2$, the $p_{j_1}^{(\ell_1,i_1)}$ message will always precede/equal the $p_{j_2-1}^{(\ell_2,n)}$ message). In particular, paths $\mathcal{P}_{is}(\overline{q}_1)$ and $\mathcal{P}_{is}(\overline{q}_2)$ are disjoint.

It follows that for every two ip-different queries, $\overline{q}_1$ and $\overline{q}_2$, subpaths $\mathcal{P}_{is}(\overline{q}_1)$ and $\mathcal{P}_{is}(\overline{q}_2)$ are disjoint, as required. ∎

Back to the proof of Claim 7.3.14, let $\overline{q}_1$ and $\overline{q}_2$ be two ip-different queries that correspond to block prefix $\overline{bp}_T$ (as guaranteed by the hypothesis of Claim 7.3.14), and let $\mathcal{P}_{is}(\overline{q}_1)$ and $\mathcal{P}_{is}(\overline{q}_2)$ be as above. Consider the two subtrees, T_1 and T_2, of T that are rooted at the starting point of subpaths $\mathcal{P}_{is}(\overline{q}_1)$ and $\mathcal{P}_{is}(\overline{q}_2)$ respectively (note that, by Fact 7.3.16, T_1 and T_2 are indeed subtrees of T). By definition of our recursive schedule, T_1 and T_2 correspond to $\frac{m-n}{k}$ sessions one level down in the recursive construction (i.e., to an instance of $\mathcal{R}_{\frac{m-n}{k}}$). Using Fact 7.3.16 we infer that subpath $\mathcal{P}_{is}(\overline{q}_1)$ (resp., $\mathcal{P}_{is}(\overline{q}_2)$) contains all messages of all sessions in T_1 (resp., T_2), and so the subtree T_1 (resp., T_2), is $\frac{m-n}{k}$-good. In addition, since subpaths $\mathcal{P}_{is}(\overline{q}_1)$ and $\mathcal{P}_{is}(\overline{q}_2)$ are disjoint (by Fact 7.3.17) and since, by definition of an $\frac{m-n}{k}$-good tree, two different $\frac{m-n}{k}$-good trees are always disjoint, then T_1 and T_2 (which, being rooted at different vertices, must be different) are also disjoint. It follows that for every pair of different queries that correspond to block prefix $\overline{bp}_T$, the subtree T contains two disjoint $\frac{m-n}{k}$-good subtrees. ∎

We are finally ready to establish Lemma 7.3.10 (using Claims 7.3.13 and 7.3.14). By Claim 7.3.13, we have that the number of different queries that correspond to block prefix $\overline{bp}_T$ is at least k^{c+1}. Since (by Claim 7.3.14), for every pair

---

[25]That is, unless $bp(\overline{q}_1) \neq bp(\overline{q}_2)$. But in such a case, paths $\mathcal{P}_{ip}(\overline{q}_1)$ and $\mathcal{P}_{ip}(\overline{q}_2)$ must split from each other (since they differ in some message that belongs to their block prefix), and we are back to Case 1.

of different queries that correspond to block prefix $\overline{bp}_T$ the subtree T contains two disjoint $\frac{m-n}{k}$-good subtrees, we infer that T contains a total of at least k^{c+1} disjoint $\frac{m-n}{k}$-good subtrees (corresponding to the (at least) k^{c+1} different queries mentioned above). Lemma 7.3.10 follows. ∎

7.3.5 Existence of Useful Block Prefixes

Now that the correctness of Lemma 7.3.9 is established, we may go back to the proof of Lemma 7.3.7 and proceed with its proof. Let $x \in \{0,1\}^n$, and fix $\sigma \in \{0,1\}^*$, $h \in H$. We bound from above the probability, taken over the choice of $g \xleftarrow{\text{R}} G$, that $(\sigma, g, h) \in \mathsf{AC}$ and that for all $\ell \in \{1, \ldots, t_S(n)\}$ and all $i \in \{1, \ldots, n\}$, the ℓth distinct block prefix in $\mathrm{EXEC}_x(\sigma, g, h)$ is not i-useful. Specifically, we would like to show that:

$$\Pr_g \left[(\forall \ell, i \; \neg\mathsf{useful}_{\ell,i}(\sigma, g, h)) \; \& \; ((\sigma, g, h) \in \mathsf{AC}) \right] \tag{7.10}$$

is negligible. Define a Boolean indicator $\mathsf{pot\text{-}use}_\ell(\sigma, g, h)$ to be true if and only if the ℓth distinct block prefix in $\mathrm{EXEC}_x(\sigma, g, h)$ is potentially useful. As proved in Lemma 7.3.9, for any $(\sigma, g, h) \in \mathsf{AC}$ there exists an index $\ell \in \{1, \ldots, t_S(n)\}$, so that the ℓth block prefix in $\mathrm{EXEC}_x(\sigma, g, h)$ is potentially useful. In other words, for every $(\sigma, g, h) \in \mathsf{AC}$, $\mathsf{pot\text{-}use}_\ell(\sigma, g, h)$ holds for some value of ℓ. Thus, (7.10) is upper bounded by:

$$\Pr_g \left[\bigvee_{\ell=1}^{t_S(n)} \mathsf{pot\text{-}use}_\ell(\sigma, g, h) \; \& \; (\forall i \in \{1, \ldots, n\} \; \neg\mathsf{useful}_{\ell,i}(\sigma, g, h)) \right]. \tag{7.11}$$

Consider a specific $\ell \in \{1, \ldots, t_S(n)\}$ so that $\mathsf{pot\text{-}use}_\ell(\sigma, g, h)$ is satisfied (i.e., the ℓth block prefix in $\mathrm{EXEC}_x(\sigma, g, h)$ is potentially useful). By Condition 2 in the definition of a potentially useful block prefix (Definition 7.3.8), the execution of the simulator reaches the end of the corresponding block in the schedule. In other words, there exists a query $\overline{q} \in \mathrm{EXEC}_x(\sigma, g, h)$ that ends with the $(k+1)^{\text{st}}$ prover message in the nth main session of recursive block number $\ell^{(\overline{bp}_\ell)}$, where $\overline{bp}_\ell$ denotes the ℓth distinct block prefix in $\mathrm{EXEC}_x(\sigma, g, h)$, and $\ell^{(\overline{bp}_\ell)}$ denotes the index of the recursive block that corresponds to block prefix $\overline{bp}_\ell$ in $\mathrm{EXEC}_x(\sigma, g, h)$. Since, by our convention and the modification of the simulator, S never generates a query that is answered with a `DEVIATION` message, we have that the partial execution transcript induced by query $\overline{q}$ must contain the accepting conversations of at least $\frac{n^{1/2}}{4}$ main sessions in block number $\ell^{(\overline{bp}_\ell)}$ (as otherwise query $\overline{q}$ would have been answered with the `DEVIATION` message in Step 1' of $V_{g,h}$).

Let $\overline{q}^{(\overline{bp}_\ell)} = \overline{q}^{(\overline{bp}_\ell)}(\sigma, g, h)$ denote the first query in $\mathrm{EXEC}_x(\sigma, g, h)$ that is as above (i.e., that ends with the $(k+1)^{\text{st}}$ prover message in the nth main session of recursive block number $\ell^{(\overline{bp}_\ell)}$, where $\overline{bp}_\ell$ denotes the dth block prefix appearing in $\text{EXEC}_x(\sigma, g, h)$).[26]

Define an additional Boolean indicator $\text{accept}_{\ell,i}(\sigma, g, h)$ to be true if and only if query $\overline{q}^{(\overline{bp}_\ell)}$ contains an accepting conversation for session $(\ell^{(\overline{bp}_\ell)}, i)$ (that is, no prover message in session $(\ell^{(\overline{bp}_\ell)}, i)$ is answered with ABORT, and the last verifier message of this session equals ACCEPT).[27] It follows that for every $\ell \in \{1, \dots, t_S(n)\}$ that satisfies $\text{pot-use}_\ell(\sigma, g, h)$, there must exist a set $\mathcal{S} \subset \{1, \dots, n\}$ of size $\frac{n^{1/2}}{4}$ such that $\text{accept}_{\ell,i}(\sigma, g, h)$ holds for every $i \in \mathcal{S}$.

For simplicity, rewrite $\text{pot-use}_\ell(\sigma, g, h)$, $\text{useful}_{\ell,i}(\sigma, g, h)$, $\text{accept}_{\ell,i}(\sigma, g, h)$ as $\text{pot-use}_\ell(g)$, $\text{useful}_{\ell,i}(g)$ and $\text{accept}_{\ell,i}(g)$ (notice that σ, h are fixed anyway at this point). We thus get that (7.11) is upper bounded by:

$$\Pr_g \left[\bigvee_{\ell=1}^{t_S(n)} \bigvee_{\substack{\mathcal{S} \subset \{1,\dots,n\} \\ |\mathcal{S}| = \frac{n^{1/2}}{4}}} \left(\text{pot-use}_\ell(g) \ \& \ \left(\forall i \in \mathcal{S}, \ \neg\text{useful}_{\ell,i}(g) \ \& \ \text{accept}_{\ell,i}(g) \right) \right) \right]. \tag{7.12}$$

Using the union bound, we upper bound (7.12) by:

$$\sum_{\ell=1}^{t_S(n)} \sum_{\substack{\mathcal{S} \subset \{1,\dots,n\} \\ |\mathcal{S}| = \frac{n^{1/2}}{4}}} \Pr_g \left[\text{pot-use}_\ell(g) \ \& \ \left(\forall i \in \mathcal{S}, \ \neg\text{useful}_{\ell,i}(g) \ \& \ \text{accept}_{\ell,i}(g) \right) \right]. \tag{7.13}$$

The last expression is upper bounded using the following lemma, that bounds the probability that a specific set of different sessions corresponding to the same (in index) potentially useful block prefix are accepted (at the first time that the recursive block to which they belong is completed), but still do not turn it into a useful block prefix.

---

[26]Since the simulator is allowed to feed $V_{g,h}$ with different queries of the same length, we have that the execution of the simulator may reach the end of the corresponding block more than once (and thus, $\text{EXEC}_x(\sigma, g, h)$ may contain more than a single query that ends with the $(k+1)^{\text{st}}$ prover message in the nth main session of block number $\ell^{(\overline{bp}_\ell)}$). Since each time that the simulator reaches the end of the corresponding block, the above set of accepted sessions may be different, we are not able to pinpoint a specific set of accepted sessions without explicitly specifying to which one of the above queries we are referring. We solve this problem by explicitly referring to the first query that satisfies the above conditions (note that, in our case, such a query is always guaranteed to exist).

[27]Note that the second condition implies the first one. Namely, if the last verifier message of session $(\ell^{(\overline{bp}_\ell)}, i)$ equals ACCEPT, then no prover message in this session could have been answered with ABORT.

Lemma 7.3.18 *For every $\ell \in \{1, \ldots, t_S(n)\}$, and every $S \subset \{1, \ldots, n\}$, so that $|S| > k$:*

$$\Pr_g \left[\textsf{pot–use}_\ell(g) \ \& \ \left(\forall i \in S, \ \neg \textsf{useful}_{\ell,i}(g) \ \& \ \textsf{accept}_{\ell,i}(g) \right) \right] < \left(n^{-\left(\frac{1}{2} + \frac{1}{4k}\right)} \right)^{|S|}.$$

Proof Let $x \in \{0,1\}^*$. Fix some $\ell \in \{1, \ldots, t_S(n)\}$ and a set $S \subset \{1, \ldots, n\}$. Denote by $\overline{bp}_\ell = \overline{bp}_\ell(g)$ the ℓth distinct block prefix in $\text{EXEC}_x(\sigma, h, g)$, and by $\ell^{(\overline{bp}_\ell)}$ the index of its corresponding recursive block in the schedule. Recall that $\sigma \in \{0,1\}^*$ and $h \in H$ are fixed.

We bound the probability, taken over the choice of $g \xleftarrow{\text{R}} G$, that for all $i \in S$ block prefix $\overline{bp}_\ell$ is not i-useful, even though it is potentially useful and for all $i \in S$ the query $\overline{q}^{(\overline{bp}_\ell)}$ contains an accepting conversation for session $(\ell^{(\overline{bp}_\ell)}, i)$.

A Technical Problem Resolved. In order to prove Lemma 7.3.18 we need to focus on the ℓth distinct block prefix in $\text{EXEC}_x(\sigma, h, g)$ (denoted by $\overline{bp}_\ell$) and analyze the behavior of a uniformly chosen g when applied to the various iteration prefixes that correspond to $\overline{bp}_\ell$. However, trying to do so we encounter a technical problem. This problem is caused by the fact that the contents of block prefix $\overline{bp}_\ell$ depends on g.[28] In particular, it does not make sense to analyze the behavior of a uniformly chosen g on iteration prefixes that correspond to an "undetermined" block prefix (since it is not possible to determine the iteration prefixes that correspond to $\overline{bp}_\ell$ when $\overline{bp}_\ell$ itself is not determined). To overcome the above problem, we rely on the following observations:

1. Whenever σ, h and ℓ are fixed, the contents of block prefix $\overline{bp}_\ell$ is completely determined by the output of g on inputs that have occurred *before $\overline{bp}_\ell$ has been reached* (i.e., has appeared as a block prefix of some query) for the first time.
2. All iteration prefixes that correspond to block prefix $\overline{bp}_\ell$ occur *after $\overline{bp}_\ell$ has been reached* for the first time.

It is thus possible to carry out the analysis by considering the output of g only on inputs that have occurred *after $\overline{bp}_\ell$ has been determined*. That is, fixing σ, h and ℓ we distinguish between: (a) the outputs of g that have occurred *before* the ℓth distinct block prefix in $\text{EXEC}_x(\sigma, g, h)$ (i.e., $\overline{bp}_\ell$) has been reached, and (b) the outputs of g that have occurred *after* $\overline{bp}_\ell$ has been reached. For every possible outcome of (a) we will analyze the (probabilistic) behavior of g only over the outcomes of (b). (Recall that once (a)'s outcome has been determined, the identities (but not the contents) of all relevant prefixes are

---

[28] Clearly, the contents of queries that appear in $\text{EXEC}_x(\sigma, g, h)$ may depend on the choice of the hash function g. (This is because the simulator may dynamically adapt its queries depending on the outcome of g on iteration prefixes of past queries.) As a consequence, the contents of $\overline{bp}_\ell = \overline{bp}_\ell(g)$ may vary together with the choice of g.

well defined.) Since for *every* possible outcome of (a) the analysis will hold, it will in particular hold over all choices of g.

More formally, consider the following (alternative) way of describing a uniformly chosen $g \in G$ (at least as far as $\text{EXEC}_x(\sigma, g, h)$ is concerned). Let g_1, g_2 be two $t_S(n)$-wise independent hash functions uniformly chosen from G and let σ, h, ℓ be as above. We define $g^{(g_1,g_2)} = g^{(\sigma,h,\ell,g_1,g_2)}$ to be uniformly distributed among the functions g' that satisfy the following conditions: the value of g' when applied to an input α that has occurred *before* $\overline{bp}_\ell$ has been reached (in $\text{EXEC}_x(\sigma, g, h)$) is equal to $g_1(\alpha)$, whereas the value of g' when applied to an input α that has occurred *after* $\overline{bp}_\ell$ has been reached is equal to $g_2(\alpha)$.

Similarly to the proof of Claim 7.3.2 it can be shown that for every σ, h, ℓ as above, if g_1 and g_2 are uniformly distributed then so is $g^{(g_1,g_2)}$. In particular:

$$\Pr_g \left[\text{pot--use}_\ell(g) \ \& \ \left(\forall i \in S, \ \neg \text{useful}_{\ell,i}(g) \ \& \ \text{accept}_{\ell,i}(g) \right) \right]$$

equals

$$\Pr_{g_1,g_2} \left[\text{pot--use}_\ell(g^{(g_1,g_2)}) \ \& \ \left(\forall i \in S, \neg \text{useful}_{\ell,i}(g^{(g_1,g_2)}) \ \& \ \text{accept}_{\ell,i}(g^{(g_1,g_2)}) \right) \right].$$

By fixing g_1 and then analyzing the behavior of a uniformly chosen g_2 on the relevant iteration prefixes the above technical problem is resolved. This is due to the following two reasons: (1) For every choice of σ, h, ℓ and for *every* fixed value of g_1, the block prefix $\overline{bp}_\ell$ is completely determined (and the corresponding iteration prefixes are well defined). (2) Once $\overline{bp}_\ell$ has been reached, the outcome of $g^{(g_1,g_2)}$ when applied to the *relevant* iteration prefixes is completely determined by the choice of g_2. Thus, all we need to show to prove Lemma 7.3.18 is that for *every* choice of g_1

$$\Pr_{g_2} \left[\text{pot--use}_\ell(g^{(g_1,g_2)}) \ \& \ \left(\forall i \in S, \ \neg \text{useful}_{\ell,i}(g^{(g_1,g_2)}) \ \& \ \text{accept}_{\ell,i}(g^{(g_1,g_2)}) \right) \right] \tag{7.14}$$

is upper bounded by $(n^{-(1/2+1/4k)})^{|S|}$.

Back to the Actual Proof of Lemma 7.3.18. Consider the block prefix $\overline{bp}_\ell$, as determined by the choices of σ, h, ℓ and g_1, and focus on the iteration prefixes that correspond to $\overline{bp}_\ell$ in $\text{EXEC}_x(\sigma, g, h)$. We next analyze the implications of $\overline{bp}_\ell$ being not i-useful, even though it is potentially useful and for all $i \in S$ query $\overline{q}^{(\overline{bp}_\ell)}$ contains an accepting conversation for session $(\ell^{(\overline{bp}_\ell)}, i)$.

Claim 7.3.19 *Let* $\sigma \in \{0,1\}^*$, $g \in G$, $h \in H$, $d \in \{1, \ldots, t_S(n)\}$ *and* $S \subset \{1, \ldots, n\}$. *Suppose that the indicator*

$$\text{pot--use}_\ell(\sigma, g, h) \ \& \ \left(\forall i \in S, \neg \text{useful}_{\ell,i}(\sigma, g, h) \ \& \ \text{accept}_{\ell,i}(\sigma, g, h) \right)$$

is true. Then:

1. *The number of different iteration prefixes that correspond to block prefix $\overline{bp}_\ell$ is at most k^{c+1}.*

2. *For every $j \in \{2, \dots, k+1\}$, there exists an iteration prefix $\overline{ip}_j$ (corresponding to block prefix $\overline{bp}_\ell$), so that for every $i \in S$ we have $g(i, \overline{ip}_j) = 1$.*

3. *For every $i \in S$, there exists an (additional) iteration prefix $\overline{ip}^{(i)}$ (corresponding to block prefix $\overline{bp}_\ell$), so that for every $j \in \{2, \dots, k+1\}$, we have $\overline{ip}^{(i)} \neq \overline{ip}_j$, and $g(i, \overline{ip}^{(i)}) = 1$.*

In accordance with the discussion above, Claim 7.3.19 will be invoked with $g = g^{(g_1, g_2)}$.

Proof Loosely speaking, item (1) follows directly from the hypothesis that block prefix $\overline{bp}_\ell$ is potentially useful. In order to prove item (2) we also use the hypothesis that for all $i \in S$ query $\overline{q}^{(\overline{bp}_\ell)}$ contains an accepting conversation for session $(\ell^{(\overline{bp}_\ell)}, i)$, and in order to prove Item (3) we additionally use the hypothesis that for all $i \in S$ block prefix $\overline{bp}_\ell$ is not i-useful. Details follow.

Proof of Item 1. The hypothesis that block prefix $\overline{bp}_\ell$ is potentially useful (i.e., pot–use$_\ell(\sigma, g, h)$ holds), implies that the number of iteration prefixes that correspond to block prefix $\overline{bp}_\ell$ is at most k^{c+1} (as otherwise, the number of ip-different queries that correspond to $\overline{bp}_\ell$ would have been greater than k^{c+1}).

Proof of Item 2. Let $i \in S$ and recall that accept$_{\ell,i}(\sigma, g, h)$ holds. In particular, we have that query $\overline{q}^{(\overline{bp}_\ell)}$ (i.e., the first query in EXEC$_x(\sigma, g, h)$ that ends with the $(k+1)^{\text{st}}$ prover message in the nth main session of recursive block number $\ell^{(\overline{bp}_\ell)}$) contains an accepting conversation for session $(\ell^{(\overline{bp}_\ell)}, i)$. That is, no prover message in session $(\ell^{(\overline{bp}_\ell)}, i)$ is answered with ABORT, and the last verifier message of this session equals ACCEPT. Since by our conventions regarding the simulator, before making query $\overline{q}^{(\overline{bp}_\ell)}$ the simulator has made queries to all relevant prefixes, then it must be the case that all prefixes of query $\overline{q}^{(\overline{bp}_\ell)}$ have previously occurred as queries in EXEC$_x(\sigma, g, h)$. In particular, for every $i \in S$ and for every $j \in \{2, \dots, k+1\}$, the execution of the simulator must contain a query $\overline{q}_{i,j}$ that is a prefix of $\overline{q}^{(\overline{bp}_\ell)}$ and that satisfies $bp(\overline{q}_{i,j}) = \overline{bp}_\ell$, $\pi_{\text{sn}}(\overline{q}_{i,j}) = (\ell^{(\overline{bp}_\ell)}, i)$, $\pi_{\text{msg}}(\overline{q}_{i,j}) = j$, and $g(i, ip(\overline{q}_{i,j})) = 1$. (If $g(i, ip(\overline{q}_{i,j}))$ would have been equal to 0, query $\overline{q}^{(\overline{bp}_\ell)}$ would have contained a prover message in session $(\ell^{(\overline{bp}_\ell)}, i)$ that is answered with ABORT, in contradiction to the fact that accept$_{\ell,i}(\sigma, g, h)$ holds.) Since for every $j \in \{2, \dots, k+1\}$ and for every $i_1, i_2 \in S$ we have that $ip(\overline{q}_{i_1,j}) = ip(\overline{q}_{i_2,j})$ (as queries $\overline{q}_{i,j}$ are all prefixes of $\overline{q}_\ell$ and $|ip(\overline{q}_{i_1,j})| = |ip(\overline{q}_{i_2,j})|$), we can set $\overline{ip}_j = ip(\overline{q}_{i,j})$. It follows that for every $j \in \{2, \dots, k+1\}$, iteration prefix $\overline{ip}_j$ corresponds to block prefix $\overline{bp}_\ell$ (as queries $\overline{q}_{i,j}$ all have block prefix $\overline{bp}_\ell$), and for every $i \in S$ we have that $g(i, \overline{ip}_j) = 1$.

Proof of Item 3. Let $i \in S$ and recall that in addition to the fact that accept$_{\ell,i}(\sigma, g, h)$ holds, we have that useful$_{\ell,i}(\sigma, g, h)$ does not hold. Notice that the only reason for which $\mathsf{useful}_{\ell,i}(\sigma, g, h)$ can be false (i.e., the ℓth block prefix is not i-useful), is that Condition 1 in Definition 7.3.4 is violated by $\mathrm{EXEC}_x(\sigma, g, h)$. (Recall that $\mathsf{accept}_{\ell,i}(\sigma, g, h)$ holds, and so Condition 2 in Definition 7.3.4 is indeed satisfied by query $\overline{q}_{i,k+1}$ (as defined above): This query corresponds to block prefix $\overline{bp}_\ell$, satisfies $\pi_{\mathrm{sn}}(\overline{q}_{i,k+1}) = (\ell^{(\overline{bp}_\ell)}, i)$, $\pi_{\mathrm{msg}}(\overline{q}_{i,k+1}) = k + 1$, $g(i, ip(\overline{q}_{i,k+1})) = 1$, and is answered with ACCEPT.)

For Condition 1 in Definition 7.3.4 to be violated, there must exist a $j \in \{2, \ldots, k+1\}$, with two ip-different queries, $\overline{q}_1$ and $\overline{q}_2$, that correspond to block prefix $\overline{bp}_\ell$, satisfy $\pi_{\mathrm{sn}}(\overline{q}_1) = \pi_{\mathrm{sn}}(\overline{q}_2) = (\ell^{(\overline{bp}_\ell)}, i)$, $\pi_{\mathrm{msg}}(\overline{q}_1) = \pi_{\mathrm{msg}}(\overline{q}_2) = j$, and $g(i, ip(\overline{q}_1)) = g(i, ip(\overline{q}_2)) = 1$. Since, by definition, two queries are considered ip-different only if they differ in their iteration prefixes, we have that there exist two different iteration prefixes $\overline{ip}(\overline{q}_1)$ and $\overline{ip}(\overline{q}_2)$ (of the same length) that correspond to block prefix $\overline{bp}_\ell$ and satisfy $g(i, \overline{ip}(\overline{q}_1)) = g(i, \overline{ip}(\overline{q}_2)) = 1$. Since iteration prefixes $\overline{ip}_2, \ldots, \overline{ip}_{k+1}$ (from Item 2 above) are all of distinct length, and since the only iteration prefix in $\overline{ip}_2, \ldots, \overline{ip}_{k+1}$ that can be equal to either $\overline{ip}(\overline{q}_1)$ or $\overline{ip}(\overline{q}_2)$ is $\overline{ip}_j$ (note that this is the only iteration prefix having the same length as $\overline{ip}(\overline{q}_1)$ and $\overline{ip}(\overline{q}_2)$), then it must be the case that at least one of $\overline{ip}(\overline{q}_1), \overline{ip}(\overline{q}_2)$ is different from all of $\overline{ip}_2, \ldots, \overline{ip}_{k+1}$ (recall that $\overline{ip}(\overline{q}_1)$ and $\overline{ip}(\overline{q}_2)$ are different, which means that they cannot be both equal to $\overline{ip}_j$). In particular, for every $i \in S$ (that satisfies $\mathsf{useful}_{\ell,i}(\sigma, g, h)$ & $\mathsf{accept}_{\ell,i}(\sigma, g, h)$), there exists at least one (extra) iteration prefix, $\overline{ip}^{(i)} \in \{\overline{ip}(\overline{q}_1), \overline{ip}(\overline{q}_2)\}$, that corresponds to block prefix $\overline{bp}_\ell$, differs from $\overline{ip}_j$ for every $j \in \{2, \ldots, k+1\}$, and satisfies $g_2(i, \overline{ip}^{(i)}) = 1$.

This completes the proof of Claim 7.3.19. ∎

Recall that the hash function g_2 is chosen at random from a $t_S(n)$-wise independent family. Since for every pair of different iteration prefixes the function g_2 will have different inputs, then g_2 will have independent outputs when applied to different iteration prefixes (since no more than $t_S(n)$ queries are made by the simulator). Similarly, for every pair of different $i, i' \in S$, g_2 will have different input, and thus independent output. Put in other words, all outcomes of g_2 that are relevant to block prefix $\overline{bp}_\ell$ are independent of each other. Since a uniformly chosen g_2 will output 1 with probability $n^{-1/2k}$, we may view every application of g_2 on iteration prefixes that correspond to $\overline{bp}_\ell$ as an independently executed experiment that succeeds with probability $n^{-1/2k}$.[29]

Using Claim 7.3.19.1 (i.e., Item 1 of Claim 7.3.19), the applications of g_2 which are relevant to sessions $\{(\ell^{(\overline{bp}_\ell)}, i)\}_{i \in S}$ can be viewed as a sequence of at

---

[29]We may describe the process of picking $g_2 \overset{\text{R}}{\leftarrow} G$ as the process of independently letting the output of g_2 be equal to 1 with probability $n^{-1/2k}$ (each time a new input is introduced). Note that we will be doing so only for inputs that occur after block prefix $\overline{bp}_\ell$ has been determined (as, in the above case, all inputs for g_2 are iteration prefixes that correspond to block prefix $\overline{bp}_\ell$, and such iteration prefixes will occur only after $\overline{bp}_\ell$ has already been determined).

most k^{c+1} experiments (corresponding to at most k^{c+1} different iteration prefixes). Each of these experiments consists of $|S|$ independent sub-experiments (corresponding to the different $i \in S$), and each sub-experiment succeeds with probability $n^{-1/2k}$. Claim 7.3.19.2 now implies that at least k of the above experiments will fully succeed (that is, all of their sub-experiments will succeed), while Claim 7.3.19.3 implies that for every $i \in S$ there exists an additional successful sub-experiment (that is, a sub-experiment of one of the $k^{c+1} - k$ remaining experiments). Using the fact that the probability that a sub-experiment succeeds is $n^{-1/2k}$, we infer that the probability that an experiment fully succeeds is equal to $(n^{-1/2k})^{|S|}$. In particular, the probability in (7.14) is upper bounded by the probability that the following two events occur (these events correspond to Claims 7.3.19.2 and 7.3.19.3, respectively):

Event 1: *In a sequence of (at most k^{c+1}) experiments, each succeeding with probability $(n^{-1/2k})^{|S|}$, there exist k successful experiments.* (The success probability corresponds to the probability that for every $i \in S$, we have $g_2(i, \overline{ip}_j) = 1$ (see Claim 7.3.19.2).)

Event 2: *For every one out of $|S|$ sequences of the remaining (at most $k^{c+1} - k$) subexperiments, each succeeding with probability $n^{-1/2k}$, there exists at least one successful experiment.* (In this case, the success probability corresponds to the probability that iteration prefix $\overline{ip}^{(i)}$ satisfies $g_2(i, \overline{ip}^{(i)}) = 1$ (see Claim 7.3.19.3).)

For $i \in |S|$ and $j \in [k^{c+1}]$, denote the success of the ith sub-experiment in the jth experiment by $\chi_{i,j}$. By the above discussion for every i, j, the probability that $\chi_{i,j}$ holds is $n^{-1/2k}$ (independently of other $\chi_{i,j}$'s). So for Event 1 above to succeed, there must exist a set of k experiments, $K \subseteq [k^{c+1}]$, so that for all $(i, j) \in S \times K$, the event $\chi_{i,j}$ holds. For Event 2 to succeed, it must be the case that, for every $i \in S$, there exists one additional experiment (i.e., some $j \in [k^{c+1}] \setminus K$) so that $\chi_{i,j}$ holds. It follows that (7.14) is upper bounded by:

$$\sum_{\substack{K \subseteq [k^{c+1}] \\ |K|=k}} \Pr\left[\forall j \in K, \forall i \in S \text{ s.t. } \chi_{i,j}\right] \cdot \Pr\left[\forall i \in S, \exists j \in [k^{c+1}] \setminus K \text{ s.t. } \chi_{i,j}\right]$$

$$= \binom{k^{c+1}}{k} \cdot \left(\left(n^{-\frac{1}{2k}}\right)^{|S|}\right)^k \cdot \left(1 - \left(1 - n^{-\frac{1}{2k}}\right)^{k^{c+1}-k}\right)^{|S|}$$

$$< \left(k^{c+1}\right)^k \cdot \left(\left(n^{-\frac{1}{2k}}\right)^{|S|}\right)^k \cdot \left(k^{c+1} \cdot n^{-\frac{1}{2k}}\right)^{|S|} \tag{7.15}$$

$$= \left(k^{c+1}\right)^{k+|S|} \cdot \left(n^{-\frac{1}{2k}}\right)^{k \cdot |S| + |S|}$$

$$= \left(k^{c+1}\right)^{k+|S|} \cdot \left(n^{-\frac{1}{4k}}\right)^{|S|} \left(n^{-\left(\frac{1}{2}+\frac{1}{4k}\right)}\right)^{|S|}$$

$$< \left(n^{-\left(\frac{1}{2}+\frac{1}{4k}\right)}\right)^{|S|} \tag{7.16}$$

where (7.15) holds whenever $k^{c+1} - k = o(n^{1/2k})$ (which is satisfied if $k = o(\frac{\log n}{\log \log n})$), and (7.16) holds whenever $(k^{c+1})^{k+|S|} \cdot (n^{-1/4k})^{|S|} < 1$ (which is satisfied if both $|S| > k$ and $k = o(\frac{\log n}{\log \log n})$). This means that (7.14) is upper bounded by $(n^{-(1/2+1/4k)})^{|S|}$. The proof of Lemma 7.3.18 is complete. ∎

Using Lemma 7.3.18, we upper bound (7.13) by

$$t_S(n) \cdot \binom{n}{\frac{n^{1/2}}{4}} \cdot \left(n^{-\left(\frac{1}{2}+\frac{1}{4k}\right)}\right)^{\frac{n^{1/2}}{4}} < t_S(n) \cdot \left(\frac{4 \cdot e \cdot n}{n^{1/2}}\right)^{\frac{n^{1/2}}{4}} \cdot \left(n^{-\left(\frac{1}{2}+\frac{1}{4k}\right)}\right)^{\frac{n^{1/2}}{4}}$$

$$= t_S(n) \cdot \left(\frac{4 \cdot e}{n^{1/4k}}\right)^{\frac{n^{1/2}}{4}}$$

$$< t_S(n) \cdot 2^{-\frac{n^{1/2}}{4}} \tag{7.17}$$

where (7.17) holds whenever $8 \cdot e < n^{1/4k}$ (which holds for $k < \frac{\log n}{4 \cdot (3+\log e)}$). This completes the proof of Lemma 7.3.7 (since $\mathrm{poly}(n) \cdot 2^{-\Omega(n^{1/2})}$ is negligible).

8

Conclusions and Open Problems

8.1 Avoiding the Lower Bounds of Chapter 7

The lower bound presented in Chap. 7 draws severe limitations on the ability of black-box simulators to cope with the standard concurrent zero-knowledge setting. This suggests two main directions for further research in the area.

Alternative Models. One first possibility that comes into mind would be to consider relaxations of and augmentations to the standard model. Indeed, several works have managed to "bypass" the difficulty in constructing concurrent zero-knowledge protocols by modifying the standard model in a number of ways. Dwork, Naor and Sahai augment the communication model with assumptions on the maximum delay of messages and skews of local clocks of parties [39, 41]. Damgård uses a common reference string [34], and Canetti et al. use a public registry file [28].

A different approach would be to try and achieve security properties that are weaker than zero-knowledge but are still useful. For example, Feige and Shamir consider the notion of *witness indistinguishability* [42, 48], which is preserved under concurrent composition.

Beyond Black-Box Simulation. Loosely speaking, the only advantage that a black-box simulator may have over the honest prover is the ability to "rewind" the interaction and explore different execution paths before proceeding with the simulation (as its access to the verifier's strategy is restricted to the examination of input/output behavior). As we show in Chap. 7, such a mode of operation (i.e., the necessity to rewind every session) is a major contributor to the hardness of simulating many concurrent sessions. It is thus natural to think that a simulator that deviates from this paradigm (i.e., is non-black-box, in the sense that is does not have to rewind the adversary in order to obtain a faithful simulation of the conversation), would essentially bypass the main problem that arises while trying to simulate many concurrent sessions.

Hada and Tanaka [75] have considered some weaker variants of zero-knowledge, and exhibited a three-round protocol for $\mathcal{NP}$ (whereas only $\mathcal{BPP}$ has three-round block-box zero-knowledge [63]). Their protocol was an example for a zero-knowledge protocol not proven secure via black-box simulation. However, their analysis was based in an essential way on a strong and highly non-standard hardness assumption.

As mentioned before, Barak [8] constructs a constant-round protocol for all languages in $\mathcal{NP}$ whose zero-knowledge property is proved using a *non black-box* simulator. It should be noted, however, that Barak's new techniques are still not known to yield a satisfactory solution to the problem of "full-fledged" concurrent composition (even when allowing arbitrarily many rounds in the protocol).

8.2 Open Problems

The main conclusion from the results presented in this book is that the round-complexity of black-box $c\mathcal{ZK}$ is essentially logarithmic. Specifically, by combining Theorem 7.1 with Theorem 5.1, we have:

Corollary *The round-complexity of black-box concurrent zero-knowledge is* $\tilde{\Theta}(\log n)$ *rounds.*[1]

Still, in light of Barak's recent result [8], constant-round $c\mathcal{ZK}$ protocols (with non-black-box simulators) do not seem out of reach. A natural open question is whether there exists a constant-round (non black-box) $c\mathcal{ZK}$ protocol for all languages in $\mathcal{NP}$.

Open Problem 1 *Is there a $c\mathcal{ZK}$ protocol for $\mathcal{NP}$ with a constant number of rounds?*

As a first step, it would be interesting to determine whether non-black-box simulation techniques can at all improve over black-box simulation techniques in the context of concurrent composition.

Open Problem 2 *Is there a $c\mathcal{ZK}$ protocol for $\mathcal{NP}$ with a sublogarithmic number of rounds?*

It would be in fact interesting to see whether Barak's non-black-box simulation techniques can at all be extended to handle unbounded concurrency (regardless of the number of rounds).

The lower bound presented in Chap. 7 heavily relies on the fact that the malicious verifier is allowed to prematurely abort the interaction with some (predetermined) probability. A natural scenario to be considered is one in

---

[1] $f(n) = \tilde{\Theta}(h(n))$ if both $f(n) = \tilde{O}(h(n))$ and $f(n) = \tilde{\Omega}(h(n))$. $f(n) = \tilde{O}(h(n))$ (resp. $f(n) = \tilde{\Omega}(h(n))$) if there exist constants $c_1, c_2 > 0$ so that for all sufficiently large n, $f(n) \leq c_1 \cdot h(n)/(\log h(n))^{c_2}$ (resp. $f(n) \geq c_1 \cdot h(n)/(\log h(n))^{c_2}$).

which the verifier never aborts the interaction. That is, the simulator is required to succeed in its task only for verifiers that do not deviate from the prescribed strategy in a *detectable* manner (see [96], Chap. 5 for a more detailed treatment of non aborting verifiers). We note that in the case of non-aborting verifiers the situation is far from being resolved. In particular, assuming that the verifier never aborts is not known to enable any improvement in the round-complexity of $c\mathcal{ZK}$ protocols. On the other hand, the best lower bound to date shows that 7 rounds are not sufficient for black-box simulation [97]. It would be interesting to close the gap between the currently known upper and lower bounds (where the best known upper bound is the one presented in Chap. 5 of this book).

Open Problem 3 *Determine the exact round-complexity of $c\mathcal{ZK}$ without aborts.*

The latter question mainly refers to black-box simulation, though it is also interesting (and open) in the context of non-black-box simulation. In fact, we feel that investigation of the above question is likely to shed light on the issue of non-black-box simulation in the concurrent setting.

A Brief Account of Other Developments
(by Oded Goldreich)

As noted in Chap. 1, zero-knowledge proofs are typically used to force malicious parties to behave according to a predetermined protocol. This general principle, which is based on the fact that zero-knowledge proofs can be constructed for any NP-set, has been utilized in numerous different settings. Indeed, this general principle is the basis for the wide applicability of zero-knowledge protocols in cryptography. In particular, zero-knowledge proofs of various types were explicitly used (as a tool) in a variety of applications. In addition to their direct applicability in cryptography, zero-knowledge protocols serve as a good benchmark for the study of various problems regarding cryptographic protocols (see below). Thus, zero-knowledge protocols have had a vast impact on the development of cryptography.

In view of the above, it is not surprising that zero-knowledge protocols have attracted a lot of attention in the last two decades (following their introduction). The study of zero-knowledge protocols has taken numerous directions, ranging from the abstract study of their general properties, through the introduction of various variants of zero-knowledge proofs, to the developement of methods for constructing zero-knowledge protocols. In this chapter we attempt to provide a brief account of these directions, while certainly neglecting to even mention many important works.

We start by considering two basic problems regarding zero-knowledge, which actually arise also with respect to the security of other cryptographic primitives. Specifically, we consider the "preservation of security under various forms of protocol composition" and the "use of of the adversary's program within the proof of security". The first question, as applied to the preservation of zero-knowledge under various types of composition operations, is discussed in Sect. 1.4. Recall that the main facts regarding this question are:

- Zero-knowledge (with respect to auxiliary inputs) is closed under sequential composition.
- In general, zero-knowledge is not closed under parallel composition. Yet, some zero-knowledge proofs (for NP) preserve their security when many

copies are executed in parallel. Furthermore, some of these protocols use a constant number of rounds, and this result extends to a restricted notion of concurrent executions (cf. the timing model).

- Some zero-knowledge proofs (for NP) preserve their security when many copies are executed concurrently, but such a result is not known for constant-round protocols. (Recall that most of this book is devoted to the study of the round-complexity of concurrent zero-knowledge protocols.)

The second basic question regarding zero-knowledge refers to the usage of the adversary's program within the proof of security (i.e., demonstration of the zero-knowledge property). For 15 years, all known proofs of security used the adversary's program as a black-box (i.e., a universal simulator was presented using the adversary's program as an oracle). Furthermore, it was believed that there is no advantage in having access to the code of the adversary's program. Consequently it was conjectured that negative results regarding black-box simulation represent an inherent limitation of zero-knowledge. This believe has been refuted recently by the presentation of a zero-knowledge argument (for NP) that has important properties that are unachievable by black-box simulation. For example, this zero-knowledge argument uses a constant number of rounds and preserves its security when an (a priori fixed polynomial) number of copies are executed concurrently.[1]

The aforementioned zero-knowledge argument, developed by Barak [8], makes crucial use of a technique introduced by Feige, Lapidot and Shamir [46], which in turn is based on the notion of witness indistinguishability (introduced by Feige and Shamir [47]). This technique, hereafter referred to as the FLS technique, has been used in several other sophisticated constructions of zero-knowledge protocols and is briefly surveyed in this chapter. Other topics treated in this chapter include

- *Proofs of knowledge*: This is a related fascinating notion of vast applicability (especially in the case of zero-knowledge proof of knowledge).
- *Non-interactive zero-knowledge proofs*: This model assumes also the existence of a random (reference) string, and yet retains the zero-knowledge flavor and makes it available to non-interactive applications (e.g., public-key encryption schemes).
- *Statistical zero-knowledge proofs*: Here the zero-knowledge condition is stronger, and the resulting proof is "secure" also in an information theoretic sense.

Finally, we mention the indirect impact of zero-knowledge on the definitional approach underlying the foundations of cryptography (cf. Sect. 1.2.1). In addition, zero-knowledge has served as a source of inspiration for complexity

---

[1] This result falls short of achieving a fully concurrent zero-knowledge argument, because the number of concurrent copies must be fixed before the protocol is presented. Specifically, the protocol uses messages that are longer than the allowed number of concurrent copies.

theory. In particular, it served as the main motivation towards the introduction of interactive proof systems [72] and multi-prover interactive proof systems [17].

Organization of This Chapter. The use of the adversary's program within the proof of security is discussed in Sect. 9.1. In Sect. 9.2, we briefly survey the FLS technique (as well as the underlying notion of witness indistinguishability). Other topics treated in this chapter include proofs of knowledge (Sect. 9.3), non-interactive zero-knowledge proofs (Sect. 9.4), statistical zero-knowledge (Sect. 9.5), resettability of a party's random-tape (Sect. 9.6), and zero-knowledge in other models (Sect. 9.7).

Suggestions for Further Reading. For further details regarding the material presented in Sects. 9.2–9.4, the reader is referred to [57, Chap. 4]. For further details regarding Sect. 9.5, the reader is referred to [101]. For the rest, unless suggested differently, the reader is referred to the original papers.

9.1 Using the Adversary's Program in the Proof of Security

As discussed in Chapter 1, zero-knowledge is defined by following the simulation paradigm, which in turn underlies many other central definitions in cryptography. Recall that the definition of zero-knowledge proofs states that whatever an efficient adversary can compute after interacting with the prover can actually be efficiently computed from scratch by a so-called *simulator* (which works without interacting with the prover). Although the simulator may depend arbitrarily on the adversary, the need to present a simulator for each feasible adversary seems to require the presentation of a universal simulator that is given the adversary's strategy (or program) as another auxiliary input. The question addressed in this section is how can the universal simulator use the adversary's program.

The adversary's program (or strategy) is actually a function determining for each possible view of the adversary (i.e., its input, random choices and the message it has received so far) which message will be sent next. Thus, we identify the adversary's program with this next-message function. As stated in Sect. 1.2.3, until very recently, all universal simulators (constructed towards demonstrating zero-knowledge properties) used the adversary's program (or rather its next-message function) as a black-box (i.e., the simulator invoked the next-message function on a sequence of arguments of its choice). Furthermore, in view of the presumed difficulty of "reverse engineering" programs, it was commonly believed that nothing is lost by restricting attention to simulators, called black-box simulators, that only make black-box usage of the adversary's program. Consequently, Goldreich and Krawczyk conjectured that impossibility results regarding black-box simulation represent inherent limitations of zero-knowledge itself, and studied the limitations of the former [62].

In particular, they showed that parallel composition of the protocol of Fig. 1.2 (as well as of any constant-round public-coin protocol) *cannot be proven to be zero-knowledge using a black-box simulator*, unless the language (i.e., 3-colorability) is in $\mathcal{BPP}$. In fact their result refers to any constant-round public-coin protocol with negligible soundness error, regardless of how such a protocol is obtained. This result was taken as strong evidence towards the conjecture that constant-round public-coin protocol with negligible soundness error *cannot be zero-knowledge* (unless the language is in $\mathcal{BPP}$).

Similarly, as mentioned in Sect. 1.4.3, it was shown that protocols of sublogarithmic number of rounds *cannot be proven to be concurrent zero-knowledge via a black-box simulator* [30], and this was taken as evidence towards the conjecture that such protocols cannot be *concurrent zero-knowledge*.

In contrast to these conjectures and supportive evidence, Barak showed how to construct non-black-box simulators and obtained several results that were known to be unachievable via black-box simulators [8]. In particular, under a standard intractability assumption (see also [10]), he presented constant-round public-coin zero-knowledge arguments with negligible soundness error for any language in $\mathcal{NP}$. (Moreover, the simulator runs in strict polynomial-time, which is impossible for black-box simulators of non-trivial constant-round protocols [12].) Furthermore, this protocol preserves zero-knowledge under a fixed[2] polynomial number of concurrent executions, in contrast to the result of [30] (regarding black-box simulators) that holds also in that restricted case. Thus, Barak's result calls for the re-evaluation of many common beliefs. Most concretely, it says that results regarding black-box simulators do not reflect inherent limitations of zero-knowledge (but rather an inherent limitation of a natural way of demonstrating the zero-knowledge property). Most abstractly, it says that there are meaningful ways of using a program other than merely invoking it as a black-box.

Does this means that a method was found to "reverse engineer" programs or to "understand" them? We believe that the answer is negative. Barak [8] is using the adversary's program in a significant way (i.e., more significant than just invoking it), without "understanding" it. *So how does he use the program?*

The key idea underlying Barak's protocol [8] is to have the prover prove that either the original NP-assertion is valid or that he (i.e., the prover) "knows the verifier's residual strategy" (in the sense that it can predict the next verifier message). Indeed, in a real interaction (with the honest verifier), it is infeasible for the prover to predict the next verifier message, and so

---

[2] The protocol depends on the polynomial bounding the number of executions, and thus is not known to be concurrent zero-knowledge (because the latter requires to fix the protocol and then consider any polynomial number of concurrent executions).

computational soundness of the protocol follows. However, a simulator that is given the code of the verifier's strategy (and not merely oracle access to that code) can produce a valid proof of the disjunction by properly executing the subprotocol using its knowledge of an NP-witness for the second disjunctive. The simulation is computational indistinguishable from the real execution, provided that one cannot distinguish an execution of the subprotocol in which one NP-witness (i.e., an NP-witness for the original assertion) is used from an execution in which the second NP-witness (i.e., an NP-witness for the auxiliary assertion) is used. That is, the subprotocol should be a *witness-indistinguishable* argument system (see Sect. 9.2 for further discussion). We warn the reader that the actual implementation of the above idea requires overcoming several technical difficulties (cf. [8, 10]).

Perspective. In retrospect, taking a wide perspective, it should not come as a surprise that the program's code yields extra power beyond black-box access to it. Feeding a program with its own code (or part of it) is the essence of the diagonalization technique, and this too is done without "reverse engineering". Furthermore, various non-black-box techniques have appeared before in the cryptographic setting, but they were used in the more natural context of *devising an attack* on an (artificial) insecure scheme (e.g., towards proving the failure of the "random oracle methodology" [29] and the impossibility of software obfuscation [11]). In contrast, in [8] (and [9]) the code of the adversary is being used within a sophisticated proof of security. What we wish to highlight here is that *non-black-box usage of programs is relevant also to proving* (rather than to disproving) *the security of systems.*

9.2 Witness Indistinguishability and the FLS-Technique

The description of [8] provided in Sect. 9.1, as well as several other sophisticated constructions of zero-knowledge protocols (e.g., [46, 94]), makes crucial use of a technique introduced by Feige, Lapidot and Shamir [46], which we briefly survey below. This technique is based on the notion of witness indistinguishability, introduced by Feige and Shamir [47] (cf. [57, Sect. 4.6]) and briefly described next.

Witness Indistinguishability. Let R be any NP-relation and L_R denote the corresponding language. An argument system for L_R is called witness indistinguishable if no feasible verifier may distinguish the case in which the (prescribed) prover uses one NP-witness to x (i.e., w_1 such that $(x, w_1) \in R$) from the case where this prover is using a different NP-witness to the same input x (i.e., w_2 such that $(x, w_2) \in R$). Indeed, witness indistinguishability is interesting mainly when applied to prescribed provers that can be implemented in polynomial-time (when given a corresponding NP-witness as an auxiliary input). Thus, we adopt the common convention of confining the discussion to such prescribed provers.

Any zero-knowledge protocol is witness indistinguishable, but the converse does not necessarily hold. Furthermore, it seems that witness-indistinguishable protocols are easier to construct than zero-knowledge ones. In particular, witness-indistinguishable protocols are closed under parallel (and even concurrent) composition [47], and so constant-round witness-indistinguishable protocols of negligible soundness error can be obtained by parallel composition of corresponding protocols (of, say, constant soundness error). (Recall that, in general, zero-knowledge is not preserved under parallel composition and so the aforementioned methodology cannot be applied in that context.)

The FLS Technique. Following is a sketchy description of a special case of the FLS technique, whereas the application in Sect. 9.1 uses a more general version (which refers to proofs of knowledge, as defined in Sect. 9.3).[3] In this special case, the technique consists of the following construction schema, which uses witness-indistinguishable protocols for $\mathcal{NP}$ in order to obtain zero-knowledge protocols for $\mathcal{NP}$. On common input $x \in L$, where $L = L_R$ is the NP-set defined by the witness relation R, the following two steps are performed:

1. The parties generate an instance x' for an auxiliary NP-set L', where L' is defined by a witness relation R'. The generation protocol in use must satisfy the following two conditions:
   a) If the verifier follows its prescribed strategy then no matter which feasible strategy is used by the prover, with high probability, the protocol's outcome is a NO-instance of L'.
   b) Loosely speaking, there exists an efficient (non-interactive) procedure for producing a (random) transcript of the generation protocol *along with an NP-witness for the corresponding outcome* such that the produced transcript is computationally indistinguishable from the transcript of a real execution of the protocol.
2. The parties execute a witness-indistinguishable protocol for the set L'' defined by the witness relation $R'' = \{((\alpha, \alpha'), (\beta, \beta')) : (\alpha, \beta) \in R \vee (\alpha', \beta') \in R'\}$. The subprotocol is such that the corresponding prover can be implemented in probabilistic polynomial-time given an NP-witness for $(\alpha, \alpha') \in L''$. The subprotocol is invoked on common input (x, x'), where x' is the outcome of Step 1, and the subprover is invoked with the corresponding NP-witness as auxiliary input (i.e., with (w, λ), where w is the NP-witness for x given to the main prover).

The computational-soundness of the above protocol follows from Property (a) of the generation protocol (i.e., with high probability $x' \notin L'$, and so $x \in L$

---

[3] In the general case, the generation protocol may generate an instance x' in L', but it is infeasible for the prover to obtain a corresponding witness (i.e., a w' such that $(x', w') \in R'$). In the second step, the subprotocol in use ought to be a proof of knowledge, and computational soundness of the main protocol will follow (because otherwise the prover, using a knowledge extractor, can obtain a witness for $x' \in L'$).

follows from the soundness of the protocol used in Step 2). To demonstrate the zero-knowledge property, we first generate a simulated transcript of Step 1 (with outcome $x' \in L'$) along with an adequate NP-witness (i.e., w' such that $(x', w') \in L'$), and then emulate Step 2 by feeding the subprover strategy with the NP-witness (λ, w'). Combining Property (b) of the generation protocol and the witness indistinguishability property of the protocol used in Step 2, the simulation is indistinguishable from the real execution.

9.3 Proofs of Knowledge

This section addresses the concept of "proofs of knowledge". Loosely speaking, these are proofs in which the prover asserts "knowledge" of some object (e.g., a 3-coloring of a graph), and not merely its existence (e.g., the existence of a 3-coloring of the graph, which in turn implies that the graph is 3-colorable). But what is meant by saying that a machine knows something? Indeed the main thrust of this section is in addressing this question. Before doing so we point out that proofs of knowledge, and in particular zero-knowledge proofs of knowledge, have many applications to the design of cryptographic schemes and cryptographic protocols. In fact, we have already referred to proofs of knowledge in Sect. 9.2.

9.3.1 How to Define Proofs of Knowledge

What does it mean to say that a *machine* knows something? Any standard dictionary suggests several meanings for the verb to **know**, and most meanings are phrased with reference to *awareness*, a notion which is certainly inapplicable in the context of machines. We must look for a *behavioristic* interpretation of the verb to **know**. Indeed, it is reasonable to link knowledge with ability to do something (e.g., the ability to write down whatever one knows). Hence, we will say that a machine knows a string α if it *can* output the string α. But this seems to be total nonsense too: a machine has a well-defined output – either the output equals α or it does not. So what can be meant by saying that *a machine can do something?* Loosely speaking, it may mean that the machine can be *easily modified* so that it does whatever is claimed. More precisely, it may mean that there exists an *efficient* machine that, using the original machine as a black-box (or given its code as an input), outputs whatever is claimed.

So much for defining the "knowledge of machines". Yet, whatever a machine knows or does not know is "its own business". What can be of interest and reference *to the outside* is the question of what can be deduced about the knowledge of a machine after interacting with it. Hence, we are interested in proofs of knowledge (rather than in mere knowledge).

For sake of simplicity let us consider a concrete question: *how can a machine prove that it knows a 3-coloring of a graph?* An obvious way is just to send the 3-coloring to the verifier. Yet, we claim that applying the protocol in Fig. 1.2 (i.e., the zero-knowledge proof system for 3-colorability) is an alternative way of proving knowledge of a 3-coloring of the graph.

Loosely speaking, we may say that an interactive machine, V, constitutes a verifier for knowledge of 3-coloring if the probability that the verifier is convinced by a machine P to accept the graph G is inversely proportional to the difficulty of extracting a 3-coloring of G when using machine P as a "black box".[4] Namely, the extraction of the 3-coloring is done by an oracle machine, called an *extractor*, that is given access to a function specifying the behavior P (i.e., the messages it sends in response to particular messages it may receive). We require that the (expected) running time of the extractor, on input G and access to an oracle specifying P's messages, be inversely related (by a factor polynomial in $|G|$) to the probability that P convinces V to accept G. In case P always convinces V to accept G, the extractor runs in expected polynomial-time. The same holds in case P convinces V to accept with noticeable probability. (We stress that the latter special cases do not suffice for a satisfactory definition; see discussion in [57, Sect. 4.7.1].)[5]

We mention that the concept of proofs of knowledge was first introduced in [72], but the above formulation is based mostly on [14]. A famous application of zero-knowledge proofs of knowledge is to the construction of identification schemes (e.g., the Fiat–Shamir scheme [49]).

9.3.2 How to Construct Proofs of Knowledge

As hinted above, many of the known proof systems are in fact proofs of knowledge. Furthermore, some (but not all) known zero-knowledge proofs (resp., arguments) are in fact proofs (resp., arguments) of knowledge.[6] Indeed, a notable example is the zero-knowledge proof depicted in Fig. 1.2. For further discussion, see [57, Sect. 4.7] and [12].

---

[4] Indeed, as hinted above, one may consider also non-black-box extractors as done in [12]. However, this limits the applicability of the definitions to provers that are implemented by polynomial-size circuits.

[5] In particular, note that the latter probability (i.e., of being convinced) may be neither noticeable (i.e., bounded below by the reciprocal of some polynomial) nor negligible (i.e., bounded above by the reciprocal of every polynomial). Thus, events that occur with probability that is neither noticeable nor negligible cannot neither be ignored nor occur with high probability when the experiment is repeated for an a priori bounded polynomial number of times.

[6] Arguments of knowledge are defined analogous to proofs of knowledge, while limiting the extraction requirement to provers that are implemented by polynomial-size circuits. In this case, it is natural to allow also non-black-box extraction, as discussed in Footnote 4.

9.4 Non-interactive Zero-Knowledge

In this section we consider non-interactive zero-knowledge proof systems. The model, introduced in [20], consists of three entities: a prover, a verifier and a uniformly selected reference string (which can be thought of as being selected by a trusted third party). Both verifier and prover can read the reference string, and each can toss additional coins. The interaction consists of a single message sent from the prover to the verifier, who then is left with the final decision (whether to accept or not). The (basic) zero-knowledge requirement refers to a simulator that outputs pairs that should be computationally indistinguishable from the distribution (of pairs consisting of a uniformly selected reference string and a random prover message) seen in the real model.[7] Non-interactive zero-knowledge proof systems have numerous applications (e.g., to the construction of public-key encryption and signature schemes, where the reference string may be incorporated in the public key). Several different definitions of non-interactive zero-knowledge proofs were considered in the literature.

- In the *basic definition*, one considers proving a single assertion of a priori bounded length, where this length may be smaller than the length of the reference string.
- A natural extension, required in many applications, is the ability to prove multiple assertions of varying length, where the total length of these assertions may exceed the length of the reference string (as long as the total length is polynomial in the length of the reference string). This definition is sometimes referred to as the *unbounded definition*, because the total length of the assertions to be proven is not a priori bounded.
- Other natural extensions refer to the preservation of security (i.e., both soundness and zero-knowledge) when the assertions to be proven are selected *adaptively* (based on the reference string and possibly even based on previous proofs).
- Finally, we mention the notion of *simulation-soundness*, which is related to *non-malleability*. This extension, which mixes the zero-knowledge and soundness conditions, refers to the soundness of proofs presented by an adversary after it obtains proofs of assertions of its own choice (with respect to the same reference string). This notion is important in applications of non-interactive zero-knowledge proofs to the construction of public-key encryption schemes secure against chosen ciphertext attacks (see [58, Sect. 5.4.4.4]).

Constructing non-interactive zero-knowledge proofs seems more difficult than constructing interactive zero-knowledge proofs. Still, based on standard in-

---

[7] Note that the verifier does not affect the distribution seen in the real model, and so the basic definition of (non-interactive) zero-knowledge does not refer to it. The verifier (or rather a process of adaptively selecting assertions to be proven) will be referred to in the adaptive variants of the definition.

tractability assumptions (e.g., intractability of factoring), it is known how to construct a non-interactive zero-knowledge proof (even in the adaptive and non-malleable sense) for any NP-set.

Suggestions for Further Reading. For a definitional treatment of the basic, unbounded and adaptive definitions see [57, Sect. 4.10]. Increasingly stronger variants of the non-malleable definition are presented in [36] and [58, Sect. 5.4.4.4]. A relatively simple construction for the basic model is presented in [46] (see also [57, Sect. 4.10.2]). (A more efficient construction can be found in [81].) A transformation of systems for the basic model into systems for the unbounded model is also presented in [46] (and [57, Sect. 4.10.3]). Constructions for increasingly stronger variants of the (adaptive) non-malleable definition are presented in [58, Sect. 5.4.4.4] and [36].

9.5 Statistical Zero-Knowledge

Recall that statistical zero-knowledge protocols are such in which the distribution ensembles referred to in Definition 1.2.1 are required to be *statistically indistinguishable* (rather than *computationally indistinguishable*). Under standard intractability assumptions, every NP-set has a *statistical* zero-knowledge *argument* [23]. On the other hand, it is unlikely that all NP-sets have *statistical* zero-knowledge *proofs* [50, 1]. Currently, the intractability assumption used for constructing *statistical* zero-knowledge *arguments* (for $\mathcal{NP}$) seems stronger than the assumption used for constructing *computational* zero-knowledge *proofs* (for $\mathcal{NP}$). Assuming both constructs exist, the question of which to prefer depends on the application (e.g., is it more important to protect the prover's secrets or to protect the verifier from being convinced of false assertions). In contrast, *statistical* zero-knowledge *proofs*, whenever they exist, free us from this dilemma. Indeed, this is one out of several reasons for studying these objects. That is:

- Statistical zero-knowledge proofs offer information-theoretic security to both parties. Thus, whenever they exist, statistical zero-knowledge proofs may be preferred over computational zero-knowledge proofs (which only offer computational security to the prover) and over statistical zero-knowledge arguments (which only offer computational security to the verifier).
- Statistical zero-knowledge proofs provide a clean model for the study of various questions regarding zero-knowledge. Often, this study results in techniques that are applicable also for computational zero-knowledge; one example is mentioned below.
- The class of problems having statistical zero-knowledge proofs is interesting from a complexity theoretic point of view. On one hand, this class is likely to be a proper superset of $\mathcal{BPP}$ (e.g., it contains seemingly hard problems such as quadratic residuosity [72], graph isomorphism [65], and

a promise problem equivalent to the discrete logarithm problem [64]). On the other hand, this class is contained in $\mathcal{AM} \cap \mathrm{co}\mathcal{AM}$ (cf. [1, 50]), which is believed not to extend much beyond $\mathcal{NP} \cap \mathrm{co}\mathcal{NP}$. ($\mathcal{AM}$ is the class of sets having two-round public-coin interactive proofs.)

In the rest of this section, we survey the main results regarding the internal structure of the class of sets having statistical zero-knowledge proofs. This study was initiated to a large extent by Okamoto [90]. We first present *transformations* that, when applied to certain statistical zero-knowledge protocols, yield protocols with additional properties. Next, we consider several structural properties of the class, most notably the existence of *natural* complete problems (discovered by Sahai and Vadhan [99]). For further details see [101].

9.5.1 Transformations

The first transformation takes any public-coin interactive proof that is statistical zero-knowledge with respect to the honest verifier, and returns a (public-coin) statistical zero-knowledge [68]. When applied to a public-coin interactive proof that is (computational) zero-knowledge with respect to the honest verifier, the transformation yields a (computational) zero-knowledge proof. Thus, this transformation "amplifies the security" of (public-coin) protocols, from leaking nothing to the prescribed verifier into leaking nothing to any cheating verifier.

The heart of the transformation is a suitable random selection protocol, which is used to emulate the verifier's messages in the original protocol. Loosely speaking, the random selection protocol is zero-knowledge in a strong sense, and the effect of each of the parties on the protocol's outcome is adequately bounded. For example, it is impossible for the verifier to affect the protocol's outcome (by more than a negligible amount), whereas the prover cannot increase the probability that the outcome hits any set by more than some specific (super-polynomial) factor.

The first transformation calls our attention to public-coin interactive proofs that are statistical zero-knowledge (with respect to the honest verifier). In general, public-coin interactive proofs are easier to manipulate than general interactive proofs. The second transformation takes any statistical zero-knowledge (with respect to the honest verifier) proof and returns one that is of the public-coin type (see [70], which builds on [90]). Unfortunately, the second transformation, which is analogous to a previously known result regarding interactive proofs [74], does *not* extend to computational zero-knowledge,

Combined together, the two transformations imply that the class of sets (or promise problems) having interactive proofs that are statistical zero-knowledge with respect to the honest verifier equals the class of sets having (general) statistical zero-knowledge proofs.

9.5.2 Complete Problems and Structural Properties

In the rest of this section we consider classes of *promise problems* (rather than classes of decision problems or sets). Specifically, we denote by $\mathcal{SZK}$ the class of problems having a statistical zero-knowledge proof. Recall that $\mathcal{BPP} \subseteq \mathcal{SZK} \subseteq \mathcal{AM} \cap \text{co}\mathcal{AM}$, and that the first inclusion is believed to be strict.

One remarkable property of the class $\mathcal{SZK}$ is that it has natural complete problems (i.e., problems in $\mathcal{SZK}$ such that any problem in $\mathcal{SZK}$ is Karp-reducible to them). One such problem is to distinguish pairs of distributions (given via sampling circuits) that are statistically close from pairs that are statistically far apart [99]. Another such problem is, given two distributions of sufficiently different entropy, to tell which has higher entropy [70]. It is indeed interesting that "the class statistical zero-knowledge is all about statistics (or probability)".

Another remarkable property of $\mathcal{SZK}$ is the fact that it is closed under complementation (see [99], which builds on [90]). In fact, $\mathcal{SZK}$ is closed under $\mathcal{NC}_1$-truth-table reductions [99].

Non-interactive SZK. A systematic study of non-interactive statistical zero-knowledge proof systems was conducted in [69]. The main result is evidence to the non-triviality of the class (i.e., it contains sets outside $\mathcal{BPP}$ if and only if $\mathcal{SZK} \neq \mathcal{BPP}$).

9.6 Resettability of a Party's Random-Tape (rZK and rsZK)

Having gained a reasonable understanding of the security of cryptographic schemes and protocols as stand-alone, cryptographic research is moving towards the study of stronger notions of security. Examples include the effect of executing several instances of the same protocol concurrently (e.g., the malleability of an individual protocol [38]) as well as the effect of executing the protocol concurrently to any other activity (or set of protocols) [27]. Another example of a stronger notion of security, which is of theoretical and practical interest, is the security of protocols under a "resetting" attack. In such an attack a party may be forced to *execute a protocol several times while using the same random-tape* and *without coordinating these executions* (e.g., by maintaining a joint state). The theoretical interest in this notion stems from the fact that randomness plays a pivotal role in cryptography, and thus the question of whether one needs fresh randomness in each invocation of a cryptographic protocol is very natural. The practical importance is due to the fact that in many settings it is impossible or undesirable to generate fresh randomness on the fly (or to maintain a state between executions).

Resettable Zero-Knowledge (rZK). Resettability of players in a cryptographic protocol was first considered in [28], which studies what happens to the security of zero-knowledge interactive proofs and arguments *when the verifier can reset the prover to use the same random tape in multiple concurrent executions*. Protocols that remain zero-knowledge against such a verifier are called resettable zero-knowledge (rZK). Put differently, the question of prover resettability is whether zero-knowledge is achievable when the prover cannot use fresh randomness in new interactions, but is rather restricted to (re-)using a fixed number of coins. Resettability implies security under concurrent executions: As shown in [28], any rZK protocol constitutes a concurrent zero-knowledge protocol. The opposite direction does not hold (in general), and indeed it was not a priori clear whether (non-trivial) rZK protocols may at all exist. Under standard intractability assumptions, it was shown that resettable zero-knowledge interactive proofs for any NP-set do exist [28]. (For related models and efficiency improvements, see [28] and Sect. 5.5.3, respectively.)

Resettably Sound Zero-Knowledge (rsZK). Resettably sound proofs and arguments maintain soundness even *when the prover can reset the verifier to use the same random coins in repeated executions of the protocol.* This notion was studied in [13], where the authors obtained the following results: On one hand, under standard intractability assumptions, any NP-set has a (constant-round) resettably sound zero-knowledge *argument*. On the other hand, resettably sound zero-knowledge *proofs* are possible only for languages in $\mathcal{P}/\text{poly}$. The question of whether a protocol for $\mathcal{NP}$ can be both resettably sound and resettable-zero-knowledge is still open.

9.7 Zero-Knowledge in Other Models

As stated above, zero-knowledge is a property of some interactive strategies, regardless of the goal (or other properties) of these strategies. We have seen that zero-knowledge can be meaningfully applied in the context of interactive proofs and arguments. Here we briefly discuss the applicability of zero-knowledge to other settings in which, as in the case of arguments, there are restrictions on the type of prover strategies. We stress that the restrictions discussed here refer to the strategies employed by the prover both in case it tries to prove valid assertions (i.e., the completeness condition) and in case it tries to fool the verifier to believe false statements (i.e., the soundness condition). Thus, the validity of the verifier decision (concerning false statements) depends on whether this restriction (concerning potential "cheating" prover strategies) really holds. The reason to consider these restricted models is that they enable us to achieve results that are not possible in the general model of interactive proofs (cf., [17, 23, 80, 86]). We consider restrictions of two types: computational and physical. We start with the latter.

Multiprover Interactive Proofs (MIP). In the so-called *multiprover interactive proof* model, denoted MIP (cf., [17]), the prover is split into several (say, two) entities and the restriction (or assumption) is that these entities cannot interact with each other. Actually, the formulation allows them to coordinate their strategies prior to interacting with the verifier[8] but it is crucial that they don't exchange messages among themselves while interacting with the verifier. The multiprover model is reminiscent of the common police procedure of isolating collaborating suspects and interrogating each of them separately. A typical application in which the two-prover model may be assumed is an ATM that verifies the validity of a pair of smart-cards inserted in two isolated slots of the ATM. The advantage in using such a split system is that it enables the presentation of (perfect) zero-knowledge proof systems for any set in $\mathcal{NP}$, while *using no intractability assumptions* [17]. For further details see [57, Sect. 4.11].

Strict Computational Soundness (a.k.a. Timed-ZK). Recall that we have already discussed one model of computational-soundness; that is, the model of arguments refers to prover strategies that are implementable by probabilistic polynomial-time machines with adequate auxiliary input.[9] A more strict restriction, studied in [41], refers to prover strategies that are implementable within an a priori fixed number of computation steps (where this number is a fixed polynomial in the length of the common input). In reality, the prover's actual running time is monitored by the verifier that may run for a longer time, and the prover's utility is due to an auxiliary input that it has. (An analogous model, where the length of the auxiliary input is a priori fixed, was also considered in [41].)

---

[8] This is implicit in the universal quantifier used in the soundness condition.

[9] A related model is that of CS-proofs, where the prover's strategy is allowed to run in time that is polynomial in the time it takes to decide membership of the common input via a canonical decision procedure for the language [86].

References

1. W. Aiello and J. Håstad. Perfect Zero-Knowledge Languages Can Be Recognized in Two Rounds. In *28th IEEE Symposium on Foundations of Computer Science*, pages 439–448, 1987.
2. N. Alon, L. Babai and A. Itai A Fast and Simple Randomized Parallel Algorithm for the Maximal Independent Set Problem. *J. Algorithms*, 7, pages 567–583, 1986.
3. S. Arora, C. Lund, R. Motwani, M. Sudan and M. Szegedy. Proof Verification and Intractability of Approximation Problems. *Journal of the ACM*, 45, pages 501–555, 1998. Preliminary version in *33rd FOCS*, 1992.
4. S. Arora and S. Safra. Probabilistic Checkable Proofs: A New Characterization of NP. *Journal of the ACM*, 45, pages 70–122, 1998. Preliminary version in *33rd FOCS*, 1992.
5. L. Babai. Trading Group Theory for Randomness. In *17th ACM Symposium on the Theory of Computing*, pages 421–420, 1985.
6. L. Babai, L. Fortnow, L. Levin and M. Szegedy. Checking Computations in Polylogarithmic Time. In *23rd ACM Symposium on the Theory of Computing*, pages 21–31, 1991.
7. L. Babai, L. Fortnow, N. Nisan and A. Wigderson. BPP has Subexponential Time Simulations Unless EXPTIME Has Publishable Proofs. *Complexity Theory*, 3, pages 307–318, 1993.
8. B. Barak. How to Go Beyond the Black-Box Simulation Barrier. In *42nd FOCS*, pages 106–115, 2001.
9. B. Barak. Constant-Round Coin-Tossing with a Man in the Middle or Realizing the Shared Random String Model. In *43th IEEE Symposium on Foundations of Computer Science*, pages 345–355, 2002.
10. B. Barak and O. Goldreich, Universal Arguments and Their Applications. In the *17th IEEE Conference on Computational Complexity*, pages 194–203, 2002.
11. B. Barak, O. Goldreich, R. Impagliazzo, S. Rudich, A. Sahai, S. Vadhan, and K. Yang. On the (Im)Possibility of Software Obfuscation. In *Crypto01*, *Springer-Verlag Lecture Notes in Computer Science*, 2139, pages 1–18.
12. B. Barak and Y. Lindell. Strict Polynomial-Time in Simulation and Extraction. In *34th STOC*, pages 484–493, 2002.

13. B. Barak, O. Goldreich, S. Goldwasser and Y. Lindell, Resettably-Sound Zero-Knowledge and Its Applications. In *42th IEEE Symposium on Foundations of Computer Science*, pages 116–125, 2001.

14. M. Bellare, O. Goldreich. On Defining Proofs of Knowledge. In *CRYPTO92*. *Springer-Verlag Lecture Notes in Computer Science*, 740, pages 390–420, 1992.

15. M. Bellare, R. Impagliazzo and M. Naor. Does Parallel Repetition Lower the Error in Computationally Sound Protocols? In *38th FOCS*, pages 374–383, 1997.

16. M. Ben-Or, O. Goldreich, S. Goldwasser, J. Håstad, J. Kilian, S. Micali and P. Rogaway. Everything Provable Is Provable in Zero-Knowledge. In *Crypto88*, *Springer-Verlag Lecture Notes in Computer Science*, 403, pages 37–56, 1990.

17. M. Ben-Or, S. Goldwasser, J. Kilian and A. Wigderson. Multi-prover Interactive Proofs: How to Remove Intractability. In *20th ACM Symposium on the Theory of Computing*, pages 113–131, 1988.

18. M. Blum. How to Prove a Theorem So No One Else Can Claim It. *Proc. of the International Congress of Mathematicians,* Berkeley, California, USA, pages 1444–1451, 1986.

19. M. Blum, A. De Santis, S. Micali, and G. Persiano. Non-interactive Zero-Knowledge Proof Systems. *SIAM Journal on Computing*, 20(6), pages 1084–1118, 1991. (Considered the journal version of [20].)

20. M. Blum, P. Feldman and S. Micali. Non-Interactive Zero-Knowledge and its Applications. In *20th ACM Symposium on the Theory of Computing*, pages 103–112, 1988. See [19].

21. M. Blum and S. Micali. How to Generate Cryptographically Strong Sequences of Pseudo-Random Bits. *SIAM Journal on Computing*, 13, pages 850–864, 1984. Preliminary version in *23rd FOCS*, 1982.

22. R. Boppana, J. Håstad, and S. Zachos. Does Co-NP Have Short Interactive Proofs? *Information Processing Letters*, 25, pages 127–132, May 1987.

23. G. Brassard, D. Chaum and C. Crépeau. Minimum Disclosure Proofs of Knowledge. *Journal of Computer and System Science*, 37(2), pages 156–189, 1988.

24. G. Brassard and C. Crépeau. Zero-Knowledge Simulation of Boolean Circuits. In *Crypto86, Springer-Verlag Lecture Notes in Computer Science*, 263, pages 223–233, 1987.

25. G. Brassard, C. Crépeau and M. Yung. Constant-Round Perfect Zero-Knowledge Computationally Convincing Protocols. *Theoretical Computer Science*, 84, pages 23–52, 1991.

26. R. Canetti. Security and Composition of Multi-party Cryptographic Protocols. *Journal of Cryptology*, 13(1), pages 143–202, 2000.

27. R. Canetti. Universally Composable Security: A New Paradigm for Cryptographic Protocols. In *42nd IEEE Symposium on Foundations of Computer Science*, pages 136–145, 2001. Full version (with different title) is available from *Cryptology ePrint Archive*, Report 2000/067.

28. R. Canetti, O. Goldreich, S. Goldwasser and S. Micali. Resettable Zero-Knowledge. In *32nd STOC*, pages 235–244, 2000.

29. R. Canetti, O. Goldreich and S. Halevi. The Random Oracle Methodology, Revisited. In *30th ACM Symposium on the Theory of Computing*, pages 209–218, 1998. Full version available on-line from http://eprint.iacr.org/1998/011.

30. R. Canetti, J. Kilian, E. Petrank and A. Rosen. Black-Box Concurrent Zero-Knowledge Requires (Almost) Logarithmically Many Rounds. In *SIAM Jour-*

nal on Computing, 32(1), pages 1–47, 2002. Preliminary version (titled Black-Box Concurrent Zero-Knowledge Requires $\tilde{\Omega}(\log n)$ Rounds) appeared in *33rd STOC*, pages 570–579 2001.

31. R. Canetti, Y. Lindell, R. Ostrovsky and A. Sahai. Universally Composable Two-Party and Multi-party Secure Computation. In *34th ACM Symposium on the Theory of Computing*, pages 494–503, 2002.

32. M.N. Wegman, and J.L. Carter. New Hash Functions and Their Use in Authentication and Set Equality. *JCSS 22*, pages 265–279, 1981.

33. B. Chor, and O. Goldreich On the Power of Two-Point Based Sampling. *Jour. of Complexity*, 5, 1989, pages 96–106.

34. I. Damgard. Efficient Concurrent Zero-Knowledge in the Auxiliary String Model. In *EuroCrypt2000, Springer-Verlag Lecture Notes in Computer Science*, 1807, pages 418–430, 2000.

35. I. Damgard, T. Pedersen and B. Pfitzmann. On the Existence of Statistically Hiding Bit Commitment Schemes and Fail-Stop Signatures. In *Crypto93*, Springer-Verlag Lecture Notes in Computer Science, 773, pages 250–265, 1993.

36. A. De Santis, G. Di Crescenzo, R. Ostrovsky, G. Persiano and A. Sahai. Robust Non-interactive Zero-Knowledge. In *Crypto01, Springer-Verlag Lecture Notes in Computer Science*, 2139, pages 566–598, 2001.

37. W. Diffie, and M.E. Hellman. New Directions in Cryptography. *IEEE Trans. on Info. Theory*, IT-22, pages 644–654, Nov. 1976.

38. D. Dolev, C. Dwork, and M. Naor. Non-malleable Cryptography. *SIAM Journal on Computing*, 30(2), pages 391–437, 2000. Preliminary version in *23rd STOC*, 1991.

39. C. Dwork, M. Naor and A. Sahai. Concurrent Zero-Knowledge. In *30th STOC*, pages 409–418, 1998.

40. C. Dwork, and A. Sahai. Concurrent Zero-Knowledge: Reducing the Need for Timing Constraints. In *Crypto98, Springer-Verlag Lecture Notes in Computer Science*, 1462, pages 442–457, 1998.

41. C. Dwork and L. Stockmeyer. 2-Round Zero-Knowledge and Proof Auditors. In *34th ACM Symposium on the Theory of Computing*, pages 322–331, 2004.

42. U. Feige. Ph.D. thesis, Alternative Models for Zero Knowledge Interactive Proofs. Weizmann Institute of Science, 1990.

43. U. Feige, A. Fiat and A. Shamir. Zero Knowledge Proofs of Identity. *JofC*, 1(2), pages 77–94, 1988.

44. U. Feige, S. Goldwasser, L. Lovász, S. Safra, and M. Szegedy. Approximating Clique is Almost NP-complete. *Journal of the ACM*, 43, pages 268–292, 1996. Preliminary version in *32nd FOCS*, 1991.

45. U. Feige and J. Kilian. Zero Knowledge and the Chromatic Number. In *11th IEEE Conference on Computational Complexity*, pages 278–287, 1996.

46. U. Feige, D. Lapidot, and A. Shamir. Multiple Non-interactive Zero-Knowledge Proofs Under General Assumptions. *SIAM Journal on Computing*, 29(1), pages 1–28, 1999.

47. U. Feige and A. Shamir. Witness Indistinguishability and Witness Hiding Protocols. In *22nd ACM Symposium on the Theory of Computing*, pages 416–426, 1990.

48. U. Feige and A. Shamir. Zero-Knowledge Proofs of Knowledge in Two Rounds. In *Crypto'89, Springer-Verlag Lecture Notes in Computer Science*, 435, pages 526–544, 1990.

49. A. Fiat and A. Shamir. How to Prove Yourself: Practical Solution to Identification and Signature Problems. In *Crypto86,Springer-Verlag Lecture Notes in Computer Science*, 263, pages 186–189, 1987.
50. L. Fortnow, The Complexity of Perfect Zero-Knowledge. In *19th ACM Symposium on the Theory of Computing*, pages 204–209, 1987.
51. L. Fortnow, J. Rompel and M. Sipser. On the power of multi-prover interactive protocols. In *Proc. 3rd IEEE Symp. on Structure in Complexity Theory*, pages 156–161, 1988.
52. M. Fürer, O. Goldreich, Y. Mansour, M. Sipser, and S. Zachos. On Completeness and Soundness in Interactive Proof Systems. *Advances in Computing Research: a Research Annual*, 5, Randomness and Computation, S. Micali, ed., pages 429–442, 1989.
53. O. Goldreich. A Uniform Complexity Treatment of Encryption and Zero-Knowledge. *JofC*, 6(1), pages 21–53, 1993.
54. O. Goldreich. Notes on Levin's Theory of Average-Case Complexity. *ECCC*, TR97-058, Dec. 1997.
55. O. Goldreich. *Secure Multi-party Computation*. Working draft, June 1998. Available from http://www.wisdom.weizmann.ac.il/~oded/pp.html.
56. O. Goldreich. *Modern Cryptography, Probabilistic Proofs and Pseudorandomness*. Algorithms and Combinatorics series 17, *Springer*, 1998.
57. O. Goldreich. *Foundations of Cryptography – Basic Tools*. Cambridge University Press, 2001.
58. O. Goldreich. *Foundations of Cryptography – Basic Applications*. Cambridge University Press, 2004.
59. O. Goldreich. Concurrent Zero-Knowledge With Timing, Revisited. In *34th ACM Symposium on the Theory of Computing*, pages 332–340, 2002.
60. O. Goldreich, S. Goldwasser, and S. Micali. How to Construct Random Functions. *Journal of the ACM*, 33(4), pages 792–807, 1986.
61. O. Goldreich and J. Håstad. On the Complexity of Interactive Proofs with Bounded Communication. *IPL*, 67(4), pages 205–214, 1998.
62. O. Goldreich and A. Kahan. How to Construct Constant-Round Zero-Knowledge Proof Systems for NP. *JofC*, 9(2), pages 167–189, 1996.
63. O. Goldreich and H. Krawczyk. On the Composition of Zero-Knowledge Proof Systems. *SIAM J. Computing*, 25(1), pages 169–192, 1996.
64. O. Goldreich and E. Kushilevitz. A Perfect Zero-Knowledge Proof for a Decision Problem Equivalent to Discrete Logarithm. *Journal of Cryptology*, 6(2), pages 97–116, 1993.
65. O. Goldreich, S. Micali and A. Wigderson. Proofs that Yield Nothing but Their Validity or All Languages in NP Have Zero-Knowledge Proof Systems. *Journal of the ACM*, 38(1), pages 691–729, 1991. Preliminary version in *27th FOCS*, 1986.
66. O. Goldreich, S. Micali and A. Wigderson. How to Play Any Mental Game – A Completeness Theorem for Protocols with Honest Majority. In *19th ACM Symposium on the Theory of Computing*, pages 218–229, 1987. See details in [55].
67. O. Goldreich and Y. Oren. Definitions and Properties of Zero-Knowledge Proof Systems. *JofC*, 7(1), pages 1–32, 1994.
68. O. Goldreich, A. Sahai, and S. Vadhan. Honest-Verifier Statistical Zero-Knowledge Equals General Statistical Zero-Knowledge. In *30th ACM Symposium on the Theory of Computing*, pages 399–408, 1998.

69. O. Goldreich, A. Sahai, and S. Vadhan. Can Statistical Zero-Knowledge Be Made Non-interactive? or On the Relationship of SZK and NISZK. In *Crypto99*, *Springer-Verlag Lecture Notes in Computer Science*, 1666, pages 467–484.

70. O. Goldreich and S. Vadhan. Comparing Entropies in Statistical Zero-Knowledge with Applications to the Structure of SZK. In *14th IEEE Conference on Computational Complexity*, pages 54–73, 1999.

71. S. Goldwasser and S. Micali. Probabilistic Encryption. *Journal of Computer and System Science*, 28(2), pages 270–299, 1984. Preliminary version in *14th STOC*, 1982.

72. S. Goldwasser, S. Micali and C. Rackoff. The Knowledge Complexity of Interactive Proof Systems. *SIAM J. Comput.*, 18(1), pages 186–208, 1989.

73. S. Goldwasser, S. Micali and R.L. Rivest. A Digital Signature Scheme Secure Against Adaptive Chosen Message Attacks. *SIAM J. Comput.*, 17(2), pages 281–308, 1988.

74. S. Goldwasser and M. Sipser. Private Coins Versus Public Coins in Interactive Proof Systems. *Advances in Computing Research: a Research Annual*, 5 (Randomness and Computation, S. Micali, ed.), pages 73–90, 1989. Extended abstract in *18th STOC*, pages 59–68, 1986.

75. S. Hada and T. Tanaka. On the Existence of 3-Round Zero-Knowledge Protocols. In *Crypto98*, *Springer-Verlag Lecture Notes in Computer Science*, 1462, pages 408–423, 1998.

76. D. Harnik, M. Naor, O. Reingold and A. Rosen. Completeness in Two-Party Secure Computation Revisited. Unpublished manuscript.

77. J. Hastad, R. Impagliazzo, L.A. Levin and M. Luby. Construction of Pseudorandom Generator from any One-Way Function. *SIAM Journal on Computing*, 28(4), pages 1364–1396, 1999.

78. R. Impagliazzo and M. Yung. Direct Zero-Knowledge Computations. In *Crypto87*, *Springer-Verlag Lecture Notes in Computer Science*, 293, pages 40–51, 1987.

79. A. Joffe. On a Set of Almost Deterministic k-Independent Random Variables. *The Annals of Probability*, 2(1), pages 161–162, 1974.

80. J. Kilian. A Note on Efficient Zero-Knowledge Proofs and Arguments. In *24th STOC*, pages 723–732, 1992.

81. J. Kilian and E. Petrank. An Efficient Non-interactive Zero-Knowledge Proof System for NP with General Assumptions. *Journal of Cryptology*, 11, pages 1–27, 1998.

82. J. Kilian and E. Petrank. Concurrent and Resettable Zero-Knowledge in Polylogarithmic Rounds. In *33rd STOC*, pages 560–569, 2001.

83. J. Kilian, E. Petrank, and C. Rackoff. Lower Bounds for Zero-Knowledge on the Internet. In *39th FOCS*, pages 484–492, 1998.

84. L.A. Levin. Average Case Complete Problems. *SIAM Journal on Computing*, 15, pages 285–286, 1986.

85. C. Lund, L. Fortnow, H. Karloff, and N. Nisan. Algebraic Methods for Interactive Proof Systems. *Journal of the ACM*, 39(4), pages 859–868, 1992. Preliminary version in *31st FOCS*, 1990.

86. S. Micali. Computationally Sound Proofs. *SICOMP*, 30(4), pages 1253–1298, 2000. Preliminary version in *35th FOCS*, 1994.

87. M. Naor. Bit Commitment Using Pseudorandomness. *JofC*, 4, pages 151–158, 1991.

88. M. Naor, R. Ostrovsky, R. Venkatesan and M. Yung. Zero-Knowledge Arguments for NP Can Be Based on General Assumptions. *JofC*, 11, pages 87–108, 1998.

89. M. Naor and M. Yung. Universal One-Way Hash Functions and Their Cryptographic Applications. In *21st STOC*, pages 33–43, 1989.

90. T. Okamoto. On Relationships Between Statistical Zero-Knowledge Proofs. In *28th ACM Symposium on the Theory of Computing*, pages 649–658, 1996.

91. R. Ostrovsky and A. Wigderson. One-Way Functions Are Essential for Nontrivial Zero-Knowledge. In *2nd Israel Symp. on Theory of Computing and Systems*, IEEE Comp. Soc. Press, pages 3–17, 1993.

92. R. Pass. Simulation in Quasi-polynomial Time and Its Application to Protocol Composition. In *EuroCrypt2003, Springer-Verlag Lecture Notes in Computer Science*, 2656, pages 160–176, 2003.

93. M. Prabhakaran, A. Rosen and A. Sahai. Concurrent Zero-Knowledge Proofs in Logarithmic Number of Rounds. In *43rd IEEE Symposium on Foundations of Computer Science*, pages 366–375, 2002.

94. R. Richardson and J. Kilian. On the Concurrent Composition of Zero-Knowledge Proofs. In *EuroCrypt99, Springer-Verlag Lecture Notes in Computer Science*, 1592, pages 415–431, 1999.

95. R. Rivest, A. Shamir and L. Adleman. A Method for Obtaining Digital Signatures and Public Key Cryptosystems. *Communications of the ACM*, 21, pages 120–126, Feb. 1978.

96. A. Rosen. Ph.D. thesis, The Round-Complexity of Black-Box Concurrent Zero-Knowledge. Weizmann Institute of Science, 2003.

97. A. Rosen. A Note on the Round-Complexity of Concurrent Zero-Knowledge. In *Crypto2000, Springer Lecture Notes in Computer Science*, 1880, pages 451–468, 2000.

98. C.P. Schnorr. Efficient Signature Generation by Smart Cards. *JofC* 4(3), pages 161-174, 1991.

99. A. Sahai and S. Vadhan. A Complete Promise Problem for Statistical Zero-Knowledge. In *38th IEEE Symposium on Foundations of Computer Science*, pages 448–457, 1997.

100. A. Shamir. IP = PSPACE. *Journal of the ACM*, 39(4), pages 869–877, 1992. Preliminary version in *31st FOCS*, 1990.

101. S. Vadhan. A Study of Statistical Zero-Knowledge Proofs. PhD Thesis, Department of Mathematics, MIT, 1999. *ACM Doctoral Dissertation Award 2000*.

102. A.C. Yao. Theory and Application of Trapdoor Functions. In *23rd IEEE Symposium on Foundations of Computer Science*, pages 80–91, 1982.

103. A.C. Yao. How to Generate and Exchange Secrets. In *27th IEEE Symposium on Foundations of Computer Science*, pages 162–167, 1986.